UNPACKING PARTICIPATORY DEMOCRACY

Unpacking Participatory Democracy

From Theory to Practice

Edited by

Aruna Roy
Suchi Pande

Orient BlackSwan

All rights reserved. No part of this book may be (i) modified, reproduced or utilised in any form, or by any means, electronic or mechanical, including photocopying, recording or by any information storage and retrieval system, in any form of binding or cover other than in which it is published, without permission in writing from the publisher; or (ii) used or reproduced in any manner for the purpose of training, development or operation of artificial intelligence (AI) technologies and systems, including generative AI technologies, without permission in writing from the copyright holder.

UNPACKING PARTICIPATORY DEMOCRACY:
FROM THEORY TO PRACTICE

ORIENT BLACKSWAN PRIVATE LIMITED

Registered Office
3-6-752 Himayatnagar, Hyderabad 500 029, Telangana, India
e-mail: centraloffice@orientblackswan.com

Other Offices
Bengaluru, Chennai, Guwahati, Hyderabad, Kolkata,
Mumbai, New Delhi, Noida, Patna

© Aruna Roy and Suchi Pande 2025
First published by Orient Blackswan Pvt. Ltd. 2025
First published 2025

ISBN 978-93-6973-299-9

041003

Typeset in
Cochin LT Std 11.5/13.5
by Le Studio Graphique, Gurgaon 122 007

Printed in India at
Akash Press, Delhi

Published by
Orient Blackswan Private Limited
3-6-752 Himayatnagar, Hyderabad 500 029, Telangana, India
e-mail: info@orientblackswan.com

Contents

Abbreviations	*vii*
Acknowledgements	*xi*
Preface	*xiii*
Prabhat Patnaik	

    INTRODUCTION   1
    Aruna Roy and *Suchi Pande*

    OHEN:TON KARIHWATEHKWEN   10
    Thanksgiving from the Mohawk
    Otsi'tsaken:ra (Charles Patton)

1. UNPACKING PARTICIPATORY DEMOCRACY IN AN AGE OF REACTION   17
   Patrick Heller

2. PARTICIPATION, CITIZENSHIP, AND THE RENEWAL OF SOCIAL DEMOCRACY IN THE TIME OF COVID-19   31
   John Harriss

3. DECENTRALISATION FOR CREATING LOCAL DEMOCRATIC SPACE   49
   The Case of the People's Plan Campaign in Kerala
   T. M. Thomas Isaac

4. POPULISM, INFORMATION DISORDERS, AND EROSION OF DEMOCRACY   72
   The Case of Brazil
   Nandini Ramanujam and *Paula Martins*

5.	DEMOCRACY UPENDED Lessons from Afghanistan *Pearl Eliadis* and *Lucile Martin*	99
6.	CAN INFORMATION MAKE THE SUBALTERN SPEAK? *Rajesh Veeraraghavan*	139
7.	KNOWLEDGE PANCHAYATS *Shiv Visvanathan*	165
8.	THE FISCAL DIMENSION OF JUSTICE From Inequality, the Consequences of COVID, and Systemic Racism *Vivek Ramkumar*	191
9.	DO INDIANS HAVE A RIGHT TO KNOW THEIR FOREIGN DONORS? *Inayat Sabhikhi*	202
10.	SPEAK FOR US Democracy, Digital Media, and the Politics of Voice *Sohini Sengupta*	219
11.	SAFEGUARDING DEMOCRACY FROM ORGANISED INFORMATION MANIPULATIONS Paid News, Fake News, and Hate Speech in India *Vipul Mudgal*	235
12.	FLOWERING OF INDIA'S DEMOCRACY *Wajahat Habibullah*	266
13.	WHEN WE THOUGHT WE HAD ALL THE ANSWERS, HINDU SUPREMACY CHANGED THE QUESTIONS *Moyukh Chatterjee*	284
	A CODA *Aruna Roy*	299

Notes on the Contributors   301
Index   306

Abbreviations

ADR	Association for Democratic Reforms
APPRO	Afghanistan Public Policy Research Organization
ARC	Administrative Reforms Committee
BCCL	Bennett, Coleman & Co. Ltd.
BDO	Block Development Officer
BJP	Bharatiya Janata Party
CAA	Citizenship Amendment Act
CAG	Comptroller and Auditor General
CPI(M)	Communist Party of India (Marxist)
CPMI	Comissão Parlamentar Mista de Inquérito
DAPP	Department of Public Policy (Brazil)
DFRLab	Digital Forensic Research Lab
DPC	District Planning Committee
DRDA	District Rural Development Agency
DSP	Dangerous Speech Project
EC	Election Commission (of India)
FCRA	Foreign Contributions Regulation Act
FDI	foreign direct investment
FGV	Fundacao Getulio Vargas
GDP	Gross Domestic Product
GMO	Genetically Modified Organism
GOP	Grand Old Party
GST	Goods and Services Tax
IBP	International Budget Partnership

ICCPR	International Covenant on Civil and Political Rights
ICIJ	International Consortium of Investigative Journalists
IFES	International Foundation for Electoral Systems
IMG	Institute of Management in Governance
IMR	infant mortality rate
INC	Indian National Congress
INTOSAI	International Organization of Supreme Audit Institutions
IPU	Inter-Parliamentary Union
ISID	Institute for the Study of International Development
LG	local government
LSGI	local self-government institution
MIT	Massachusetts Institute of Technology
MKSS	Mazdoor Kisan Shakti Sangathan
MLA	Member of Legislative Assembly
MoU	Memorandum of Understanding
MP	Member of Parliament
MPI	Multidimensional Poverty Index
NAC	National Advisory Committee
NDA	National Democratic Alliance
NGO	non-government organisation
NHGs	Neighbourhood Groups
NREGA	National Rural Employment Guarantee Act
NSSO	National Sample Survey Organisation
NUJ	National Union of Journalists
OBS	Open Budget Survey
OECD	Organisation for Economic Co-operation and Development
PB	Participatory Budgeting
PCI	Press Council of India

PLSI	People's Linguistic Survey of India
PMO	Prime Minister's Office
PPC	People's Plan Campaign
PRI	Panchayati Raj Institutions
RBI	Reserve Bank of India
RDR	Ranking Digital Rights
RSF	Reporters Without Borders (or, *Reporters Sans Frontières* [in French])
RTI	Right to Information Act
SEBI	Securities and Exchange Board of India
SFC	State Finance Commission
SFDAs	Small Farmers Development Agencies
SHGs	Self-Help Groups
UNDP	United Nations Development Programme
UPA	United Progressive Alliance
VLW	Village Level Worker
VTC	Volunteer Technical Corps
ZP	Zilla Parishad

Acknowledgements

First, and most importantly, our thanks to the authors who spared the time and effort to patiently help put this volume together. Their contributions have enriched this selection of writings with the inclusion of diverse and important experiences, perspectives, and analyses, which have considerably informed our understanding of participatory democracy.

We would like to particularly thank the participants from the Montreal and Kerala Workshops (2016–2017) for making the time to share their invaluable perspectives on and grounded insights into participatory democracy. Their contributions and deliberations have collectively enriched the ideas advanced in this volume.

This selection would not have been possible without the unstinting support of the Institute for the Study of International Development and McGill University, which invited and hosted Aruna Roy as Professor of Practice in Global Governance in 2016. The students in Aruna's class, 'Transparency, Accountability and Participatory Governance: Lessons from People's Movements in India', were accomplished interlocutors who energetically debated crucial ideas. They also reflected on critical concepts from their varied experiences, highlighting the essential contributions that young minds can make in questioning and expanding our viewpoints on participation in democracies.

Acknowledgements

We would like to acknowledge and thank the Institute of Management in Governance (IMG), Government of Kerala, and to the dedicated staff, who were generous hosts. They also opened up the premises for workshop activities and arranged trips to the panchayat to learn about participation in action. We would also like to thank the Tata Institute of Social Sciences for coordinating and providing logistical support for the Kerala workshop.

The Kerala workshop would not have been possible without the extensive support of the dedicated teams from the School for Democracy, Mazdoor Kisan Shakti Sangathan (MKSS), and the National Campaign for People's Right to Information (NCPRI).

The difficult task of collating documents was facilitated by our colleagues and friends, including Cheryl Dsouza, Moyukh Chatterjee, Nachiket Udupa, Nikhil Dey, Sara Mahboob, and Siddhartha Sharma. They graciously helped to compile the Montreal and Kerala workshop reports and read early drafts of the chapters. The students of Aruna's McGill class and of the Tata Institute of Social Sciences (Mumbai), were excellent rapporteurs and note-takers. Without their notes on the different breakout sessions, the workshop reports would not have been possible.

We would like to thank Saba Kohli Dave for coordinating and helping with the collation of this volume.

Aruna Roy and Suchi Pande
Rajastha, India and Washington, D.C., USA
August 2025

Preface

PRABHAT PATNAIK

Democracy envisages people becoming 'subjects' shaping their own destiny, rather than mere 'objects' whose destiny is shaped by others. For the last century-and-a-half, there has been a debate over whether such 'de-objectification' of human beings is possible within capitalism. Capitalism unleashes indescribable oppression on the people of the 'outlying regions' (such as in the colonies of conquest), on indigenous communities, and on enslaved populations; in addition, it also brings unanticipated misery to the workers employed by it, because of its being a spontaneous, or self-driven, system. Nobody consciously wants an economic slump and mass unemployment; but slumps and mass unemployment occur nonetheless under capitalism, because of its spontaneous working. This is why it is argued that socialism, which overcomes spontaneity, constitutes a *necessary* condition for the realisation of democracy.

The years following World War II, which saw significant State intervention in the functioning of capitalism, appeared to belie this proposition. It seemed that even under capitalism, people could collectively intervene, through political means within a democratic set-up, to take control of their lives; that capitalism was a malleable system after all, and not spontaneous as had been argued by socialist writers earlier.

But the emergence of neoliberal capitalism has created a new situation. The relatively unfettered cross-border mobility of capital, including finance, under neoliberalism, has meant that the *nation*-State is now confronted with *globalised* capital. Because of this, the nation-State has to pursue willy-nilly only those policies that are acceptable to finance, rather than those that are in the interests of the people; if it does not do this, then it risks triggering a capital flight and hence an economic crisis.

Neoliberal capitalism thus entails a prioritisation of the interests of big capital over those of the people, which leads to a transformation of economic policy. The State *inter alia* withdraws from its earlier role of defending, supporting, and protecting petty production, especially peasant agriculture, from encroachments by big capital; it also pursues a policy of 'fiscal austerity', thereby compressing the magnitude of purchasing power with the people. The result is a distressed peasant agriculture, as evident from the fact that over three lakh peasants in India have committed suicide over the past two-and-a-half decades; and an increase in the incidence of hunger even though the government holds surplus foodstocks.

This constitutes a *de facto* negation of democracy. But it becomes infinitely worse as neoliberal capitalism gets into a crisis, as it has done after 2008. The crisis means that it can no longer promise a better tomorrow for *all*, by claiming that the fruits of high growth would eventually 'trickle down' to *everyone*. With high growth itself having disappeared, such a claim loses its credibility. For its political viability, therefore, neoliberalism now enters into an alliance with neo-fascist elements to bring about a shift in discourse. The discourse now shifts away from the material aspects of quotidian life, which are amenable to an analysis through *reason*, to a fomenting of hatred towards the 'other', typically some hapless ethnic or religious minority, which involves the promotion of *unreason*. The shift in discourse is thus a shift from reason to unreason.

This is a phenomenon occurring all over the world. Neo-fascism has triumphed across a swathe of the globe, from Turkey to Poland, Hungary, the US (under Donald Trump), Brazil, and India; even where it has not yet captured State power, it is nonetheless in the ascendant, such as in France, Germany, and Italy. The neoliberal-neofascist alliance in India has taken the form of a corporate-Hindutva alliance.

This assault on democracy takes the form not necessarily of an abrogation of formal democratic procedures (although that too happens), but of inculcating an incapacity among people to play any 'subject' role. To play this role, people need, apart from formal democratic procedures, correct information, freedom from fear of harassment, freedom to discuss, and above all, the exercise of *reason*. The neo-fascist elements assault democracy, even while formally sticking to democratic procedures, *on every one of these other counts*. Fake news meant to arouse hatred against the targeted minority circulates on social media and even in print and electronic media; people are cowed down by the use of draconian laws that incarcerate for years, without trial, anyone critical of the government; free discussion is negated by this atmosphere of fear and the unleashing of street gangs; and the exercise of 'reason' is replaced by an arousal of passions that get a fillip from the competitive desire within the power elite to please the 'leader'. The net result is to reduce people to being mere 'objects'. But this assault on democracy involves above all an assault on participatory democracy.

II

The superiority of participatory democracy over representative democracy arises from the fact that people's actual preferences are not adequately reflected through the process of representation. For obvious practical reasons, however, participatory democracy can function primarily at the local level, which is why a devolution of resources and powers to local self-government institutions (LSGI) is considered essential.

It is important, though, to distinguish between *this* argument and another one that is also advanced for such devolution. Even reputed and well-meaning scholars often argue for a devolution of powers and resources to lower-level elected bodies in India, such as panchayats, on the grounds that they are a continuation of the old village community; since the village community was the centre of social life in rural India earlier; its successor, the panchayat, they argue, should be similarly empowered.

This argument, however, is *completely* invalid. The village community was a hierarchical institution characterised not only by caste oppression, but also by ruthless class exploitation (which had a strong overlap with caste oppression) and gender discrimination. By contrast, today's local self-government institutions exist as an instrument of participatory *democracy* that is fundamentally antithetical to the oppressive hierarchism of the old village community. The LSGIs cannot therefore be a continuation of the old village community. On the contrary, they have to free themselves *completely* from the shadow of the old village community.

In fact, the apprehension that the LSGIs may not break out of the shadow of the old village community is what had made Dr Ambedkar oppose the very idea of decentralisation. He had seen in decentralisation the danger of a regression to the past from which our modern Constitution was trying to extricate us.

But if participatory democracy is to have any meaning, then there must be appropriate devolution of powers and resources to the LSGIs. This devolution had gone the furthest in Kerala because even plan funds were devolved to LSGIs in accordance with the recommendations of the State Finance Commissions. But the centralisation of powers and resources that has occurred, especially under the neoliberal-neofascist regime, has strangulated the state governments, and hence the LSGIs as well.

A series of measures under the NDA-II government, from demonetisation to the Goods and Services Tax (GST), have severely hurt the informal sector of the economy that includes peasant agriculture; even the impact of the pandemic has been felt disproportionately by this sector, which therefore requires assistance from the LSGIs. The demand for resources by the LSGIs has gone up for these reasons. At the same time, however, the availability of resources with the LSGIs has gone down because of the process of centralisation; this happened even before the pandemic, but the pandemic has worsened things.

The substitution of the GST for the sales tax that used to provide the bulk (nearly 80 per cent) of state revenues has reduced states' taxing powers. They cannot raise taxes on particular commodities as they wish; they would now have to come as supplicants before the GST Council, where the Centre is also represented and has a dominant say. Thus, the rights enjoyed earlier by the state governments under the Constitution have been surrendered. At the same time, the GST compensation promised by the Centre, on the basis of which the states had agreed to surrender their rights, is not being paid, which leaves state finances in a precarious position and reduces in turn the devolution from the state governments to the LSGIs. Hence, at precisely the time when the LSGIs need more resources, the flow of resources to them has become even thinner than before.

But going beyond the current context of neo-fascism, the deeper issue that Ambedkar had raised remains: How can such decentralisation be kept free of the shadow of the oppressive village community? After all, the ideas of equality and democracy do not spontaneously spring up within a 'closed' village community; they are brought to the village from 'outside'. How can this opening to the 'outside', this non-'closure' of the village, be maintained without too many bureaucratic fiats from outside that also have the effect of stultifying democracy within the LSGIs?

This problem had featured in discussions in Kerala when the 'People's Plan' campaign was being launched, and the view at the time was that since the mass and class organisations (of agricultural labourers, coir workers, and so on) were powerful in Kerala and had penetrated to the village level, they could provide a counter to hierarchism. Democratic decentralisation, it was felt, would strengthen the 'subjecthood' of the people because of the existence of class and mass organisations at the village level.

The promises of participatory democracy and the challenges it faces are covered in the present volume. Since the knowledge of a problem itself goes a long way towards overcoming it, this volume is an invaluable one.

Introduction

Aruna Roy and Suchi Pande

This edited volume is based on the discussions and deliberations that took place in two seminars between scholars and practitioners on participatory democracy. The decision to hold two seminars on 'Unpacking Participatory Democracy' was part of an academic brief designed by McGill University's Institute for the Study of International Development (ISID) for the course design of the Professor of Practice. The ISID agreed to have the seminar in two parts. The first was held in Montreal, Canada to look more specifically at the theory of democratic practice, and the second, held in Kerala, India, planned to inject a contrasting set of inputs that would add to the rich tapestry of democracy in practice. Aruna Roy, who held the chair of Professor of Practice for a term in 2016–2017, organised the first phase of the dialogue in Montreal, and dialogued for the second with the Government of Kerala, famous for initiating the 'People's Plan', a widely acclaimed participatory democratic exercise, to co-host the Indian seminar in Thiruvananthapuram, Kerala.

How did this somewhat unusual design, of having two connected seminars located in two distant cities on the globe, come about? The 'Montreal–Trivandrum' North–South dialogue took place 13,500 kms apart, separated by much more than weather, food, and language. And yet, the focus on participatory democracy made it not only relevant to different parts of the world, but also allowed for a much richer examination of the similarities and differences in democratic practice, and the challenges to it in different parts of the world.

In Montreal and in Thiruvananthapuram, theoreticians—academics, political thinkers, economists, policymakers—gathered with practitioners of democracy, covering a large spectrum of interests. In Kerala, the range of practitioners also included government executives, who took the responsibility to put democratic theory into practice.

People and their movements form the crux of practice. Indian sociologist Shiv Visvanathan, who came to the Kerala seminar, described it as an 'intellectual commons'. Both the seminars tried to include the voiceless as an important thread in discussions on the nature of democratic action—from the idiom of the indigenous people in Canada to the Dalits and Adivasis (tribals) of India. The idiom included the written and spoken word, but went beyond to cultural expression—invocations, songs, and poetry.

The varied perspectives, the richness of the dialogue, and the experiences of different actors from different sectors (government, academia, civil society, and politics) that shape democracy in practice came together to critically introspect and dialogue about the nature of democratic practice and culture. The range of discussions reflected their concerns as part of an inclusive agenda. The remarkable thing about the two seminars was that the principles of democracy—dissent and disagreement—were both seen in action.

Participants came with varied hopes and expectations, united by a common desire to exchange ideas and share as equals. These hopes and expectations were more than met in the discourse that emerged, as the chapters in this volume will prove. Although the ideas in this volume do not provide a comprehensive assessment of the state of participatory democracy, they are intended to inform further discussion, dialogue, and debate.

The chapters in this volume have been written by the participants of the two seminars, and explore the realities of democratic practice. Some combine theoretical perspectives with empirical case studies (see Chapters 1, 2, and 6). They helped enable a deeper critical enquiry into some of the contemporary theories and practice of democracy. The two seminars looked at democracy *beyond* the vote. They accepted the power of 'one person one vote', but also recognised it as the narrowest form of political participation. Drawing on their varied experiences as women, indigenous people, Dalits, and religious and ethnic minorities (see Chapter 13; also see Chapter 5, in Vol. II), who are always at the margins of democratic power, the seminar participants interrogated the contested concepts of democracy and participation in light of the rising global threat of authoritarian regimes in their democracies, and the state of democracy in fragile conflict-ridden contexts (see Chapter 5). They were not merely people who watched and analysed, but they were also concerned about the outcomes and impact of electoral autocracies on the lives of the people, the erosion of democracy through information disorders (see Chapters 4 and 11), and their relationship with neoliberal capitalism (see Chapter 2).

The Montreal seminar took place not long after the 2016 US election. The mood of the participants was sombre, but it also provoked a critical deliberation on the relationship between participation and democracy today. Although Donald Trump's presidency was perceived by many as a threat to American democracy, as one of the speakers at the Montreal seminar noted, liberal democracy is 'perfectly compatible with genocide and forcible dispossession of indigenous people in North America'.[1] While the 2016 US presidential election was the culmination of a long and unprecedented campaign year,[2] it was representative of a global trend that forced academics and practitioners alike to confront the inherent tension between (electoral) representation and participation. Those of us who came together in Montreal shared a common concern about the obvious and dangerous rise and spread of authoritarianism. It was also clear to most that extant democratic theories of checks and balances were unequal to the task of being able to effectively control these prejudiced, majoritarian leaders. The legitimacy of the 'vote' and its basic and fundamental role in deciding who would come to power made all other critiques seem like weak liberal excuses for an inability to accept the 'will of the people'.

Most authors in this volume agree that democratic practice implies an intrinsic link between participation and an informed citizenry. Yet, in the past decade, many elected governments have acted to curb participation and dissent globally. The contributors to this volume posit important questions about the transformatory power of information, and the role of private actors and new forms of media on State-citizen relations. As Nandini Ramanujam and Paula Martins (Chapter 4) and Vipul Mudgal (Chapter 11) note, elected authoritarian governments in Brazil and India have resorted to 'information disorders'—'fake' and 'paid' news—to win elections, and continue to manipulate information beyond election cycles. Instigating hatred and harm towards and between citizens based on race, religion, class, and caste, silencing dissent, and spreading disinformation have become the new normal in these and several other democracies (see also Chapter 10). Many in this volume have touched upon the role of intermediaries in civil society in channelling the demands from marginalised citizens. But what about the role of civil society in the service of authoritarian governments? Inayat Sabhikhi (Chapter 9) discusses the role and growing influence of the Indian diaspora in galvanising resources to support the Hindu right. This kind of diasporic nationalism, which foregrounds a unified 'nation outside the nation' to overcome the social dislocation that comes with migration to foreign countries, previously aided anti-colonial struggles, and in its current form works as an extension of the ruling establishment to curb dissent. To have 'democratic participation' without dissent is the most obvious sign of a crude majoritarianism, and some of the worst extremes of such a framework showed how much farther this took governments on the path to fascism.

In the US and India, two disparate democracies, Chatterjee (Chapter 13) argues that the 'politics of exposure'—of wrongdoing, complicity, corruption, violence—that would perhaps lead to outrage in liberal democracies has instead given rise to 'new publics', who thrive on violence and disinformation and 'cheer the death' of liberal democracy. In this 'age of reaction', formal electoral democracy is in suspension. It is therefore even more important to distinguish between formal electoral democracy and participatory democracy. Many populist leaders have attacked both the foundations of democracy and also its ideals and values. The assault on democratic institutions follows a familiar 'strategic repertoire': loyalty to an individual rather than an office, centralisation of power, outsourcing of violence, and politicisation of the rule of law. Drawing on the experiences of people's movements from Brazil and India, Patrick Heller (Chapter 1) offers insights into concerted efforts to expand participatory democracy and the challenges to the longer-term project of building participatory democracy.

Long after the seminars, the challenges to formal electoral democracy from populists were further exacerbated by the global coronavirus pandemic. Many elected authoritarian leaders usurped greater powers under the pretext of protecting citizens. The social and economic trends during the pandemic also underscored the conflict between capitalism and the values of solidarity, freedom, and justice. With strict quarantine mandates, human suffering and inequality increased globally. Many millionaires in India and across the world became significantly richer during the pandemic. Citizen-led solidarity networks—not governments or corporations—provided the necessary humanitarian response. As John Harriss notes in Chapter 2, there were of course outliers to the global trend—social democracies with strong welfare states. In Chapter 2, Harriss asks what we can learn from global experiences with social democracy (in Scandinavia) and from social struggles to strengthen the welfare arm of the government in Brazil, India, and South Africa under capitalism. The current moment requires a web of collective actors committed to dismantling capitalism. Contributors to this volume look to contemporary struggles for the realisation of social and economic rights in countries like India and South Africa, which offer the 'potential of building a broad-based political movement' and hopefully 'creating an active democratic society'.

Similar demands for the expansion of social and economic rights, and frustration with corrupt elites and elected leaders were visible in protests throughout the pandemic in countries like Chile, Ecuador, Lebanon, Haiti, Iraq, and France. Further alienated by the fiscal policy responses during the pandemic, in these countries, the voiceless took to the streets at great personal risk and out of helplessness. Drawing on global good practices, the contributors to this volume offer a strong case for public participation in budget processes as one of many pathways to justice. A more effective and inclusive policy response to ensure fiscal justice is the participation of impacted communities, particularly those at the margins of society, in budget decisions.

India has a range of practitioners who have spent decades of their lives building organisations and collectives that have been engaging with the practice of democracy, for equality and justice. Many of the community-based initiatives had worked on outlining the modes of participation and faced immense challenges even at a 'micro level'. Their attempts to carry these modes to a macro level had very limited success. There were clearly some outstanding examples where the principles adopted and used at a micro level had been picked up and made sacrosanct even at the state and national levels, like the rights-based legislations passed by the Indian Parliament in the decade beginning 2005 (see Chapters 3, 7, and 10, in Vol. II). Some of these had subsequently caused a great deal of upheaval in the settled modes of democratic governance, and were captured by political and social elites who tried to usurp rights-based gains for private and electoral gain. Inevitably, people's protests and their role in democracy have been resisted by such established centres of power, and the strong democratic assertions of people were unable to find 'mainstream acceptance' in the bulk of academic theory or democratic institutions. Some of these initiatives were the knowledge banks of community practice, with immense potential for wider institutionalisation (see Chapter 7, Vol. II). However, sceptics dismissed the utopian idealism of community practice, and insisted that there was no choice but to settle for the practical realpolitik of representational democratic practice. These efforts remained at a stage where they raised many fundamental questions, but were not seen as solutions.

In Kerala, democratic theory and practice came together in the People's Planning Campaign which made a giant leap in democratic decentralised planning and implementation. Chapter 3 in Vol. I (by T. M. Thomas Isaac) and Chapter 2 in Vol. II (by S. M. Vijayanand) reflect on the Kerala experience. The People's Planning Campaign created sufficient institutionalised support, and facilitated its spread into every aspect of local governance. Inevitably, the local self-government institutions where this was embedded and the people's campaigns created a synergy and support for each other that led to Kerala's Panchayati Raj standing head and shoulders above the rest of the country, as well as internationally. After twenty-five years, though, there have been challenges to this radical project of decentralised democracy. Greater participation and universalisation of participatory oversight through social audits can help address some of the weaknesses of the Kerala model (see Chapter 2, Vol. II).

This volume adds to the examination of possibilities to recapture the lost power of democratic dissent, dialogue, and disagreement, and the platforms for debate in the last decade all over the world. We hope that these chapters will rekindle the debate in the public domain and in academia, so that participatory democratic practice regains lost ground.

We would like, in conclusion, to acknowledge the invaluable contribution of time and effort of all our contributors. Their perspectives, despite COVID-19 and the bleakest of periods in global democratic practice, give us hope for a change for the better. This volume brings together contributions from the intersections between the theory and practice of democracy. The tonal variations and different styles in the chapters reflect the plurality in perceptions of democracy's complexity, its present predicament, and its future. A special thanks to Otsi'tsaken:ra (Charles Patton) and Niioie:ren (Eileen Sawyer Patton), who gave their consent to print the invocation read out at the Montreal seminar, Ohen:ton Karihwatehkwen (Thanksgiving from the Mohawk). Ira Anjali Anwar, S. Anandalakshmy, and T. M. Krishna brought out the understanding of democracy from a culturally rich lens. The music performance at the end of the first day in Thiruvananthapuram brought in a different idiom of communication to enrich the discussion. The seminar, as revealed in the chapters of this volume, connected the strength in the complexity of a democracy, which allows for freedom of expression, yet demands a consensus to apply universal principles with equality, equity, and justice in practice.

Theoretical understandings across the spectrum were deepened by academic scholars, including John Harriss, Patrick Heller, Kenneth Winston, Shiv Visvanathan, Nandini Ramanujam and Paula Martins, Pearl Eliadis and Lucile Martin, Moyukh Chatterjee, Rajesh Veeraraghavan, Sohini

Sengupta, Vivek Ramkumar, and Inayat Sabikhi. Current as well as former members of the bureaucracy and/or government system, including commissions, have brought to the fore the practical aspects of the systemic implementation of rights in a democracy, including Thomas Isaac, S. M. Vijayanand, Wajahat Habibullah, C. K. Mathew, M. Sridhar Acharyulu, and Shailesh Gandhi. Activists and practitioners working on issues of advocacy, rights, and public action in democracy include Teesta Setalvad, Mamta Jaitly, Shaheen Anam, Nikhil Dey and Rakshita Swamy, Anita Gurumurthy and Nandini Chami, Vipul Mudgal, Kathyayini Chamaraj, and Rosamma Thomas.

The varied tones, perceptions, and idioms of the writers bring home the strengths and challenges in a democracy. We, as editors, look forward to sharing this volume and invite you to step into this 'intellectual commons'.

Notes

1. Ellen Gabreil, indigenous activist from Kanehsatà:ke Mohawk territory (Canada).
2. By unprecedented, we refer both (*a*) to the candidacy of a democratic socialist, Bernie Sanders, which forced the Democratic Party to programmatically align with the working class, youth, and other racial and sexual minorities; and (*b*) to the language and open endorsement of bigotry and racial slurs by a presidential candidate.

Ohen:ton Karihwatehkwen
Thanksgiving from the Mohawk

Otsi'tsaken:ra (Charles Patton)

Greetings to the Natural World

The Haudenosaunee (Iroquois) people (our elders) have taught us that whenever people gather for any occasion, the first thing that we acknowledge is the forces that have given us life at this time and continue to support us into the future. This ceremony has been done since the beginning of time and its purpose is to remind all those listening to never forget to be thankful for all that is in place to help us accomplish the work at hand using a good mind.

So, with this in mind, we use these 'words that come before all things' and turn our greetings to all of the natural world. We put our minds together as one as we offer greetings to our Creator, because all is put before us on the Earth and in the Universe:

The People

Today we have gathered and we see that the cycles of life continue. We have been given the duty to live in balance and harmony with each other and all living things. So now, we bring our minds together as one as we give greetings and thanks to one another as people.

Now our minds are one.

The Earth Mother

We are all thankful to our Mother, the Earth, for she gives us all that we need for life. She supports our feet as we walk about upon her. We must every day honour her as she continues to care for us as she has from the beginning of time. To our Mother, we send greetings and thanks.

Now our minds are one.

The Waters

We give thanks to all the Waters of the world for quenching our thirst and providing us with strength. Water is life. We know its power in many forms—waterfalls and rain, mists and streams, rivers, oceans, and even within our own bodies. We must also not forget our tears. With one mind, we send greetings and thanks to the spirit of Water.

Now our minds are one.

The Fish

We turn our minds to all the Fish life in the water. They were instructed to cleanse and purify the water. They are trying to do the best job they can. They also give themselves to us as food. We are grateful that we can still find pure water. So, we turn now to the Fish and send our greetings and thanks.

Now our minds are one.

The Plants

Now we turn toward the vast fields of Plant life. As far as the eye can see, the Plants grow, working many wonders. They sustain many life forms. They continue to thrive and fulfil their duties. With our minds gathered together, we give thanks and look forward to seeing Plant life for many generations to come.

Now our minds are one.

The Food Plants

With one mind, we turn to honour and thank all the Food Plants we harvest from the garden, our life sustainers. Since the beginning of time, the grains, vegetables, beans, and berries have helped the people survive. Many other living things draw strength from them too. We gather all the Plant Foods together as one and send them a greeting of thanks.

Now our minds are one.

The Medicine Herbs

Now we turn to all the Medicine herbs of the world. From the beginning, they were instructed to help with sickness. They are always waiting and ready to heal us. We are happy there are still among us those special few who remember how to use these plants for healing. We take only what we need and ensure they continue to grow. With one mind, we send greetings and thanks to the Medicines and to the keepers of the Medicines.

Now our minds are one.

The Insects

We gather our minds together to send greetings and thanks to all the Insects, the crawlers, the flyers, big and small, seen and unseen. They continue busily about fulfilling their duties. We see them and may be startled, but we are glad that they are still here and will remain.

Now our minds are one.

The Animals

We gather our minds together to send greetings and thanks to all the Animal life in the world. They have many things to teach us as people. We are honoured by them when they give up their lives so we may use their bodies as food for our people. We see them near our homes, and wild and free in the fields and forests. We are glad they are still here and we hope that it will always be so.

Now our minds are one.

The Trees

We now turn our thoughts to the Trees. The Earth is bountiful with many different Trees who have their own instructions and uses. Some provide us with shelter and shade, others with fruit, sap, and beauty. They are quite useful and the Maple is the leader of the trees. There is the Tree of life, the Tree is a symbol of peace and strength. With one mind, we greet and thank the Tree life.

Now our minds are one.

The Birds

We put our minds together as one and thank all the Birds who move and fly about over our heads. The Creator gave them beautiful songs. Each day they remind us to enjoy and appreciate life. The Eagle sits atop of the Tree of Peace and was chosen to be the guardian. To all the Birds—from the tiniest to the largest—we send joyful greetings and thanks.

    Now our minds are one.

The Four Winds

We are all thankful to the powers we know as the Four Winds. We hear their voices in the moving air as they refresh us and purify the air we breathe. They help us to bring the change of seasons. From the four directions they come, bringing us messages and giving us strength. With one mind, we send our greetings and thanks to the Four Winds.

    Now our minds are one.

The Thunders

Now we turn to the west where our grandfathers, the Thunder Beings, live. With lightning and thundering voices, they bring with them the water that renews life. The lightning strikes the ground and renews the earth. The roaring thunders keep the giant beings underground. We bring our minds together as one to send greetings and thanks to our Grandfathers, the Thunders.

    Now our minds are one.

The Sun

We now send greetings and thanks to our eldest Brother, the Sun. Each day without fail he travels the sky from east to west, bringing the light of a new day. He is the source of all the fires of life. He lights the earth. With one mind, we send greetings and thanks to our Brother, the Sun.

Now our minds are one.

Grandmother Moon

We put our minds together to give thanks to our oldest Grandmother, the Moon, who lights the night-time sky. She is the leader of woman, and she also directs the movement of the ocean tides. By her changing face we measure time. It is our beautiful Grandmother Moon who watches over the arrival of children here on Earth. With one mind, we send greetings and thanks to our Grandmother, the Moon.

Now our minds are one.

The Stars

We give thanks to the Stars who are spread across the sky like jewellery. We see them in the night, helping the Moon to light the darkness. They bring the morning dew to the gardens, which also helps things to grow. When we travel at night, they guide us home. With our minds gathered together as one, we send greetings and thanks to the Stars.

Now our minds are one.

The Four Enlightened Protectors

We gather our minds to greet and thank the Enlightened Protectors who have come to help throughout the ages. When we forget how to live in harmony, they remind us of the way we were instructed to live as people. They also help us through trying times and shield us. With one mind, we send greetings and thanks to these caring beings.

    Now our minds are one.

The Creator

Now we turn our thoughts to the Creator, Great Mystery, the one who made us, and send greetings and thanks for all the gifts of Creation. Everything we need to live a good life is here on this Mother Earth. For all the love that is still around us, we gather our minds together as one and send our most beautiful words of thankfulness to the Creator.

    Now our minds are one.

Closing Words

We have now arrived at the place where we end our words. Of all the things we have named, it was not our intention to leave anything out. If something was forgotten, we leave it to each individual to send such greetings and thanks in their own way.

    Now our minds are one.

Unpacking Participatory Democracy in an Age of Reaction

Patrick Heller

We live in an age of reaction. Not since the inter-war period that saw the rise of fascism have we seen so many democracies in retreat, led no less by democratically elected leaders. From the USA to India and Brazil (representing three of the four most populous democracies in the world), duly elected leaders have attacked not only the foundational institutions of democracy but also its most defining ideals and values. In every case of reaction, populist leaders, in the name of an electoral plurality and posturing as the people incarnate, have assaulted the separation of powers (including the independence of the judiciary) and the autonomy of civil society, and eviscerated the very idea of citizenship by promoting the supremacy of a core, primary, nationalist identity (Heller 2020). This assault on institutions and citizenship has taken the form of a depressingly familiar strategic repertoire: demanding the loyalty of public officials to the person and not to the office of the executive, the politicisation of the rule of law, the demonisation of the other, the outsourcing of violence, the centralisation of power, and the wholesale substitution of democratic authority with rejuvenated forms of traditional class, ethnic, religious, and patriarchal power. These reactive regimes may never regress into authoritarian rule, that is, the actual suspension of formal electoral democracy. But they are nonetheless an assertion of authoritarian power marked by the executive capture of balancing institutions, the narrowing of spaces of open deliberation, and the closure of channels of participation for opposition forces. Which is precisely why it becomes so important to clearly and purposefully spell out the differences between formal electoral democracy and participatory democracy, and identify what a resurrected and more robust form of participatory democracy would actually look like. Many of the contributions to this volume do just that by pointing to real world cases. My goal is simply to provide some basic conceptual tools for thinking about participatory democracy in an age of reaction.

Democracy and Power

Definitions of democracy abound, but in a normative and procedural sense there is broad agreement that democracy is about popular control (*the people* are the sovereign) over public affairs on the basis of political equality. As anodyne as this definition might be, a closer scrutiny of these three defining elements immediately raises critical questions: Who are the people; what counts as public affairs; and what does political equality actually look like? All three of these concepts are fraught because by definition, any change or shift in their parameters marks a change in the distribution of power. The norm of universal suffrage (who gets to vote), so taken for granted today, was the outcome of extended struggle and conflict against fierce resistance from landed, gendered, and racial elites. And today, in all the reactive democracies, who even counts as a citizen is now being challenged, as in the case of Brexit, Donald Trump's assault on immigrants, Rodrigo Duterte's extra-judicial killings in the Philippines, and the Citizenship Amendment Act (CAA) in India. The central question of political economy—what counts as public affairs—has always been how far and how deeply democratic authority should extend in managing welfare and the economy, and in particular, redistributing wealth and opportunity. In an era of globalisation, that authority has been sharply compromised by the increasing sway of market forces. And there is probably no issue more challenging to the baseline definition of all modern democracies than the sobering recognition that the ideal of political equality—the principle of one person, one vote—is being profoundly and increasingly distorted by money and power in politics.

Highlighting these basic tensions between power and democracy brings us back to four very basic constitutive tensions of all democracies that make, and will always make, democracy an object of contention. *First*, all democracies that were not just imposed by external powers are basically born of revolutionary moments. This is because democracy, even in its most restricted baseline form (extending electoral representation to a newly empowered group) is a radical shift in the balance of power. The European democracies of the nineteenth century marked the political defeat of the aristocracy at the hands of an emerging bourgeoisie, and in the Global South, democracy was driven by liberation from colonialism. *Second*, the very idea at the core of democracy—putting power in the hands of the people through electoral accountability—represents a direct challenge to the entrenched and accumulated powers of dominant groups, and as such had to be continuously defended, and ideally, extended. This is because all powerful status or class groups, animated as they are by the logic of group reproduction, will always strive to capture political power to protect their interests and privileges. To the extent that democracy can block, or at least significantly increase, the costs of that capture, it is a radical event, a circuit breaker in a long history of elite hegemony.

Third, democracy can serve governance and justice only to the extent that it effectively authorises legitimate power. Large, complex societies have to be governed, and governing means leveraging power. The universal ideal of the autonomous and aspiring individual (and the groups they belong to) declares that when the people wield the formidable power of the State, that power must be carefully de-limited (the rule of law and constitutional protections), specifically and clearly authorised (the procedural requirements of the electoral and legislative process), and must be normatively grounded, that is, based on a process of decision-making that is open, inclusive, and deliberative. This requirement of normative grounding, which takes the law beyond its minimalist procedural correctness and endows it with normative legitimacy (the law becomes the *correct* and the *right* thing to do), requires a participatory democracy (Habermas 1996). *Fourth*, the original and necessary sin of all democracies was to have declared the legal equality of all against the sociological reality of deep inequalities of class and identity. Democracy was from the outset, as Martin Luther King famously said, a promissory note that had to be redeemed. The very idea of democracy was as such a challenge to all inequality-producing forms of power, and the project of democratic deepening can be defined as nothing less than realising the ideals of fraternity, liberty, and equality (Ambedkar 2018).

We can now return to our three defining elements of democracy: the people, public affairs, and political equality. Conventional definitions of electoral democracy take these elements for granted. The 'people' are treated as a pre-existing category, yet assaults on the very definition of who constitutes a citizen are at the heart of reaction (Hindutva, white supremacy, ethno-nationalism). The scope of public affairs is constrained by bourgeois-liberal ideas of private property and the private (patriarchal) realm. Yet the rise of the welfare

State and social rights in post-World War II Europe, and more recently in postcolonial democracies has popularised the idea of the socialisation of basic opportunities and the State's redistributive functions. It is telling that the age and wealth of a democracy are highly correlated with the share of its economy controlled by government spending (ranging from single digits in Africa and India to the 30–50 per cent in the OECD [Organisation for Economic Co-operation and Development] world). And political equality has simply been defined as the conferral of basic constitutional rights of speech, association, and public engagement, a premise that confuses legal status with actual practices. The problem here is not only the increasingly common problem of voter suppression and civil society repression (developments that clearly violate the most basic constitutional foundations of formal democracy), but the sociological reality that basic associational and deliberative resources are unevenly distributed across social and economic groups. Not all groups can organise and be heard collectively as effectively. As Schattschneider (1960) once famously quipped, the heavenly chorus of democracy has a strong upper-class (or caste) accent.

Given these challenges, both the classic ones of democratic deepening and the very current challenge of protecting even the most basic foundations of contemporary democracies, what lessons can we learn from experiences with participatory democracy?

We should begin with a definition. An increase in participatory democracy is defined by any increase in popular sovereignty. This, of course, begs the question of how 'the people' become empowered. This can happen along three axes. The *first* is simply expanding the demos itself, that is, the share of citizens, and in particular the share of those traditionally excluded or marginalised, that are active in democratic politics. The *second* is expanding the range of practices and settings in which participation can meaningfully take place.

The *third* is translating the expansion of the demos and the expansion of participatory inputs into tangible outcomes.

Let me elaborate on each of these three axes. Increasing the size and depth of the demos is the most basic and mainstream understanding of participatory democracy. This means quite literally increasing the percentage of citizens who actually participate in the democratic process and begins of course with voting and an electoral system that is representative. The common challenges here are tackling problems of pervasive malapportionment (the uneven electoral representation of different constituencies, such as the electoral college in the US), direct efforts at voter suppression, and low rates of electoral participation by subordinate groups. Some democracies such as India's do not have a problem with under-participation by subordinate groups as such, but do have a problem of subordinate groups lacking the resources, the networks, and the cultural capital to effectively organise collectively and build party organisations that represent their interests.

Political parties, regardless of their programmatic or ideological positions, tend to be dominated by elites. Historically, the exception to this has been the mass-based parties that emerged out of social movements. The early socialist parties in Europe were built on the strength of the union movement, the Workers' Party in Brazil emerged out of the broad and diverse civil society organisations, and the Communist Party of India (Marxist) (CPI[M]) in Kerala has deep roots in agrarian, caste, and worker movements. What these examples underscore is the importance of a robust subaltern civil society that prefigures political organisation. That is, it is in the trenches of local associational life — unions, women's groups, consumer groups, student associations — that the subaltern cultivate the organisational and discursive skills that can make them effective political actors (Roychowdhury 2020; Sanyal 2014).

This point ties directly into the second axis, which is expanding participatory spaces. In a robust constitutional democracy, citizens have associational and political rights, but where and how do they actually get to use those rights? Citizens can participate through social movements and in the trenches of civil society, but can they also participate in both formal and informal public spaces? The first, and maybe the most impaired, public space in the postcolonial South is local government. Colonial States were extractive and centralised and ruled through local elites, entrenching what Mamdani (1996) has called 'decentralised despotism'. Even after the passage of the Panchayti Raj constitutional amendments that mandated elections at the local level, local government in India remains so weak and under-capacitated that it is not clear what the people have been given sovereignty over. Absent deeper forms of decentralisation, citizens are afforded little, if any, say over a range of matters that impact them directly, including basic public services, local economic development, land management, education, and basic health. Materially and politically, local citizens remain dependent on State agencies at the state and centre levels, a relationship that is more bureaucratic than democratic. Moreover, if we recall the point made by classic theorists of democracy, from Aristotle to Alexis De Tocqueville, that local government is a school for democracy, then the absence of genuine local democracy not only in effect defaults local power to traditional elites, but also deprives subordinate groups of the opportunity to develop their associational capabilities and to effectively leverage their rights.

The question of participatory spaces also extends beyond elections in two critical ways. On the one hand, citizens need to be given spaces other than just elections to shape democratic outcomes. When citizens vote in elections, they are voting to delegate power. Elections are a very blunt instrument of accountability and elected representatives and parties often have their own interests to protect. Direct citizen influence can be extended between elections by creating a wide range of participatory forums that have both indirect and direct power over policy, representatives, and officials. Indirect power or simply 'influence' consists of all the spaces of public engagement through which citizens, movements, civil society organisations, and the full range of interest groups can make their voices heard. Expanding participatory spaces—be they formal and structured (gram panchayats, social audits) or informal and contentions (protests)—can deepen and diversify the public sphere as a sounding board for new claims and as a court of public opinion for adjudicating the 'rightness' of these claims. Although politicians and officials have their own priorities, it is difficult to discount or ignore issues that garner significant public attention. Its gelatinous qualities aside, the public sphere can play a key role in problematising previously unproblematised issues, generate new information, expose malfeasance, invigorate new norms, and put pressure on power centres. The history of the Mazdoor Kisan Shakti Sangathan (MKSS), which scaled up from village-level protests against corruption into a full-blown constitutional reform, the Right to Information Act, all through the classic communicative and mobilisational repertoires of a social movement, is a case in point (Roy 2018).

Of course, the public sphere is no panacea, just a bullhorn for accentuated voices, which in its routinised form reflects the greater resources and symbolic power of dominant groups. But in any democracy with a vibrant civil society that nurtures a wide range of contestatory mini-publics (Fraser 1992), the public sphere can be readily disrupted by subaltern voices. As the history of social movements has shown, the public sphere can amplify the one resource all subordinate groups have, namely communicative power, and in particular the power to make claims based on moral suasion. The recent CAA protests are a case in point, a classic instance of communicative action organised around public displays of principled commitment to core democratic values. As

Habermas (1996) has argued, democratic public spheres are always predicated on exclusions, but by their own bourgeois constitutional normative pretensions, are always open to arguments by the excluded demanding inclusion.

Beyond the public sphere, there are also more formal and power-conferring participatory spaces. Indeed, in the past three decades we have seen a proliferation of important initiatives to expand points of direct citizen or civil society access to decision-making. This includes participatory budgeting, which started in Brazil but has spread widely, as well as a range of participatory forums in health, education, and other sectors (Baiocchi, et al. 2011). In India, the People's Campaign for Decentralized Planning in Kerala is one of the best documented and deepest expansions in participatory government anywhere in the world, and the social audits first pioneered by MKSS as part of the movement for the Right To Information (RTI) have now become a critical part of the machinery for strengthening local democracy in many Indian states. Beyond these well-known cases, there has been an explosion of ad-hoc or localised efforts to give citizens or civil society organisations a greater say in shaping public policy, from the now ubiquitous stakeholder forums in the environmental sector to mandated citizen inputs in policymaking arenas (see collected cases in Fung and Wright 2003). In the European Union, across a wide range of sectors, civil society participation has become the norm in developing new regulatory structures. During the United Progressive Alliance (UPA) government in India (2004–2014), the National Advisory Committee (NAC) created a unique and highly effective channel through which movements and civil society actors could take a direct role in shaping transformative national legislation. Finally, a third set of participatory spaces takes the form of new modes of continuous accountability that afford citizens and other actors more opportunities to hold officials accountable between elections. Most famously, this includes the Right to information Act (RTI), but across many democracies there have been sustained efforts to promote transparency, including ambitious new legal frameworks for continuous accountability and feedback.

The third axis for promoting participation is strengthening the chain of sovereignty, that is, ensuring that participatory inputs that flow from deliberation and through institutional venues are actually translated into tangible outcomes. The chain of sovereignty is about institutional design, the robustness of the State machinery, and especially its bureaucracy, and constant monitoring and accountability. The chain of sovereignty can be broken down into three stages. The first has to do with increasing the strength and weight of inputs from participatory actors, a point that begins with expanding formal participatory spaces and points of access, but then has to be translated into formal and binding decisions. This is key because all too often, what is celebrated as 'participation' is more about consultation or exercising voice without necessarily binding public officials to the participatory inputs. The second stage is about attaching and mobilising actual resources—be they fiscal, legal, or bureaucratic—to the decision. The pervasive problem here is that frequently, new policies or commitments fail to deliver simply because the necessary resources do not materialise. In the long chain of delivery that is any modern State (but especially the Indian State), fiscal and bureaucratic resources have to be mobilised across different agencies and have to flow through multiple checkpoints, and there is often a huge gap between what was originally committed (if anything) and what materialises at the point of implementation.[1]

Finally, the third and weakest chain is what is often referred to simply as the last mile. Even if participatory decisions are binding and money and resources flow, they still have to be used effectively at the point of delivery. Whether this is a matter of getting resources to specific entities or individuals or effectively coordinating the delivery of a public good, it requires intensive monitoring. This can come from above through conventional methods of bureaucratic accountability, but can also be much strengthened from below through participation by beneficiaries or civil society actors. Partners can in turn play a critical role in the co-production of the policy or service. Examples here abound: social audits to ensure that workers get their NREGA (National Rural Employment Guarantee Act) payments; unions that enforce labour standards in the workplace; citizens and environmentalists who expose polluters; and women who find a way to rouse the State into actually abiding with its own domestic violence laws (Roychowdhury 2020). The broader point about the chain of sovereignty is this: no matter how good the State machinery might be—and more often than not, it suffers from critical bottlenecks and under-capacitation when it comes to delivering effectively—resolving the last mile problem requires a lot of innovative design (for example, RTI and other measures of accountability), as well as continuous participation at all stages of delivery.

Challenges

In the literature on participatory democracy, the metaphor of the pincer movement has become common. To make effective changes, one needs a fortuitous combination of both mobilisation from below—that is, having subordinate groups organise and make claims—and openings from above—the support of reformist actors in the State, which could be officials or political parties, or both. These are contingent coalitions that can pry open new spaces and decisively effect change. The NAC is a case in point. Movements created pressure for rights-based welfare, a political party faction (Sonia Gandhi and her allies) provided an opening, and then, with help from other key elite actors in the polity and the bureaucracy, a slew of rights-based legislation was passed. But we should not confuse these successful moments of participation with the longer-term project of building participatory democracy. The latter requires simultaneous improvements in both organisation (the traditional focus of participation literature) and institutional reforms that make the State more accountable, more accessible, and more effective.

Making progress on both fronts begins with a sober appreciation of the obstacles at hand, and in particular the complex relationship between participation and power. There are two fundamental problems here. The first has to do with the horizontal problem of unequal associational capacity. These capacities are highly unevenly distributed across social groups, both in material and in organisational-cultural terms. The second has to do with the vertical problem of where and on what terms citizens and CSOs engage the State. Not only is the State often insular and secretive, but it is also sometimes just plain impossible to find. And when one does engage the State, it is often more as a client or a supplicant, rather than as a rights-bearing citizen. If the horizontal challenge calls for new modes of collective action, including developing new movement repertoires, coalition building, and exploiting openings in the political opportunity structure, the vertical challenge requires careful and often laborious institutional designs geared towards expanding the democratic institutional surface area of the State.

Calls for greater participatory democracy are often dismissed as idealistic, impractical, or just politically impossible in highly unequal societies. But in an age of reaction, when even the most basic institutional and normative foundations of democracy are under assault, it is more essential than ever to invest in strengthening the participatory basis of democratic practices. An expansion and deepening of the demos brings in new actors who have the greatest stake in democracy. Broadening the scope of public affairs democratises social and economic contexts that otherwise reproduce power. And strengthening the opportunities and effects of political participation marks not only an investment in the most fundamental of human capabilities—associational freedom—but also vitally contributes to the institutional robustness of democratic decision-making. Taken together, deepening and extending participation are critical to realising the normative promise of empowering citizens with effective rights and grounding the legitimacy of democratic rule.

Note

1. See in particular the studies conducted by the Accountability Initiative at the Centre for Policy Research.

Select References

Ambedkar, Bhimrao Ramji. 2018. 'Annihilation of Caste', in Valerian Rodrigues (ed.), *The Essential Writings of B.R. Ambedkar*, 263–305. New Delhi: Oxford University Press.

Baiocchi, Gianpaolo, Patrick Heller, and Marcelo K Silva. 2011. *Bootstrapping Democracy: Transforming Local Governance and Civil Society in Brazil*. Stanford, California: Stanford University Press.

Fraser, Nancy. 1992. 'Rethinking the Public Sphere: A Contribution to the Critique of Actually Existing Democracy', in Craig Calhoun (ed.), *Habermas and the Public Sphere*, 109–143. Cambridge: MIT Press.

Fung, Archon, and Erik O. Wright. 2003. *Deepening Democracy: Institutional Innovations in Empowered Participatory Governance*. London: Verso.

Habermas, Jürgen. 1996. *Between Facts and Norms: Contributions to a Discourse Theory of Law and Democracy*, Studies in Contemporary German Social Thought. Cambridge, Mass.: MIT Press.

Heller, Patrick. 2020. 'The Age of Reaction: Retrenchment Populism in India and Brazil', *International Sociology* 35 (6), 590–609.

Mamdani, Mahmood. 1996. *Citizen and Subject: Decentralized Despotism and the Legacy of Late Colonialism*. New Delhi: Oxford University Press.

Roy, Aruna. 2018. *The RTI Story: Power to the People*. New Delhi: Roli Books Private Limited.

Roychowdhury, Poulami. 2020. *Capable Women, Incapable States: Negotiating Violence and Rights in India*. New Delhi: Oxford University Press.

Sanyal, P. 2014. *Credit to Capabilities: A Sociological Study of Microcredit Groups in India*. Cambridge: Cambridge University Press.

Schattschneider, E. E. 1960. *The Semisovereign People: A Realist's View of Democracy in America*. New York: Holt, Rinehart, and Winston.

Participation, Citizenship, and the Renewal of Social Democracy in the Time of Covid-19

John Harriss

It has become almost commonplace to refer to the way in which the coronavirus pandemic has exposed and exacerbated deep social problems that have to do fundamentally with the ways in which capitalist development has taken place. On the one hand, there has come about a massive concentration of corporate power and soaring wealth inequality—in part, at least, the consequences of the ways in which capitalism has been 'rigged' in favour of rentier interests. In India, for example, there is a marked concentration of capital in the telecom industry, and now in the ownership of airports—both sectors in which State policy exercises considerable influence in determining the winners (see Mukherjee 2020)—and the top 1 per cent of the population has secured a greater share of national economic growth than even its peers in the United States and in China (see Therborn 2020). On the other hand, there is abundant evidence of the increasing precariousness of the lives and livelihoods of a majority of people in all our societies. In the United Kingdom, for instance, the numbers of those employed on 'zero hours contracts', with no livelihood security, have increased sharply; in India, adding to the precariousness of the 90 per cent of the labour force employed in informal activities, there is the continuing trend of increasing employment in the formal sector of contract workers who have little job security and minimal benefits. The prospects for the middle classes have dimmed, whether in the United States or the UK, or in India (ibid.); the working classes are ever more fragmented and their organisations have nothing like the clout that once they exercised. Workers very widely confront the long-term threats to meaningful employment that are presented by automation and digital technology, in addition to the consequences of the extensive privatisation of what were 'public services'.

The pandemic has brutally exacerbated these existing trends. Jeff Bezos of Amazon saw his personal wealth increase by $34.6 billion, from the start of the pandemic till 4 June 2020 (Brenner 2020, 19), and his company and just four others (Microsoft, Alphabet, Facebook, and Apple) accounted for a very large share of the surge in the US stock market in the summer of 2020 (Faroohar 2020), while the wealth of India's billionaires rose by over a third during the COVID-19 lockdown (*The Wire* 2020). At the same time, many millions have suffered the loss of their livelihoods as a result of the lockdowns imposed by governments. A telling indicator is that the World Food Program estimates that the numbers of people in the world experiencing crisis-level hunger may increase by as much as 80 per cent over the levels of 2019 (Oxfam 2020). Although the virus itself does not discriminate between rich and poor, there are, of course, big differences between them in terms of access to good healthcare, more so in some societies than in others; and there is no doubt that poorer people, depending on low-skilled and manual work, as well as young people generally, and women, suffered more than others in the circumstances of lockdown. Older men, employed in professional occupations, have usually been at a relative advantage in coping with the consequences of the pandemic. Government actions, whether in the United States or in India—although some countries have done better—have favoured big business interests, while offering relatively little help to poor people.[1]

The evidence of increasing inequality and of human suffering in the pandemic has led to a reaction against these developments among policy thinkers. One instance is in the call by the then Director of the London School of Economics, Minouche Shafik, for a new social contract. This, she argues, should include greater protection for people at work, although combined with support for labour market flexibility; universal essential healthcare coverage (estimated to require expenditure equivalent to about 5 per cent of the GDP); investment in, and improvement of, education and training (necessary to reduce the numbers of those depending on low-skill labour, for whom there will be fewer and fewer jobs); and the achievement of greater intergenerational equity by increasing the working age (Shafik 2020). Finance for measures such as these, it has been suggested, might be raised through wealth taxes (Sandhu 2020), and a striking finding in regard to India is that a tax of just 4 per cent on the wealth of the 953 wealthiest Indian entities (0.0004 per cent of all Indian households) would raise additional revenue equivalent to 1 per cent of GDP (Subramanian 2020).

The crisis has led to a recognition of the need for a shift from the almost exclusive focus on individual liberties, encouraged under neoliberalism—and reflected in a chronic form in the assertions by some people that the imposition of rules about using face masks during the pandemic represents an infringement of their personal liberties—back to the idea of our responsibilities to fellow human beings. What is needed is a renewal of the values of citizenship—the recognition that as citizens, we share in a collective endeavour, in which we have responsibilities towards each other, and in relation to the State, to which we look for our security (in a social contract).

If we recognise the ties that bind us to others, then we should be concerned about the abilities of our fellow citizens, as well as of ourselves, to lead flourishing lives.[2]

These arguments point to a politics grounded in values of equality/fairness and of community/solidarity, as well as of democracy/freedom, as these were articulated by the radical American sociologist, the late Erik Olin Wright (2019). A just society, Wright argued, is one in which all persons have broadly equal access to the material and social means necessary to live a flourishing life; they ought to cooperate with each other not simply because of how they personally benefit, but because they are committed to the well-being of others—a commitment that is of value both because of its connection to human welfare and because of its role in fostering equality and democracy. A fully democratic society is one in which people have more or less equal access to the means of participation in decisions concerning things that affect their lives. The social and economic trends that have been so exposed by the coronavirus pandemic show that capitalism (the market economy with private ownership of capital), for all its dynamism and the ways in which it has made possible remarkable innovation and enormous increases in productivity—from which human beings can benefit—also creates conditions that are in conflict with the values of fairness, solidarity, and freedom. For Wright, the task—given the history of the failure of twentieth-century revolutions to establish democratic, egalitarian, emancipatory alternatives to capitalism—is to find the political means of 'eroding' capitalism. This, he argues, may be achieved through a combination of strategies: initiatives from above, 'dismantling' (installing elements of socialism) and 'taming' capitalism (making it subject to significant regulation and redistribution—which is what actually happened in the West, after World War II, in the period that was usefully described as that of 'embedded liberalism'), together with strategies from below, 'resistance' (as has been demonstrated in the many protest movements of recent years), and 'escape' (through non-capitalist institutions such as cooperatives).

Wright's position is comparable with that of an earlier thinker, Karl Polanyi, whose ideas resonate in the context of the present crisis. Polanyi also looked to temper the capitalist market economy by regulation, not to the suppression of markets. Then, he said:

> The passing of the market economy [in our own times, we might say 'the passing of the kind of market fundamentalism associated with neoliberalism'] can become the beginning of an era of unprecedented freedom … regulation and control can achieve freedom not only for the few, but for all. Freedom not as an appurtenance of privilege, but as a prescriptive right extending far beyond the narrow confines of the political sphere into the intimate organisation of society itself. (Polanyi 2001 [1944], 265)

Polanyi thought that there was a possibility of 'the beginning of an era of unprecedented freedom' as a result of the world crisis of the years of the Great Depression and then of World War II. The crisis was caused, he believed—and as he explained in his book—by the failure, due its internal contradictions, of the effort to establish a liberal market economy that had begun in the first half of the nineteenth century.

Somewhat similarly, there are those now who think that the crisis brought about by the coronavirus pandemic has finally exposed the failure of the more contemporary effort to establish what Polanyi called the 'market economy', under neoliberalism (or 'market fundamentalism'), over the last forty years. It seemed possible to a good many observers at the time that the financial crisis of 2008 would bring about the rolling back of neoliberalism. But it did not happen then, as governments bailed out the big financial institutions that were in difficulty (they were held to be 'too big to fail'), eventually allowed bankers to continue to benefit from still enormous bonuses, and proceeded to pursue policies of austerity, trying to cut public expenditure so as to restore macroeconomic balances. Now, it seems possible, with governments having to intervene extensively and spending money as never before outside of wartime, and with so much very clearly depending on the competence of government (think, say, of the contrasts between Germany and UK in the pandemic), that at last the era of market fundamentalism is over. In Canada, certainly, the emergency benefit provided by government represents a big step toward a national guaranteed basic income — a policy that Erik Olin Wright believed was an important component of economic democracy.

The globalisation that market fundamentalism did so much to bring about has been called into question as never before, as countries (like India) seek to become more self-reliant. This crisis has also exposed the severe limitations of private provisioning of what used to be or should be public goods, including healthcare. The failings of the healthcare system in the United States, exposed by the pandemic, have 'reinforced the argument that Americans would have better health care and pay less in taxes if they had more public health care' (Micklethwaite and Wooldridge 2020). Prominent among proposals about how economies can best be rebuilt in the aftermath of the coronavirus crisis are ideas about public investment in environmental sustainability (as in the 'clean energy' agenda proposed by former US President Joe Biden; see Brower, et al. [2020]).

While there are grounds for welcoming the more assertive role that States have taken on, there is also reason to fear the ways in which the pandemic has enhanced their surveillance capacities and brought about greater centralisation of power, even alongside massive failures of coordination across levels of the State, reflected in the extent to which the responses of governments are associated with their top leaders, whether Donald Trump or Justin Trudeau, or Narendra Modi or Angela Merkel. This, even though the pandemic, has shown how important the capacities of the lower levels of government are—in India, the progress of the pandemic was crucially influenced by the differing capacities of states and city corporations, and even of panchayats. There was absolutely no certainty that once the pandemic was over, or at least clearly under control, there would not be a reversion to business as usual. Powerful voices have articulated the case for measures to cut fiscal deficits, and with widespread concerns about inflation, there are moves back to the pursuit of austerity, even while the increase in corporate concentration allows for the accumulation of rents by a few. Resistance and opposition, and efforts to reconstruct the capitalist economy through such means as introducing measures to promote competition (as, for example, by breaking up corporations that monopolise large marketplaces of their own making, as Jio threatens to do in India), have been and continue to be drained by the nationalist appeals of populist political leaders in India, whose approval ratings have continued to be extraordinarily high in spite of the suffering that has been caused to so many people by the government's handling of the coronavirus pandemic, and the evidence of its failure in regard to economic development.

For all the pressures there will be to return to 'business as usual', however, governments, whether autocratic ones or those in democracies, are not going to find it easy to deal with popular demands for change. Fairness as well as competence have risen up the hierarchy of qualities that people look for in their governments. The pandemic reminded citizens of their mutual interdependence—and of the importance for everyone, for instance, of so many 'lowly' and poorly paid service occupations, in shops and public transport as well as in hospitals and care homes. This is a moment of possibility, therefore, of movement toward what Erik Olin Wright and Karl Polanyi before him thought of as a just society, where freedom is not just an 'appurtenance of privilege', as Polanyi put it. Neither of these thinkers uses the term 'social democracy'. Wright speaks rather of 'socialism as economic democracy'. Yet both are talking about a politics that has been realised in the past by social democrats, whose aim has been to temper or to 'tame' the capitalist market economy in seeking social justice by democratic means.

Social democratic politics has been successful notably— though not exclusively—in Scandinavia. The Swedish scholar Olle Tornquist, reflecting on the Scandinavian experience, and that of some other countries (including Kerala, in India), has argued that there have been four dimensions in social democratic development (Tornquist 2016, 10):

- broad popular interests and ideas translating into the formation and organisation of democratic political collectivities;
- strong democratic linkages between State and society;
- struggle for universal civil, political, and social rights, and related welfare policies, as well as rights based on work;
- development of growth coalitions/social pacts between sections of capital and labour, as well as between labour and agricultural producers.

Social democracy builds upon and extends participatory democracy. This is what is required for the formation of what Tornquist refers to as 'democratic political collectivities', and only where there are such collectivities—democratic organisations of citizens in civil society—are there strong linkages between State and society. Patrick Heller argued in the same vein at the Montreal conference on 'Unpacking Participatory Democracy' when he spoke of the need for 'increasing the surface area of contact between citizens and the state'. The third of the dimensions that Tornquist describes—struggles for universal civil, political, and social rights—may, he has gone on to argue, be a way in which democratic political collectivities can be formed. This is a point to which we will return.

Latterly, however, social democratic parties have been in retreat, even in Scandinavia. The problems that social democrats have confronted are well summed up by Erik Olin Wright: 'Much of the progressive reformism of social democracy came from the influence of the labour movement [among Tornquist's 'democratic political collectivities'] on social democratic politics, and one of the reasons for the decline of anti-capitalism within social democracy is the decay of labour militancy in resisting capitalism' (Wright 2019, 57). The decay of labour militancy can be understood as both cause and effect of the ways in which social democratic parties in Western Europe, such as the Labour Party in the UK, have made concessions to market fundamentalism, for example by promoting further privatisation in public services. History will not be put into reverse, however, and it is most unlikely that labour organisations will ever again be able to play the central role that they had in the twentieth century in the 'taming' of capitalism. The idea of the 'working class' had meaning when large numbers of men (and it was mainly men) shared in places and conditions of work. Those conditions have changed, as the nature of work itself has changed, for example with so many more people being employed in service occupations. The Marxian expectation of the increasing homogenisation and increasing solidarity of the working class (so that it becomes a 'class-for-itself') has not been realised as labour has become increasingly segmented. The 'working class' is now fragmented. In India, for instance, it has recently been argued that the manual labour force is itself deeply divided by class differences (Parry 2019). Generally, the balance of power between capital and labour has shifted quite dramatically in favour of the former.

The fragmentation of the working class is of course not a reason for giving up on labour organisation (as Wright seemed to). There are, for instance, upstart unions in Britain and the US, which are taking on the gig economy (Staton

2020). The struggle for economic and social rights will be advanced by the development of social movement unionism, in which unions engage more directly in the public arena and form coalitions with other civil society actors, recognising that the commoditisation of society and the environment affects all strata of society. Labour organisation is under enormous pressure, but the context of the increasing precariousness of employment produces greater incentives now for higher wage employees to find common cause with contract employees and informal workers. There are signs, for example, both in India and in South Africa, of this kind of development taking place. Union action—as in the general strikes that have been called by all the major Indian trade union federations working together in the recent past—is to make demands upon the State for social rights and fair public services. A social floor of minimum income and social security benefits, such as the federations now struggle for, would have the effect of empowering informal workers, and a levelling up of the living standards of all working people would increase their market-based bargaining power. In India, and across the world, there is an even stronger case now, in the context of COVID-19, for State provision of a universal basic income that is not a substitute for the public provisioning of healthcare and other services. Mobilisation around demands for social rights supplies a better base for broad unity than the workplace issues that have been the focus of union activity in the past. And social movement unionism can also be the basis of an active democratic society, taking participation beyond the limitations of representative democracy (the central theme of the 'Unpacking Participatory Democracy' project).

But are there other collective actors with the capacity to sustain the challenge to neoliberal capitalism, which must be carried on if there is to be movement toward a more just society in a post-COVID world? This was the problem with which Erik Olin Wright struggled at the end of his life, as he battled with illness. For all the extent of protest in the world today—as has been said, 'street protests have replaced parliaments as the main arena of opposition'[3]—it remains inchoate. Wright argues, 'Ultimately ... the strategy of eroding capitalism depends upon the existence of a web of collective actors anchored in civil society *and political parties* committed to such a political project' (Wright 2019, 121; emphasis added. This recalls Tornquist's statement regarding the pillars of social democracy, referred to above). There has to be sustained and therefore organised effort to change the rules of the game by gaining State power, and this has been lacking in the many protest movements (with partial exceptions, such as that of the 'Podemos' movement that arose from the street protests in Spain in 2011, which has given rise to a radical political party; see Gari [2020]). In the past, social democratic parties built their capacity to change the rules of the game on 'a web of collective actors anchored in civil society', including trade unions, women's organisations, and a whole range of local associations—as happened notably in Scandinavia and in Kerala in India (see Tornquist and Harriss 2016). How is such a web to be constructed now?

There is no simple answer to this critically important question, and Wright does not specify any particular collective actor or combination of them, but rather discusses how identity, interests, and values, and their intersections, provide the basis for the formation of collective actors. In the end, he seems to suggest that it is the sharing of values—those of fairness, solidarity, and democracy—'that can create political unity across diverse identities and interests' (Burawoy 2019, 156). Wright argues, for instance, that although 'Oppressed racial minorities have identity-interests in ending racial discrimination and domination', which are not the same as working-class interests, and although there may be tensions between the identity interests of the two groups, 'both sets of interests share the egalitarian value of equal access to the material and social means necessary to live a flourishing life' (Wright 2019, 138). This is an important argument, certainly, although it has proven so difficult, historically, to bring together the struggles of African-Americans, say, or of Dalits, with those of other working people. And the greatest challenge that efforts to construct a web of collective actors engaged in a struggle to erode capitalism now confront is the power of exclusionary identities, fostered by populist leaders.

Wright advances another, complementary argument, however, which is that 'struggles to "democratize democracy" are pivotal in eroding capitalism' (Wright 2019, 112). This is of huge importance in the conjuncture of the pandemic, because the economic and social trends referred to at the beginning of this chapter, which have been exposed and exacerbated by the coronavirus, provided fertile ground for populist political leaders who have gone on to do a great deal to undermine democracy. The United States, India, and Brazil—countries with prominent and notably populist leaders who are strongly inclined to authoritarianism— have all been found by the V-Dem Institute, which reports each year on the state of democracy across the world, to be 'substantially declining' on its liberal democracy index. India, indeed, has by now become what V-Dem calls an 'electoral autocracy' (V-Dem Institute 2024). The prior struggle at the moment is to oppose these political trends and to work for the revitalising and deepening of democracy. This matters in turn for the erosion of neoliberal capitalism because democratic deepening has the potential to dilute the inherently capitalist character of the State apparatus, given the dependence of the State on the capitalist economy for revenues, and elite bias in the recruitment of powerful State officials. States also have to secure legitimacy, however, and the more they are subject to democratic forces, the greater the likelihood of their intervening to regulate capitalism in the interests of the wider society (indeed, to protect society against the consequences of market fundamentalism, exactly as Polanyi showed to have happened in the late nineteenth and early twentieth centuries).

An answer to the question of how the web of collective actors committed to the project of anti-capitalism can be constructed is perhaps to be found, therefore, in struggles for 'democratizing democracy'. Collective actors are formed, after all, in processes of struggle. Working together with others for democratic freedoms can build solidarity between people and further the quest for a just society. Erik Olin Wright's ideas about the means of deepening democracy resonate with those of many activists in India and elsewhere. He discusses, first, the importance of democratically empowered decentralisation, both because of its practical value in regard to effective problem-solving, and because 'meaningful popular participation is also much easier at smaller scales of government (and) likewise opens up the possibility of vigorous democratic experimentalism with high levels of citizen involvement' (Wright 2019, 113). He will certainly have had in mind the example of the People's Planning Campaign in Kerala, discussed in his earlier book, *Deepening Democracy* (2003)[4]. Decentralisation of political power, however, is not enough to deepen democracy, not least because 'local levels of government can be corrupt and authoritarian, run by political machines organized around patronage'. There has to be a deepening of democracy at these local levels, together with 'giving such units the necessary power and resources to do things' (Wright 2019, 114) within a framework of coordination between these units, and across levels of government. An innovation that accomplishes some of these objectives is that of participatory budgeting, a particular instance of a new form of citizen participation. Another to which Wright refers is the random selection of citizens to participate in decision-making bodies, extending the principle of sortition that is the basis of the jury system in many countries. A legislative body constituted by citizens selected at random would more accurately reflect the population than those formed by election, which are usually filled by people who are relatively privileged. Wright's idea here is not to do away with electoral democracy, but to supplement it (as, for example, in the suggestions in the UK for the formation of the second chamber of Parliament by sortition rather than by a combination of hereditary privilege and nepotistic appointment). Electoral rules are badly in need of reform in many countries, and perhaps nowhere more so than in the United States.

Democratic deepening and the formation of the web of collective actors committed to the erosion of capitalism are clearly interdependent. Both may gain from what is effectively a reversal of the sequence of development in Scandinavia. There, the achievement of economic and social rights followed from the mobilisation of a web of collective actors in a broad-based political movement. Now, in countries like India, Brazil, Indonesia, and South Africa, the struggle for the realisation of economic and social rights—for rights to health and education, to a livelihood, to food and decent housing—has brought together people from disparate social groups, finding common cause in placing programmatic demands upon the State. We may take heart from the fact that a common refrain in many of the protest movements in recent years has been 'We want better public services'— or, in other words, effective non-market provisioning. The struggle has to be for the establishment of the rights of all people as citizens, entitled to impartial governance and fair public services delivered by non-market means, and not for targeted interventions that have the character of charity for the poor. The struggle is important in itself, and because it has the potential of building a broad-based political movement and creating an active democratic society, it may strengthen democratic structures in society and lead to the establishing of stronger linkages between State and society.

There was a historical moment in the time of the United Progressive Alliance (UPA) government in India, between 2004 and 2014, when democratic participation in struggles over economic and social rights was encouraged, thanks to what was called 'the new rights agenda' (Ruparelia 2013), established with the passage of the Right to Information Act and the National Rural Employment Guarantee Act, both in 2005, and then the Forest Rights Act of 2006, the Right to Education Act of 2009, and the National Food Security Act of 2013. What was missing, however, was a broad, united front in which different social interests came together around an agenda of transformation, or a national political party with a thorough-going social democratic programme. The need for such a party is even greater now, to carry on the prior struggle against the ascendancy of an exclusivist, majoritarian nationalism.

Acknowledgements

For gifts of encouragement and criticism, I am grateful to Leslie Armijo, Teddy Brett, Nate Roberts, Ashwin Subramanian, and Olle Tornquist.

Notes

1. On the United States, see Brenner (2020); on India, see Harriss (2020).

2. This was the argument of the eminent *Financial Times* commentator, Martin Wolf. See Wolf (2020).

3. This is the subtitle of an article by Simon Kuper; see Kuper (2020).

4. The chapter on the Kerala case is by Thomas Isaac and Patrick Heller.

Select References

Brenner, Robert. 2020. 'Escalating Plunder', *New Left Review* 123, 5–22.

Brower, Derek, Myles McCormick, and Lauren Fedor. 2020. 'Biden promises $2tn green energy and infrastructure plan'. *Financial Times*, 15 July. Available at https://www.ft.com/content/8cae665f-4910-4cdd-91ea-f58c4ce5afbf (accessed September 2024).

Burawoy, Michael. 2019. 'Afterword', in Erik Olin Wright, *How to be an Anti-capitalist in the 21st Century*. London and New York: Verso.

Faroohar, Rana. 2020. 'Big tech, neoliberalism and what comes next'. *Financial Times*, 27 July. Available at https://www.ft.com/content/31bab53a-b27a-419f-a592-8eee6d5b860e (accessed September 2024).

Fung, Archon, and Erik Olin Wright (eds). 2003. *Deepening Democracy: Institutional Innovations in Empowered Prticipatory Governance*. London: Verso.

Gari, Manuel. 2020. 'Sunset for Podemos: A Farewell'. *The Bullet*, 1 October. Available at https://socialistproject.ca/2020/10/sunset-for-podemos-a-farewell/#more (accessed September 2024).

Harriss, John. 2020. '"Responding to an epidemic requires a compassionate State". How has the Indian State been doing in the time of covid-19?'. *Journal of Asian Studies* 79 (3).

Kuper, Simon. 2020. 'From America to Zimbabwe, the world is taking to the streets'. *Financial Times*, 20 August.

Micklethwaite, John, and Adrian Wooldridge. 2020. 'The virus should wake up the West', Bloomberg, 13 April. Available at https://www.bloomberg.com/opinion/articles/2020-04-13/coronavirus-pandemic-is-wake-up-call-to-reinvent-the-state (accessed September 2024).

Mukherjee, Andy. 2020. 'After Ambani, it's Adani who's beginning to carve up India's post-Covid business monopoly'. *The Print*, 25 August. Available at https://theprint.in/economy/after-ambani-its-adani-whos-beginning-to-carve-up-indias-post-covid-business-monopoly/488783/ (accessed September 2024).

Oxfam. 2020. 'The Hunger Virus: How Covid-19 is Fuelling Hunger in a Hungry World', 9 July. Available at https://oxfamilibrary.openrepository.com/bitstream/handle/10546/621023/mb-the-hunger-virus-090720-en.pdf (accessed September 2024).

Parry, Jonathan. 2019. *Classes of Labour: Work and Life in a Central Indian Steel Town*. New Delhi: Social Science Press.

Polanyi, Karl. 2001 [1944]. *The Great Transformation: The Political and Economic Origins of Our Times*. Boston: Beacon Press.

Ruparelia, Sanjay. 2013. 'India's New Rights Agenda: Genesis, Promises and Risks'. *Pacific Affairs* 86 (3), 569–590.

Sandbu, Martin. 2020. *The Economics of Belonging*. Princeton, NJ and London: Princeton University Press.

Shafik, Minouche. 2020. 'Redesigning society after Covid-19'. *Financial Times*, 10 July. Available at https://www.ft.com/content/0c44b7cf-b3fe-4b45-8f55-0275358b8414 (accessed September 2024).

Staton, Bethan. 2020. 'The upstart unions taking on the gig economy'. *Financial Times*, 19 January.

Subramanian, S. 2020. 'Doing the maths: Why India should introduce a Covid wealth tax on the ultra-rich'. *Scroll.in*, 16 April. Available at https://scroll.in/article/959314/doing-the-maths-why-india-should-introduce-a-covid-wealth-tax-on-=the-ultra-rich (accessed September 2024).

Therborn, Goran. 2020. 'Dreams and Nightmares of the World's Middle Classes'. *New Left Review* 124, 63–87, Table 2.

The Wire. 2020. 'Wealth of Indian Billionaires Rose by Over a Third During the Covid-19 Lockdown', 16 October. Available at https://thewire.in/business/indian-billionaires-wealth-rose-during-covid (accessed September 2024).

Tornquist, Olle. 2016. 'Social Democratic Development', in Olle Tornquist and John Harriss (eds), *Reinventing Social Democratic Development: Insights from Indian and Scadinavian Comparisons*. Copenhagen: NIAS Press.

V-Dem Institute. 2024. *Democracy Winning and Losing at the Ballot*. Democracy Report 2024, University of Gothenburg, Sweden. Available at https://www.v-dem.net/documents/44/v-dem_dr2024_highres.pdf (accessed February 2025).

Wolf, Martin. 2019. 'Why rigged capitalism is damaging liberal democracy'. *Financial Times*, 18 September. Available at https://www.ft.com/content/5a8ab27e-d470-11e9-8367-807ebd53ab77 (accessed September 2024).

_____. 2020. 'Democracy will fail if we don't think as citizens'. *Financial Times*, 6 July. Available at https://www.ft.com/content/36abf9a6-b838-4ca2-ba35-2836bd0b62e2 (accessed September 2024).

Wright, Erik Olin. 2019. *How to be an Anti-capitalist in the 21st Century*. London and New York: Verso.

DECENTRALISATION FOR CREATING LOCAL DEMOCRATIC SPACE
The Case of the People's Plan Campaign in Kerala

T. M. THOMAS ISAAC

Democratisation is the process of creating a social space for deliberation and participation in public decision-making and public action, subject to the principle of subsidiarity. Parliamentary democracy at the federal and regional levels is often limited to the right to participate in periodic elections. Importantly, it also provides a set of valuable democratic rights like freedom of expression, faith and association, and equality. These rights are important for the poor in their struggle against exploitation and in the creation of a more just socioeconomic system. E. M. S. Namboodiripad (1978), in his note of dissent to the Ashok Mehta Committee Report on Panchayati Raj Institutions, stated:

> Defense of Parliamentary democracy at Central and State level (where it exists but is very often threatened by the authoritarian forces) and its extension to the district and lower levels as envisaged in the four-pillar democracy is, therefore, of extreme importance in the advance of Indian society....

The 73rd and 74th Constitutional Amendments created a uniform national legal framework for local governments in India. They have ensured a uniform three-tier structure in the rural areas, periodic elections, reservations for women and Scheduled Caste/Scheduled Tribe (SC/ST) communities, district planning committees, and the institution of State Finance Commissions to recommend the devolution of funds to local governments. But unfortunately, devolution of the funds, functions, and functionaries are not mandatory clauses but only enabling ones that give discretionary powers to the state governments. As a result, the local governments in India at large have remained weak despite the amendments to the Constitution.

With particular reference to local governments in Kerala, the lower tier in the rural areas has been in sharp contrast with the rest of India. The state has been in the front ranks of the Devolution Index in the country. More importantly, the democratic decentralisation programme in the state has worked with a vision to encourage participation and deliberation in decision-making at the local level. The devolution necessarily works from top to bottom. However, in Kerala, decentralisation was not merely an administrative reform from above, but was also a social movement from below to create the political will in the state for radical devolution. The experience and the feedback it received from the ground have had an important influence in the making of laws and statutes.

We begin our discussion with an analysis of the radical perspective on decentralisation in the first section and then go on to describe how the People's Plan Campaign (PPC) was designed to enable greater participation and deliberation in the local decision-making process in the second section.

Twenty-five years have passed since the radical local-level reforms. Section three examines the questions: Were the processes sustained? What have the outcomes been? No doubt, in our scheme the processes are as important as the outcomes. Therefore, there is a need for a continuous modification of the theory and design of the processes based on the experience. We shall therefore describe how the laws, rules, and institutions were modified at the end of the PPC in section four. Finally, by way of conclusion, an attempt is made in section five to map out new directions to strengthen the democratic decentralisation based on twenty-five years of experience.

THE RADICAL PERSPECTIVE OF DECENTRALISATION

A wide spectrum of agencies, from radical political parties and movements to neoliberal international development agencies, has promoted decentralisation. Consequently, the conceptualisation, ideological underpinnings, design, techniques, and outcomes of decentralisation have varied across countries and over time. Where is Kerala positioned on this decentralisation spectrum?

Democratic decentralisation in Kerala draws its inspiration from the Gandhian tradition and the national movement for independence. The nationalist vision of decentralisation acquires renewed significance in the present era of globalisation. It challenges imperialist global domination. From the late 1930s, when local bodies were transferred to elected provincial governments after the Montague-Chelmsford reforms in colonial India, the Left in Kerala has consistently advocated for greater democratisation, empowerment, and autonomy for local governments (Namboodiripad 1938). Within the framework of the 73rd and 74th Constitutional Amendments, Kerala ushered in one of the most radical democratic decentralisation programmes ever seen anywhere.

From a conservative perspective, the objective of decentralisation is not relocating powers, resources, and functions within an activist state, following the principle of subsidiarity, but instead building a local apparatus that fits into the 'neoliberal' paradigm. The World Development Report 2002, titled *Building Institutions for Markets*, discusses the role of decentralisation (see World Bank 2002). By contrast, planning is the central fulcrum around which decentralisation in Kerala unfolded.

In this conservative and bureaucratic form of decentralisation, local bodies are transformed from being direct providers of services to facilitators. Participation, and not privatisation, is seen as the solution to the social infrastructure crisis in Kerala. Much of the decentralisation in developed countries is also driven by conservative attempts to downsize government support for the poor and diminish the public sector, all under the slogan of the 'post-welfare agenda' (Bennett 1990). As Joel Samoff noted (1990, 517), such approaches use the language of 'service delivery', 'efficiency', and 'cost recovery'. The Kerala experiment, by contrast, promotes popular democracy as an alternative to conservative decentralisation. It involves what Samoff calls the language of 'effective participation', 'empowerment', 'conscientization', and 'collective action'.

Devolution can be a strategic response of the 'affirmative democratic state' to the neoliberal onslaught (Fung and Wright 2003). Decentralisation of the State apparatus is essential for transforming the existing State institutions into empowered deliberative bodies. 'Empowered Deliberative Democracy' should produce superior results when compared to traditional 'Representative-Techno-Bureaucratic Democracy' in promoting equity, improving the quality of citizenship, and producing better outcomes of State action.

The neoliberal approach to 'decentralisation' visualises a substitution of the State by a set of NGOs in the implementation of local projects, especially social-sector projects, the funds for which, whether drawn from the State budget or from foreign donors, are expended through these NGOs, who need not be accountable to the people (Patnaik 2004). Civil society actors will continue to play an important role in the development process in Kerala. But their interventions must remain within the framework of the local plan. The LGs (local governments) are the central fulcrum of the decentralisation process.

The decentralisation programme in Kerala was fashioned from a theoretical understanding of the possibility of using decentralisation to advance the causes for which the Left has always struggled. Extending parliamentary democracy from the Central and state levels to the districts, blocks, and panchayats or municipalities opens possibilities for more direct participation of the masses in day-to-day governance. Grassroots democracy is favourable for mobilisations that defend the exploited and weaker sections.

The Kerala PPC is thus a part of a larger political vision as in the case of the Participatory Budgeting (PB) promoted by the Left parties and social movements during the 'pink tide' (Baiocchi 1999; Ganuza and Baiocchi 2012; Spronk 2008) in Latin America:

> It provides a legacy for the construction of a better society. Any socialist society must build on the institutions bequeathed to it by the pre-existing society. Indeed, a part of the reason for the excessive centralization, and the accompanying authoritarianism, that prevailed in the earlier socialist societies lay in the absence of any representative democratic institutions in these societies prior to the emergence of socialism on which the latter could build its foundations. In that sense the decentralization experiment, by empowering elected bodies, puts life into a whole range of institutions based on which a future society can be built. (Patnaik 2004)

However, the above claim raises an important question: If the PPC was indeed a political project of the Left in Kerala, then how did the non-Left governments in Kerala continue the project? How do the LGs under the non-Left political formations perform within the PPC framework?

This was precisely the challenge—how to design a programme platform that can accommodate a diversity of views and multiple party formations. What democratic decentralisation achieves is the creation of a democratic space at the local level for popular mobilisation and democratisation. Who will occupy this space and how they will utilise it is a matter of political contestation and the outcome will remain open.

The Design of PPC for Greater Participation and Deliberation

While in the rest of India decentralisation was implemented as administrative reforms from above, in Kerala it was implemented as part of a social movement from below. The movement was launched with the declaration of the devolution of an unprecedented amount of 35–40 per cent of the Ninth Five-Year Plan outlay as allocation to the local governments. To claim their entitlement, each local government had to prepare a local plan in a participatory and deliberative manner. The planning process was used as an instrument for social mobilisation to generate democratic ideals and create the political will for the devolution of funds, functions, and functionaries. This process was designed in such a manner as to facilitate maximum participation, deliberation, and transparency (Thomas and Franke 2021).

Planning

The needs of the people were to be identified in gram sabhas where every citizen has the right to participate. Two million people did participate. Their needs were to be prioritised at a development seminar at the gram panchayat or municipal level by the representatives of gram sabhas, officials, and experts based on an objective assessment of natural, human, and financial resources, recorded in a development report. More than 200,000 persons participated in the development seminars and every local government did produce a substantial printed status document. Over 100,000 persons were participants in the working groups which converted the prioritised needs into formal project proposals. The format of the project proposals was designed in such a manner as to ensure a thorough scrutiny of the problem, the solution, and its implementation. These projects were finally adopted by the elected representatives into a plan document. Nearly 10,000 technical experts worked voluntarily to assist the District Planning Committees (DPCs) to evaluate the plans and approve them. The plans of the higher tiers were drawn up in a similar manner, considering the plans from below. Both the Latin American PB and Kerala PPC combine direct participation with representative democracy. The final choice is made by elected representatives, but they have to follow a democratic procedure for prioritisation in which they themselves are participants.

Each phase of planning was preceded by a cascading training programme involving a state faculty comprising 100 experts, 500 state-level key resource persons, 10,000 district resource persons, and more than 50,000 local resource persons. What was remarkable was the formation of the Volunteer Technical Corps (VTC), consisting of retired technical experts who worked voluntarily with the LGs and DPC to draw up the plans and evaluate them. More than 10,000 had volunteered. Through the VTC, technical expertise of the calibre usually available at the Central and state levels was made available at the local level. They were also given an orientation in participation in the planning process. This capacity building exercise has been effective in successfully formulating local plans, not just in one year, but year after year for the past twenty-five years.

Implementation

A major difference between the Kerala PPC and Latin American PB is that the PB is limited to participation in the budgeting process and to some extent in the oversight, and none at all in the actual implementation of the projects. The PPC participation extends to the implementation stage as well. The direct participation of the people in plan implementation is facilitated through micro-organisations such as beneficiary committees in public works, parent-teacher associations, and hospital development committees in education and health, and co-operatives, self-help groups, and farming groups in the production sectors. Besides reviews in the grama sabhas and development seminars, the most important oversight mechanism in the Kerala PPC is the social auditing process, although it has not achieved widespread success yet. The direct involvement of the people in organising petty production and providing basic services would heighten the accountability, improve efficiency, and mobilise additional resources.

Santos (1998, 500) describes the PB as a movement from 'techno-bureaucracy to techno-democracy'. In a techno-bureaucracy, only the bureaucrats need training. In a techno-democracy, ordinary people must develop enough skills to understand cost-benefit analysis, choices among construction materials and techniques, and a wide array of other issues. In Porto Alegre, the birthplace of PB, the approach has been to insist that the technical staff learn to explain technical issues in a language accessible to participants in the budgeting meetings. Special training sessions were organised from 1997 to sensitise government workers to this need.

The training of participants does not appear to have been tried in Porto Alegre. But the most important element in Kerala's attempt to bridge the gap between specialisation and democracy has been the massive training programme, not only in the initial stages of campaign-based planning but also in subsequent years. Hundreds of thousands of ordinary citizens received at least some training. There does not seem to be anything in the decentralisation experiences anywhere in the world comparable to Kerala's achievements in training.

Given the similarities in these independently evolved experiments in two distant continents, Marta Harnecker tried to develop a synthesis of the two experiments in the concrete context of Venezuela. In Venezuela, activists took up the concept of 'protagonism' to describe the individual human transformations associated with democratic decentralisation. Protagonism is generally parallel to 'empowered deliberative democracy' and the cardinal principles enunciated by the Sen Committee Report that we shall refer to later in the next section (Harnecker and Bartolomé 2019, 15). Protagonism implies that ordinary people can have a meaningful impact within society. Democratic participatory decentralisation—devolving real decision-making powers to local assemblies—provides a setting in which protagonism can develop and be experienced (ibid., 71). Planning from below is an essential component in former President Hugo Chávez's '21st-century socialism' (Harnecker 2015, 60).

The Practice of Decentralisation—Sustainability of the Processes and the Outcomes

Before the achievements of the PPC could be consolidated and institutionalised, the Left lost power. Since then, decentralisation in Kerala has survived four turnovers of government, while remaining essentially intact. In the international decentralisation literature, this fact alone sets the Kerala experience apart. The PPC created an environment that made it politically inexpedient to undermine decentralisation.

As for the three great 'Fs' of decentralisation—devolution of funds, functions, functionaries—Kerala has not slipped back. In the budget of 2020–2021, the share of untied funds in the plan is 25.9 per cent of the plan outlay. The total devolution, including non-plan grants and Central and state-sponsored schemes, would be more than Rs 20,000, that is, nearly 20 per cent of the total revenue of the state government (Isaac 2021a). There has been no major erosion of functions that were devolved. On the other hand, they have recently been assigned a key role in disaster management. Finally, the number of employees under the LGs, including the transferred employees, have more than doubled. Kerala has continuously been in the front ranks in the index of decentralisation.

The basic architecture of planning from below and the implementation procedures have remained intact. The campaign mode of popular mobilisation was dismantled when the new government came to power in 2001. This has been one of the factors that weakened the level of participation in grama sabhas and the planning process. It also adversely affected the pace of institutionalisation of the processes and ideals generated by the movement.

Twenty-five years is a long enough time span to look back and make an honest assessment of the achievements of this rare experiment in democratic decentralisation in the country. What were the key outcomes?

Health

The famed public health system in Kerala was in a crisis by the 1990s, confronted with increasing demand for healthcare arising from a change in the epidemiological regime and decline in public health expenditure. When the government cut back investments in health, the private sector stepped in to meet the demand-supply gap. The percentage of persons using government facilities in 1986–1987 was only 28 per cent (Kannan, et al. 1991). The consequence was an escalation in health costs, marginalisation of the poor, and inequities in infrastructure, utilisation, and outcomes. The increase in the infant mortality rate (IMR), from 12 per 1,000 live births in 1997 to 15 per 1,000 live births in 2006, was a big embarrassment.

But decentralisation brought about a turnaround. According to the 71st round of the NSSO (2015), the proportion of the population utilising public health services increased to 34 per cent. It has further increased to 48 per cent in the 75th round of NSSO (2018). The IMR has declined to a single digit of 6, lower than UN SDG target of 8 in 2020 and far ahead of national average of 28. (Ministry of Health and Family Welfare 2020). Immunisation rates rose to nearly 100 per cent for many diseases.

Education

Free and universal school education through the public education system (government schools and private-aided schools) slipped behind popular aspiration levels as per capita incomes improved. As a result, the middle class increasingly began to shift towards unaided private schools, whose strength increased from 1.5 lakh students in 1991 to a peak of 4.1 lakhs in 2016–2017 (Vimalan 2019).

The trend has now been reversed, with more than 7.8 lakh new students of classes 1–10, with a significant percentage of them migrating back from the unaided sector during 2016–2021. The number of students in unaided schools has started to decline, and those in the public education system has increased. Kerala has emerged at the top among twenty large states, with a score of 76.6 out of 100 in the School Education Quality Index prepared for 2019 (NITI Ayog 2019).

Local Roads

The total road length under the LGs more than doubled from 115,306 km in 1995–1996 to 231,676 km in 2018–2019. There has also been a visible improvement in the condition of town and country roads because of investments in upgradation and renovation. Roads have become more evenly distributed across districts and regions.

Housing

The One Lakh Housing Scheme of the early 1970s, set up to provide houses to the beneficiaries of land reforms, is still etched in the memories of Keralites. However, the PPC surprised everyone by constructing 5.7 lakh houses. By the end of the 13th Five-Year Plan in 2021–2022, the LGs constructed a cumulative total of more than twenty lakh houses, rapidly transforming Kerala into a near universal housing state.

In 2011, 77 per cent of the houses in the state had drinking water within their premises, while in India the ratio was 51 per cent. Ninety-five per cent of the houses were electrified, as against the national average of 67 per cent. Ninety-five per cent of the houses had latrines, while in India only 47 per cent houses had such facilities. Ninety-three per cent of the houses in Kerala had more than one room, while the ratio in India was only 59 per cent (Kannan and Khan 2016).

Kudumbasree

One of the most celebrated outcomes of democratic decentralisation has been the emergence and growth of Kudumbasree Neighbourhood Groups (NHGs). They are basically a micro-finance network linked to LGs. They also function as a platform for the convergence of anti-poverty programmes, an agency for women's empowerment, and basic community organisation. At present, there are 2.77 lakh NHGs with a membership of 43 lakh households, each represented by a woman member. They have become the most accessible source of micro-credit with a fund base of more than Rs 11,000 crore—Rs 7,000 crore from live bank linkage and internal thrift of the NHGs of Rs 4,000 crore.

Poverty Alleviation

On the eve of the PPC in 1993–1994, the poverty ratio was 25.76 and 24.59 per cent in rural and urban areas, respectively. Although not strictly comparable to the earlier series according to the Rangarajan Committee Report on Poverty Estimation, in 2011–2012 the poverty ratio in Kerala had declined to 7.3 and 5.3 per cent, respectively (State Planning Board 2016).

In the Multidimensional Poverty Index (MPI) consisting of ten deprivation indicators related to health, education, and living standards as per the United Nations Development Programme (UNDP), the proportion of poor in Kerala has declined from 13 per cent to 1 per cent between 2005–2006 and 2015–2016 (UNDP 2019). Not only is the poverty ratio the lowest in India, but the annual rate of decline was also the highest in the country.

The performance of the LGs has been largely lacklustre on the production front. There are miles to go before overcoming challenges like participatory fatigue, inadequate integration of plans, nagging corruption, weakness of tribal sub-plans, and so on. Kerala's achievements in decentralisation, however fragile and incomplete, offers a sense of what is possible.

Learning from the Experience: Evolution of Law, Rules, and Institutions

The PPC was successful in empowering local governments to prepare and implement the first annual plan. It was a great learning experience; people were learning by doing. The campaign continued into subsequent years of the Ninth Five-Year Plan period. However, a governance system cannot function permanently in campaign mode. The Committee on Decentralisation of Powers (1999, 6–7) aptly described this as follows:

> A campaign by definition relies on volunteers who — basically social activists — are willing to lead from the front without any expectation of personal gain. Necessarily the campaign depends on informal and semi-formal systems and on the motive force of committed individuals. The momentum generated by the campaign has pushed this along. This is the time to internalize the essential elements of the campaign and institutionalize the procedures and systems thrown up by the process.... However much the campaign had succeeded, the challenge was to institutionalize the new system and fix the new attitudes in the public consciousness before the momentum generated by the campaign ebbed.

This task was to be undertaken by three committees set up while the campaign was on. The *first* was the Committee on Decentralisation of Powers, more popularly known as the Sen Committee after its Chairman, Satyabrata Sen; the *second* was the Second Finance Commission headed by Prabhat Patnaik; and the *third* was the Administrative Reforms Committee headed by Chief Minister E. K. Nayanar. These committees attempted to learn from concrete experience and suggest changes in the laws and rules, modify procedures, and reform the institutions so that democratic decentralisation is strengthened.

The Legislative Amendments

At the end of 1999, the government comprehensively amended the existing Kerala Panchayati Raj Act of 1994 and the Kerala Municipality Act of 1994 as per the recommendations of the Sen Committee. The objectives of these amendments and the administrative changes recommended were to realise the following cardinal principles: autonomy, subsidiarity, complementarity, uniformity, accountability, transparency, and participation.

The scope for State interference in the day-to-day functions of local bodies was drastically reduced. The resolutions of the LGs can be overridden only in extraordinary circumstances. A rigorous process must be followed for the dissolution of a local body, along with support from an independent authority like the ombudsman. The LGs were also empowered with substantial control over the staff transferred to it.

The amendments redefined the powers and functions of the different tiers, based on the principles enunciated earlier. To improve people's participation, the powers and functions of grama sabhas were enhanced and the minimum number of grama sabha meetings and quorum were raised. Enabling provisions were added to the law to encourage LGs to experiment with participatory community structures, such as neighbourhood groups and beneficiary committees.

Another major effort to enlarge the legal entitlement of LGs was the amending of thirty-six Acts that dealt with the functions devolved to LGs at one stroke. These amendments strengthened the supportive legal framework enabling the exercise of local government functions by harmonising the existing laws through the removal of contradictions, dropping anachronistic legislations, updating provisions, and demarcating functional domains more clearly.

Transparency was also incorporated into the law. All plan documents, including those related to beneficiary selection, bills and vouchers of works, etc., are to be considered public documents that any citizen can access. Social auditing was to be encouraged. A Citizen's Charter comprising the standards of service that the LG guarantees to every citizen, an ombudsman with wide powers to check malfeasance, Appellate Tribunals to reduce the delays in court cases and provide easier access to citizens seeking redress for their grievances, and independent Audit Commissions were all incorporated as well.

The amendments accept the reality of elected members affiliated to political parties in the leadership of LGs. To encourage a non-divisive style of governance, the number of standing committees was increased, and every elected member was given a role in the day-to-day transactions. With regard to defections, an attempt was made to strike a balance. The members have to abide by the decision of the affiliated parties in matters of election of officers and of no-confidence motions, but will have absolute freedom, free of party considerations, in matters relating to development. All elected members have to be included in one or the other standing committee, and standing committee chairpersons were elected under a proportional voting system so that all political parties with minimum representatives would share a leadership role in the LGs. The Election Commission was given powers to delimit ward boundaries, something formerly done through the executive.

Administrative Reforms

The Committee on Decentralisation of Powers (1999, 6–7) concluded that 'the functional responsibilities given are so wide and financial resources transferred have become so huge, [that] a mismatch has come about between the assigned responsibility and the means of carrying them out, which needs to be set right'. Even before the campaign, several grassroots-level departmental offices, including those of agriculture, veterinary, hospitals, schools, and women and child development, along with their staff, were transferred to the local governments.

The experience of four years of the campaign showed that the redeployment did not result in enhancing the local operational capacity in proportion to the scale of redeployment because of inadequate clarity about roles, an insufficient departmental reporting systems, and weakness of the core LGs official administrative leadership. Steps were taken to improve redeployment, bring clarity to the situation of dual control, and provide additional staff support. Parallel structures to LGs, such as the District Rural Development Agency (DRDA), and several development authorities were merged with the LGs. A separate mission for the computerisation of local governance was set up.

The Administrative Reforms Committee (ARC) was charged with overhauling the entire edifice of the state government to make it consistent with the transparent and participatory structures emerging at the local level. However, there has been no satisfactory follow-up in implementing its recommendations.

The Financial Devolution

The First State Finance Commission (SFC) (1994–1996) predated the PPC and had confined itself to recommendations regarding non-plan devolution. The additional finances for the LGs came from the plan devolution of the People's Campaign, an aspect on which the SFC had not given any recommendation. However, the plan grant-in-aid remained a discretionary grant recommended by the SPB and approved by the state government. Theoretically, it could be reduced or even abolished at any time by the state government. Institutionalising the devolution of plan funds to insulate them from arbitrary decisions of the state government remained an important challenge for the future of democratic decentralisation in Kerala. This task was undertaken in the Second SFC. The subsequent SFCs have all continued to uphold the fiscal autonomy and criteria-based devolution.

New Directions, 25 Years after Democratic Decentralisation

After more than two decades of practice in democratic decentralisation, it is high time to revisit the theoretical, legal, and institutional framework of the practice so far. Although the legal framework has withstood the test of time, the subsidiary rules have not yet been codified in manuals. The decentralisation has proceeded on the basis of *ad hoc* rules, which have been frequently changed with respect to beneficiary selection, financial procedures, implementation of public works, and so on. The frequency of modifications was very high in the initial years, so much so that orders during the PPC period had to be consolidated in three big volumes. Now the system has stabilised by and large, and therefore we can move on to formally adopt rules of business procedure. This has indeed been a major departure from the normal functioning of the government, where every activity is bound by rigid and tight rules, leaving little space for experimentation.

The key challenge remains how to sustain the scale and quality of participation. The large size of grama sabhas is a barrier to meaningful participation. Improving participation and deliberation in the grama sabha is a major challenge. The experience of transforming the NHGs and residence associations and similar grassroots community organisations into subsets of the grama sabhas, which would discuss the agenda in detail prior to the grama sabha, must be incorporated into the rules. The other deliberative fora of local planning, such as the development seminars, task forces, and monitoring committees, need to be revitalised. There have been a number of experiments seeking to enhance the participation of experts in planning and implementation processes, and their valuable experiences must converted into formal rules. The disbandment of VTC by the new government in 2001 was a major setback. The experience so far underlines the need for the incorporation of greater expertise in the local planning process.

As we have seen, the multi-sectoral interventions for poverty alleviation at the local level have been successful in reducing poverty. It is now possible to plan for the eradication of absolute poverty in the state through micro-level planning for each individual household in extreme poverty. This new programme would, to an extent, overcome the failure to tackle the backwardness of outlier groups such as tribals and fisherfolk.

We have already noted the positive impact of Kudumbasree and gender budgeting. But gender discrimination and violence against women continue to be a distressing feature of social life. A critical review of the gender programme is therefore necessary. The proposal for an extensive participatory crime mapping of violence against women by each panchayat and municipality and for drawing up projects to address the problems identified is indeed an innovative approach that holds much potential.

Decentralisation initially reduced corruption substantially, but over time, it has again been on the rise. An official review undertaken by M. A. Oommen (2009) took a dim view of the outcome of the battle to avoid contractors and implement public works through beneficiary committees, as despite 'all the precautions taken, the (beneficiary committee) system did not meet with great success' (ibid., 85). With this route virtually closed, the solution to putting an end to corruption lies in greater participation and universalisation of social auditing and the effective implementation of a Citizen's Charter and review of the ombudsman system.

Yet another major weakness of decentralised planning in Kerala is with regard to an integrated approach to solving local problems or integration of the plans of different tiers of government at the local level. With respect to education and healthcare, a multi-sectoral approach has been adopted by most of the LGs with positive outcomes. On the other hand, watershed planning, so vital for agricultural rejuvenation and solving the drinking water problem, has not taken off yet. The possibilities of launching a campaign—even if not on the scale of 1996—to draw up micro-watershed programmes for land and water management and integrated intervention in the agriculture sector are being explored. This can also be linked to the preparation of a local disaster management action plan, a new major activity that has recently been assigned to LGs.

Ever since the launch of the PPC, district plans have been identified as the key instrument for greater integration of the projects of different tiers. Although district plans were prepared in 2000, there were no follow-up actions subsequently. The second attempt in 2017 has also not generated the desired impact. The district plan is important, not only for integrating the plans of different tiers through interaction between them, but also as a key instrument for arriving at a consensus regarding the district-level plan guidelines to be issued by the DPC. Currently, these guidelines are formulated at the state level.

Democratic decentralisation has expanded democratic space at the local level. All the new directions that we noted above have been experimented with through local initiatives in different local governments. They have proved successful, and have therefore come to constitute items in the agenda for scaling up. Protection and expansion of the democratic space should be the most important objective for the future. Democratic decentralisation does not guarantee any particular outcome. What it promises is a democratic space in which to intervene and strive for the realisation of people's dreams.

Acknowledgements

The discussion in this chapter closely follows the analysis presented in *People's Planning Kerala: Local Democracy and Development*, co-authored with Richard W Franke. I am grateful to S. M. Vijayanand for comments on an earlier version.

Select References

Baiocchi, Gianpaolo. 1999.'Participation, Activism, and Politics: The Porto Alegre Experiment and Deliberative Democratic Theory'. Paper presented at the Real Utopias Project Conference on Experiments in Empowered Deliberative Democracy, University of Wisconsin, Madison, 14–16 January 2000.

Bennett, Robert J. (ed.). 1990. *Decentralization, Local Governments, and Markets: Towards a Post-Welfare Agenda*. Oxford: Clarendon Press.

Committee on Decentralization of Powers. 1999. *Final Report: Strengthening of Professional and Ministerial Support to Local Government* (mimeo.). Thiruvananthapuram: Government of Kerala.

E. M. S. Namboodiripad. 1938. *Madirasi Governmentum Pradeshika Swayambharanavum (Madras Government and Local Self-Government)*. Mathrubhumi, Kozhikkode, 12 July.

———. 1978. 'Note on Report of the Committee on Panchayat Raj Institutions', in *Report of the Committee on Panchayat Raj Institutions*. New Delhi: Government of India.

Fung, Archon, and Erik Olin Wright. 2003. 'Thinking about Empowered Participatory Governance', in Archon Fung and Erik Olin Wright (eds), *Deepening Democracy: Institutional Innovations in Empowered Participatory Governance*, 3–42, The Real Utopias Project, Vol. IV. London and New York: Verso.

Ganuza, Ernesto, and Gianpaolo Baiocchi. 2012. 'The Power of Ambiguity: How Participatory Budgeting Travels the Globe'. *Journal of Public Deliberation* 8 (2). doi: http://www.publicdeliberation.net/jpd/vol8/iss2/art8 (accessed October 2024).

Government of Kerala. 2016. *Report of the Expert Group on Total Housing Mission*. Thiruvananthapuram: Kerala State Planning Board.

Harnecker, Marta. 2015. *A World to Build: New Paths Toward Twenty-First Century Socialism*. New York: Monthly Review Press.

Harnecker, Marta, and José Bartolomé. 2019. *Planning from Below: A Decentralized Participatory Planning Proposal*. With the collaboration of Noel López, Federico Fuentes (trans.). New York: Monthly Review Press.

Kannan, K. P., K. R. Thankappan, V. Ramankutty, and K. P. Aravindan. 1991. *Health and Development in Rural Kerala*. Thiruvananthapuram: KSSP.

Kannan, K. P., and Imran Khan. 2016. *Housing Condition in Kerala, with Special Focus on Rural Areas and Socially Disadvantaged Sections*. Thiruvananthapuram: Laurie Baker Centre for Habitat Studies.

Kannan, K. P., and G. Raveendran. 2017. *Poverty, Women and Capability: A Study of the Impact of Kerala's Kudumbashree System on its Members and their Families*. Thiruvananthapuram: Laurie Baker Centre for Habitat.

Ministry of Health and Family Welfare. 2020. 'Health Nutrition India: The Comprehensive national Nutrition Survey'. Available at https://healthnutritionindia.in/ (accessed February 2025).

National Sample Survey Office. 2015. *Key Indicators of Social Consumption in India: Health*. NSS 71st Round, January–June. New Delhi: Ministry of Statistics and Programme Implementation, Government of India.

National Statistical Office. 2019. *Key Indicators of Social Consumption in India: Health*. NSS 75th Round, July 2017–June 2018. New Delhi: Government of India, Ministry of Statistics and Programme Implementation.

NITI Aayog. 2019. *The Success of Our Schools: School Education Quality Index*. New Delhi: Government of India.

———. 2020. 'Infant Mortality Rate'. NITI Aayog website.

Oommen, M. A., et al. 2009. *Report of the Committee for Evaluation of Decentralised Planning and Development*. Thiruvananthapuram: Government of Kerala.

Patnaik, Prabhat. 2004. 'A Theoretical Note on Kerala-Style Decentralized Planning'. Macroscan: An Alternative Economics

Webcentre, 14 April. Available at https://www.macroscan.org/fet/apr04/fet140404Theoretical_Note_1.htm (accessed October 2024).

Samoff, Joel. 1990. 'Decentralization: The Politics of Interventionism'. *Development and Change* 21 (3), 513–530.

Santos, Boaventura de Sousa. 1998. 'Participatory Budgeting in Porto Alegre: Toward a Redistributive Democracy'. *Politics and Society* 26 (4), 461–510.

Spronk, Susan. 2008. 'Review essay: Pink Tide? Neoliberalism and its Alternatives in Latin America'. *Canadian Journal of Latin American and Caribbean Studies* 33 (65), 173–186. https://doi.org/10.1080/08263663.2008.10816944 (accessed October 2024).

Isaac, Thomas. 2021. *Budget Speech 2021–22*. Thiruvananthapuram: Government of Kerala.

Isaac, Thomas, and Richard W. Franke. 2021. *People's Planning Kerala: Local Democracy and Development*. New Delhi: LeftWord Books.

United Nations Development Programme (UNDP). 2019. *Global Multidimensional Poverty Index 2019: Illuminating Inequalities*. United Nations Development Programme and Oxford Poverty and Human Development Initiative. Available at http://hdr.undp.org/en/2019-MPI (accessed October 2024).

Vimalan, K. 2019. *Karutharjikkunna Pothu Vidyabhyasam* (Public Education Empowered). Vidyarangam, 20–36. Government of Kerala: General Education Department.

World Bank. 2002. *World Development Report 2002: Building Institutions for Markets*. New York: Oxford University Press.

4

Populism, Information Disorders, and Erosion of Democracy

The Case of Brazil

Nandini Ramanujam and Paula Martins

Introduction

Access to information is at the heart of participatory democracy. Participation cannot be meaningful without informed citizens—they must be informed about their rights and obligations, as well as avenues and opportunities for participation in democratic processes. People need information from diverse and independent sources at hand to build their own positions and views on matters of public concern. Participatory democracy, therefore, is intrinsically related to the guarantee and exercise of the rights to information, opinion, and expression.

One has to look beyond formal spaces for participation in democratic processes, as the pathways to engagement in the public sphere are broader, multilayered, and contested. This is where social movements play a critical role. These movements can be seen as platforms for collective action and often take on the role of resistance and opposition through different strategies, including civil disobedience and protests.

In the current political climate, where democratic information ecosystems are being manipulated and interfered with by powerful State and non-State actors, social movements play an even more important role. The so-called 'information disorders' have demonstrably impacted electoral processes (Arnaudo 2017; Coppins 2020; Elswah and Howard 2020). This chapter posits that beyond elections, populist governments have deliberately destabilised the informational ecosystems of their countries, aggravating information disorders that are advantageous to vested interests and leadership. Insights from social movements which have operated for decades in unstable and unbalanced information ecosystems—by building resilience and counter-narratives—may provide strategies for reinforcing democratic institutions with the aim of navigating the era of information disorder.

The important role played by social movements seems to be confirmed by the fact that, in addition to the manipulation and distortion of both content and flow of information, strategies such as attacks on the press, stigmatisation of civil society groups and social movements, and the demolishing of the public information regime[1] of the country have also been very present in the digital authoritarian's playbook, with serious consequences for the health of democracies across the world.

The traditional checks and balances on information flow are no longer effective in the context of the exponential rise of new media and social medias. Amidst an overload of information, ordinary citizens are unable to distinguish between credible and false information. Fostering a climate where people cannot distinguish facts from rumours is an insidious strategy that some States use to destabilise public debate and weaken participation. The two-pronged phenomenon of restriction on the flow of information and its manipulation to justify and perpetuate undemocratic practices calls for urgent attention.

This chapter sets out to highlight this disturbing trend by illustrating the case of Brazil under the administration of Jair Bolsonaro. The distortion of information, which started from his electoral campaign of 2018, continued during the severe political crisis the country faced amidst the COVID-19 pandemic, which, at that time, had already taken over 687,000 lives in Brazil (Government of Brazil n.d.).

The use of disinformation as a cynical strategy for political gain during the COVID-19 pandemic was not a new phenomenon in the Bolsonaro administration. It aligns with his long-term communication strategy based on the creation of constant public commotion, resulting in what G. Da Empoli (2019) calls a 'saturation of the public debate'. The Bolsonaro administration was extremely dependent on an informational strategy where truth and facts no longer matter and actual meaningful discussion on public policies and projects is avoided. The regime was thriving on inciting populist and nationalist sentiments that stimulated and drove Bolsonaro's base. Consequently, a vicious cycle was created where new polemics are needed to maintain public support for his government.

The overall result is the hyper-polarisation of society and a climate of distrust undermining social cohesion and democratic processes. The significant casualties of this information chaos include declining trust in human rights, republican values, and public institutions. Understanding and mitigating the new role of information in our societies is at the centre of a strategy for safeguarding democracy itself, especially in countries like Brazil, where the building of democracy after decades of military dictatorship was still a project under consolidation.

M. Castells (2012) situates global justice movements as characteristic of societies in the information age. Their strength, in his analysis, lies in their decentralisation and loose-knit network structure, as well as their use of the internet. Although there has been much controversy concerning the role of social movements in the digital age, understanding their relationship with emerging technologies, in particular the use of social media by these groups, and their dynamics in our networked times may be a key piece of learning in order to put together effective strategies to face the prevalence of information disorders.

Disinformation and Misinformation in Brazil

The Strategic Use of Disinformation

Disinformation[2] received increased attention in Brazil prior to the impeachment of former President Dilma Roussef in 2016, finally reaching prominence in the run-off to the 2018 presidential elections. That year, the situation became so critical that Facebook, for example, proposed measures to safeguard the elections in Brazil (Meta 2018), committing to fighting disinformation; being more transparent with the platform's advertisements; removing imposter accounts; and removing 'digital pamphlets' used to deceive voters by placing a candidate's picture together with the number of a different party. These measures were taken 'to ensure the authenticity of content published on the platform'.

Despite such measures, FGV DAPP (Fundacao Getulio Vargas DAPP 2018) — FGV's Department of Public Policy — affirms that 'social networks became the axis of political discussion in the 2018 presidential campaign, with the impact of disinformation as a central theme'. FGV's research points to the massive use of social media by all political coalitions, identifying the presence of automated accounts and fake news on Twitter (now 'X'), Facebook, and YouTube.

The Atlantic Council's Digital Forensic Research Lab (DFRLab) also looked into the 2018 Brazilian elections, concluding that, in addition to social media, the electoral campaign included a significant amount of disinformation spread through encrypted messaging platforms (Bandeira, et al. 2019). Unlike disinformation circulated via internet platforms such as Facebook, where fact-checkers can spot pieces in high circulation and act upon them, WhatsApp encryption does not allow access to the content shared (Newton 2020). And because WhatsApp used to allow for the creation of large groups and the possibility of repetitive forwarding of messages, it became an ideal space for the dissemination of fake news before they reached internet platforms.[3] WhatsApp public groups often functioned as a messaging pyramid scheme. Group members received material they disseminated to their personal networks, who then shared it with other networks, rippling distribution and amplifying it to a much larger audience.

In Brazil, prior polarisation and a lack of trust in institutions, largely due to repeated corruption scandals — spanning government, media, and civil society organisations — created an atmosphere in which disinformation spread quickly, with compounding effects. Disinformation and misinformation campaigns both exploited and greatly aggravated this scenario.

Similar patterns were replicated after Bolsonaro's election and reached new levels of sophistication during the COVID-19 crisis. Since the beginning of the COVID-19 health crisis in Brazil, Bolsonaro had adopted a denialist position, downplaying the potential impact of the rapid spread of the virus and the health risks involved (Fridman 2020). Through official statements and 'live' social media broadcasts, the President first referred to the disease as a 'little flu', claiming that it would have no major effects on 90 per cent of Brazilians and that the media was creating hysteria around the issue.

The President's statements on the pandemic since then can be divided into three main categories:

- Pseudo-scientific information on the symptoms, risks of, and cures for the disease, with the content often invalid or unproven.
- Incomplete or incorrect information on preventive and protective measures adopted by other countries and recommendations by international organisations, as well as on their impact.
- Delegitimisation of those supporting isolation and quarantine, and open support to those defending the end of such restrictive measures.

Studies, including by FGV DAPP (*Observa Democracia* 2020), have pointed to a decreasing influence of the pro-Bolsonaro far-right base on social media platforms from early 2020 till mid-late March 2020 (Estado de Minas 2020). The news agency *A Publica* and others, such as *AP Exata* (2020) and political scientist Oliver Stuenkel, believe that there was a coordinated strategy linked to the use of disinformation during the COVID-19 pandemic, designed to regain space on social media for Bolsonaro.

This coordinated strategy involves the constant adoption of contentious public statements by the President; the use of key internet influencers; the employment of computational amplification;[4] the use of bots and botnets on social media platforms; and the massive distribution of messages through WhatsApp (Rudnitzki, et al. 2020). Smith (2020) affirms that 'Bolsonaro has chosen a mediated strategy that heightens political polarization and social-media "culture wars"'.

Bolsonaro's use of disinformation for political gain during the COVID-19 pandemic was not a new phenomenon. In 2019, the Brazilian National Congress created a dedicated Parliamentary Investigative Commission (Comissão Parlamentar Mista de Inquérito [CPMI]) to examine the circulation of misinformation and disinformation in the country, including its use by the current government. According to several testimonies collected by the CPMI, a core team closely linked to the President and operating from within the presidential palace coordinated the strategic spread of disinformation, including defamatory messages against opponents of Jair Bolsonaro. The team has been nicknamed the 'Hate Office'.

A former leader and ally of Bolsonaro's party in the lower chamber of Congress (Camera dos Deputados) provided extensive material in her December 2019 testimony to the CPMI (TV Senado 2019). According to her, the volume of disinformation disseminated was considerable. She affirmed that 1.4 million bots followed the official account of Jair Bolsonaro and another 468,000 followed that of Eduardo Bolsonaro, his senator son and member of the 'Hate Office'. The group also managed twenty-one profiles on Instagram, which were used to distribute memes and false content to Facebook pages (Westrup 2020).

Data provided by the fact-checking initiative of Aos Fatos suggests that the general patterns of disinformation in Brazil during the COVID-19 crisis are related to the government's efforts to control the narrative during the pandemic, *first*, to deny its seriousness, and *second*, to use it to attack its opponents. Professor Leandro Tessler from the Campinas State University (UNICAMP), who is also a member of the Study Group on Disinformation in Social Networks, affirms that there is a clear nexus between flows of disinformation in social media and the discourse of the President. He stated that the bulk of the content originates from Bolsonaro's official accounts and those of his key allies, followed by massive replication by bots (Redação RBA 2020).

Sergio Denicoli, from *AP Exata*, affirms that creating and fostering conflict is part of a communication strategy used continuously by the government to leverage social media. According to him, when things are getting 'too slow', Bolsonaro uses social media to promote division and controversy (Rudnitzki, et al. 2020).

Access to Public Information, Transparency, and Accountability

Amidst an accelerating public health crisis—when receiving accurate and timely information from official sources is critical—Brazilians faced difficulties, given the continual flow of disinformation driven by officials and a serious lack of timely and relevant public information available on the spread of the virus and government actions to address it. In parallel, the Access to Information regime established by the 2011 Freedom of Information Act and other relevant legislation was concurrently being weakened.

The right of access to public information is not limited to information requests (FoIA requests, as they are known in some countries) presented to public bodies. It includes a broader State responsibility to proactively produce relevant information; disclose such information in a meaningful, timely, and easily comprehensible fashion; and create an informational context in which official data and news are seen as credible, relevant, and accurate.

Bolsonaro's administration, however, in addition to spreading false and misleading information, attempted to discredit data circulated by official institutions responsible for providing information that it deemed unfavourable to itself. For example, during the pandemic, Bolsonaro questioned the methodology that has long been used to measure the country's unemployment rates and the number of COVID-19 deaths released by the different states of the federation (News Wires 2020). Bolsonaro affirmed that some states had been inflating the numbers of victims (*Política* 2020c). This is extremely problematic, because despite the lack of any evidence presented by the President to support his accusations, these actions were reducing the level of trust that people have in official sources.

Factual reports demonstrate that in reality, the number of coronavirus deaths is likely much higher than what were being reported, as officials faced serious challenges in accurately documenting the true extent of the crisis to citizens, while the numbers of infections and deaths are being announced daily via a dedicated webpage organised by the Ministry for Health (Government of Brazil n.d.).

In March 2020, the President passed Provisional Measure 928 (Brazil Secretary-General, 2020), which introduced important changes to the Freedom of Information Act, to be effective during the pandemic (Committee to Protect Journalists 2020). Among other measures, it suspended the rule that requests must receive answers within thirty days and halted the possibility of appeals in case of denial. More than eighty civil society organisations reacted against the measure (*Política* 2020b). The case was taken to the judiciary and the Supreme Court first suspended the effects of the Provisional Measure on 23 March (Diáro de Goiás 2020). The full plenary of the Court later upheld the decision (Supremo Tribunal Federal 2020). The Provisional Measure was ruled unconstitutional for containing generic and abusive restrictions on public transparency.

Opponents of the Provisional Measure were concerned that the restrictions imposed on the Freedom of Information Act could limit people's access to crucial health-related official information during the pandemic. They also feared that the Measure could signify further efforts to diminish the overall transparency and accountability standards of public bodies, using the pandemic as an excuse. Despite the Supreme Court decision cancelling any alterations to the Freedom of Information Act, the Brazilian Access to Information Forum (2020) monitored information requests presented between March and April 2020 and pointed out that the COVID-19 pandemic had been used in the period as a pretext to deny information requests by the federal government.

The NGO Transparency International (2020) pointed out that the Freedom of Information Act was especially important during the COVID-19 crisis because it allows for the social control of emergency public contracting and prevents the co-optation of the State by private interests that may impact the distribution of benefits and fiscal exemptions planned to minimise the economic impact of the crisis.

Media under Attack

In the midst of the pandemic, the Brazilian National Council for Human Rights, on the occasion of the World Press Freedom Day on 3 May 2020, released a statement highlighting the important work of the press in the coverage of the COVID-19 crisis, even when faced with the dangers of covering the pandemic and amid ongoing official attacks.

The critical coverage of the President's management of the pandemic crisis had witnessed a backlash in terms of attacks against the media, including verbal attacks challenging credibility as well as intimidation and online harassment. While much of the online harassment was generated by supporters of the President, a considerable amount is also directed from Bolsonaro. The NGO Reporters Without Borders (RSF) (2020b) had commented on Bolsonaro's behaviour, affirming that '[a]lthough they take many forms, these systematic attacks on the media obey a clear and increasingly well-oiled strategy—to encourage a lasting mistrust of the targeted journalists, destroy their credibility, and gradually construct a common enemy.' The attacks also served to distract public attention from important public issues. *The Wall Street Journal* has affirmed that Bolsonaro's public relations strategy was 'scold the press while pressing the flesh' (Trevisani 2020).

RSF (2020a) released the 2020 World Press Freedom Index in April. Brazil ranked 107th out of the 180 countries covered by the survey, dropping two positions since the 2019 Index. It had already dropped two positions that year since 2018.[5]

In March, seventeen Brazilian and international civil society groups requested a hearing at the OAS Inter-American Commission on Human Rights to discuss 'systematic violations to freedom of expression in the country, as well as attacks against the press, censorship of cultural and artistic expressions, shrinking of social participation spaces, and limitations on access to public information' (Paixão 2020). By September 2020, the NGO Artigo 19 (2020) had documented 449 attacks against journalists by the President, his ministers, his mandate-holding sons, and high-level allied politicians since the beginning of Bolsonaro's mandate in January 2019. Of these, 102 attacks came directly from the President (Artigo 19 2020).

The Consequences of Disinformation

After twenty months in office, Bolsonaro faced (as of 18 June 2020) at least forty-eight impeachment requests (Valfré 2020), including one from the Brazilian Press Association for his abusive use of disinformation through social media and attacks against the press (*Política* 2020a). This situation added to the political uncertainty in the country and intensified a context of growing conflicts between federal and state governments and militarisation of the federal Executive.

The critical disinformation context observed in the country, as well as the results of the CPMI (see above), had also led many Congressmen and women to propose bills aimed at legislating the issue. According to the Legislative Radar (2020) created by the organisation Coding Rights to monitor bills related to new technologies, freedom of expression and information, there were at the time thirty-nine bills in Congress seeking to regulate 'fake news', nine of which had been proposed in the context of COVID-19. Most of these bills were very restrictive and could have limited freedom of expression and information online, while failing to deal with issues of disinformation circulation and consumption.

But perhaps the most worrisome impact of the overwhelming presence of disinformation and misinformation in the country was the hyper-polarisation of public debate and the growing deterioration of confidence in public institutions.

From demonstrations against the Supreme Court, calling for its dismantling, to intimidation and direct violence against journalists critical of the regime, the campaign to discredit democratic institutions and free press was paramount. Many *Bolsonaristas* also called for the shutting down of Congress, where 'there are only thieves' (Mandl and Caverni 2020). Leaders of both Congress and the judiciary had been attacked by online harassment campaigns and targeted by an 'army of trolls' (Mello 2020).

Aside from the polarisation, this widespread disinformation and misinformation campaign has generated apathy and disillusion on a wide scale among the populace, which directly impacts participation and deliberation in democratic processes. Similar effects have been identified in a study on exposure to conspiracy theories relating to climate change — 'it found that exposure to such theories created a sense of powerlessness, resulting in disengagement from politics and a reduced likelihood of people to make small changes that would reduce their carbon footprint' (Wardle and Derakhshan 2017).

Disinformation and Technology

If there is nothing novel about rumours, conspiracy theories, and fabricated information, the complexity and scale of information pollution[6] present an unprecedented challenge today. Social media algorithms facilitated the circulation and consumption of inflammatory content and enable the creation of so-called 'echo chambers' and 'filter bubbles'.[7]

Harvard's Shorenstein Study on Media, Politics and Public Policy affirms that

> [s]ocial networks are driven by the sharing of emotional content. The architecture of these sites is designed such that every time a user posts content—and it is liked, commented upon or shared further—their brain releases a tiny hit of dopamine. As social beings, we intuit the types of posts that will conform best to the prevailing attitudes of our social circle. (Wardle and Derakhshan 2017)

In May 2020, a *Wall Street Journal* investigative piece uncovered internal Facebook documents that demonstrated that the company was aware of the impact of its platform in fostering divisive discourses. According to the article, a slide presentation to Facebook's management stated that '[o]ur algorithms exploit the human brain's attraction to divisiveness. If left unchecked', it warned, Facebook would feed users 'more and more divisive content in an effort to gain user attention & increase time on the platform' (Horwitz and Seetharaman 2020).

C. Wardle (2017) clarifies that '[w]hile confirmation bias occurs offline and the term "selective exposure" has been used by social scientists for decades to describe how information seekers use only certain sources that share their views, social media are designed to take advantage of this innate bias'. P. Carr, et al. (2020) point out that disinformation and misinformation are used in the political realm as a tool to maintain power or to gain citizens' support to controversial 'and often highly objectionable' measures. For them, such propaganda 'meshes with this tapestry of factors framing the reception, consumption, internalization and operationalization of citizen participation, engagement, agency and influence' (ibid.). Sixteen years ago, Jurgen Habermas (2006) had already called attention to how the internet had the potential to pose critical challenges to the 'public sphere', because it allows for great fragmentation and isolation of audiences and publics.

The rapid and exponential growth of available technology and the fast reduction in related costs have resulted in widespread internet use, particularly social media. Zero rating schemes[8] in low and low-middle-income countries have resulted in social media platforms becoming the entry points for access to the internet, which severely limits the sources and quality of information necessary for informed debates and deliberations.

The public sphere, considered the 'shared spaces — real, virtual or imagined — whereby social issues are discussed and public opinion is formed' (Wardle and Derakhshan 2017), is becoming increasingly less shared and more manipulated. S. Vaidhyanathan (2018) refers to Facebook, for example, as 'a sort of mediated cacophony that would hinder public deliberation about important issues, thus undermining trust in institutions and experts'.

This sphere has become a breeding ground for a new type of illiberal demagogue such as Bolsonaro, who has captured power with neither prior political experience nor any vision for democracy building. The only agenda is to maintain power by exploiting the fears and prejudices of the average voter. Da Empoli (2019) has called attention to the fact that

> behind the apparent absurdity of fake news and conspiracy theories, a very solid logic is hidden. From the point of view of populist leaders, alternative truths are not simply propaganda tools. Contrary to true information, they are a formidable vector of cohesion. (…) their refusal to accept and play by contemporary democratic and social standards is seen as an act of courage and a rupture with the 'system' instead of simple populist pyrotechnics.

Information, Technology, and Social Movements

The context presented in the preceding sections seems to contradict the idea of the internet as a democratic space, open for all, where silenced voices can find refuge and flourish. This hopeful view of the internet was prevalent amongst many practitioners and scholars during the initial years of its expansion. How can this positive take on digital technologies be reconciled with the recognition of the increasing growth in digital authoritarianism described above?

Time and space are key elements of the answer. As stated by M. Monshipouri (2016, 2), 'the emancipatory power of the Internet and other modes of digital communication has drawn attention for its unprecedented potential for social change…. By making information more accessible than ever before, digital technologies have come to shape societies and cultures in many respects.'

The result of this process, however, has been the growing privatisation, weaponisation, and commodification of the internet, particularly social media, by forces seeking to regain the terrain for authoritarianism and market fundamentalism. It is precisely because of its potential for social change that today internet ownership and regulation are at the forefront of contemporary human rights struggles. Issues such as the protection of privacy and freedom of expression online, ethical standards for the implementation of artificial intelligence, platform transparency, biased algorithms, and content moderation are prominent in the political and policymaking spaces at the national and global levels.

Looking at the past through a critical lens can provide clues to moving ahead. It is important to understand why the internet was able to develop with fewer restrictions in its early years, as well as identify when it still manages to play a pro-democracy and development role today.

The preceding sections showed how policymakers have been responding to digitalisation and disinformation with rushed and heavy-handed legal frameworks. As a rule, this will result in laws that accomplish very little to address the challenges of information disorders, and which may be used to silence contesting voices. Although there is room for adopting legal standards regarding concentration and transparency standards in the tech sector, most issues concerning content (discriminatory and harmful content, disinformation and misinformation, hate speech) are better addressed by strengthening the diversity of voices and the spaces where discussions on issues of collective interest take place in our societies.

One of the main social struggles in contemporary societies concerns access to and control over information. As made explicit by the Brazilian example above, information disorders require complex and holistic solutions centred around ensuring 'information' as a human right and a capability that should be governed as a public good.

This requires a change in paradigm and direction. The digital transformation our societies are undergoing has moved, as highlighted above, in the route towards privatisation, concentration, technical fragmentation, and political control. The paradigm of proprietary internet standards and platforms must be replaced by one that recognises the new digital public sphere. For that, much can be learnt from social movements and their role, historically and in the digital age. Digital technologies have certainly offered tools for resistance and change, and can be deployed in certain circumstances to influence power relations.

We propose that strategies and processes from social movement history ought to inform how we foster an information regime in which the right to information advances capabilities and freedoms. In particular, the following aspects of social movements could provide valuable guidance to recalibrating the information regime:

(i) social movements operate under the logic of creating trust and building linkages, in clear opposition to disinformation, which is built on the intensification of distrust and social conflict;
(ii) social movements in the digital age are decentralised and carry out *network politics*;[9]

(iii) social movements (especially those building on identity struggles) seek to create alternative and counter-narratives.

By looking at how recent social movements have used the internet, we may draw important lessons for opposing the spread of disinformation disorders and promoting an internet that can be deployed to increase people's agency and rights, counter populist authoritarian trends, and promote democracy.

As summarised by Monshipouri (2016), global social movements, such as feminist, environmental, and human rights movements, organise today around flexible, dispersed, and horizontal networks:

> By promoting horizontal links and providing a method for communication across space in real time, new technologies have bolstered decentralized network constellations, facilitating informal or underground transnational coordination and communication. This network politics involves the creation of inclusive spaces where diverse movements converge around common goals while still maintaining their autonomy.

J. Barry (2016) proposes that information and communication technologies can help mobilise and improve the salience of social movements in the following ways: they share information more efficiently and reduce the information gap; they shrink distances by allowing easier social connection across geographical locations; they enhance the types of tactics employed by movements; they increase social capital, civil society and individual connections; and they organise movements around flexible, dispersed, and horizontal networks. Castells (2012, 12) highlights the importance of developing autonomous networks for horizontal communication. By being free from the control of those holding institutional power, these networks have led to new forms of social change and political democracy.

Of course, there is also a downside to this scenario. Lack of meaningful access to the internet, and for those online, increasing surveillance, cyber attacks, and internet disruptions may compromise this strategy. Further, as indicated by M. U. D'Silva and A. Atay (2019, 3), 'social media simultaneously facilitates a vibrant public sphere and creates cultural and social cleavages'.

The struggle for network control is one for technical control, but above all, it is a struggle for governing meaning. The battle over worldviews and knowledge can no longer be separated from technological resources. Information — worldviews, knowledge — and technology have become interwoven (Monshipouri 2016).

Conclusion

The UN Secretary-General, in one of his first public addresses on the COVID-19 health crisis in March 2020, highlighted that we were not only facing a pandemic but also an 'infodemic'. Misleading, false, and conspiracy allegations flooded the internet with cures, causes, and political motivations for the health emergency, at times jeopardising efforts to curtail the spread of the disease.

COVID-19 emerged as the latest and most striking example of a world grappling with the rapid influence of information and communication technologies on our lives, particularly in how we consume and utilise information. Such technologies have facilitated people's access to both information and public debate. The rapid expansion of internet use, access to mobile technology, and social media platforms have created a world in which information has become a central part of our daily routines in unprecedented ways. Such ubiquity of information has permeated our private and public lives, possibly even blurring these borders.

The other side of this context is the hidden world of algorithms, surveillance, and content moderation. If the expansion of social media brought new opportunities for the democratisation of speech, it has also presented considerable new risks. Understanding the function of online platforms and the impact of their use is essential if we are to face their enormous powers over our rights to opinion, expression, and information. Understanding how they can be used as political weaponry is critical if we are to defend democracy and continue to promote the free flow of information, ideas, and visions, which are required for meaningful public participation and engagement in public affairs.

The authoritarian populism seen at the time of Bolsonaro's administration in Brazil—and also in many other places around the globe—represents a new form of government, based on calculated attacks against the informational ecosystem of their countries. Manipulation of information targets not only the opposition, but also seeks the delegitimisation of democratic institutions and practices.

The COVID-19 pandemic provided the 'perfect' context to demonstrate the dangers of this kind of populism. In the face of a critical health crisis that required coordination, dialogue, tolerance, and solidarity, the Brazilian government failed to manage the situation and establish a harmonised response to the emergency. Many critics have gone further, stating that several of Bolsonaro's actions aggravated the health crisis, causing the extreme numbers of infections and deaths across the country. The health crisis, despite its severity, was yet another issue caught up in political polarisation and used as a political weapon (Ricard and Medeiros 2020). The story is not much different in the United States, where President Donald Trump, who underplayed the gravity of the pandemic, undermined scientific evidence and public health guidelines to crassly pursue his re-election bid, while the country registered hundreds of thousands of COVID-19 related deaths (Observer Editorial 2020).

According to Bradshaw and Howard (2018), '[i]n an information environment characterized by high volumes of information and limited levels of user attention and trust, the tools and techniques of computational propaganda are becoming a common—and arguably essential—part of digital campaigning and public diplomacy.'

Urgent and concerted efforts are needed to find ways to counter the pandemic of disinformation. This calls for reconceptualising freedom of information, opinion, and expression in the digital context, and developing smart regulatory frameworks to respond to the serious threat that disinformation poses to democracy. But these measures need to go hand–in-hand with movement building and the strengthening of social movement strategies to promote an internet less controlled by political and economic interests. A model of governance of the internet that is centred on people and their rights and capabilities, and the characterisation of information as a public good is at the centre of these strategies.

Notes

1. Here, 'public information regime' is used to refer to the legal and policy framework established to provide individuals with access to public information and transparency on issues of collective interest. This regime normally includes Freedom of Information Acts, their oversight bodies, statistical institutes, transparency agencies, and ombudsman offices, among others.

2. For ease of reading, this chapter will refer generally to 'disinformation'. We highlight, however, that 'information disorders' refer to a complex phenomenon that has been studied and classified in different ways by researchers. For important classifications, see, for example, Neudert, et al. (2017) and Wardle and Derakhshan (2017). For a historical account of disinformation, see Uberti (2016).

3. This situation has led WhatsApp to recently add new limits on the number of times a forwarded message can be shared simultaneously; see Gold (2020).

4. 'Computational amplification' refers to the amplification of disinformation through the use of computational or automated tools, such as bots.

5. In the 2024 Index, Brazil's position was shown to have improved. It is now ranked at 82, out of 180 countries. See https://rsf.org/en/index (accessed February 2025).

6. The term 'information pollution' was first used by Jakob Nielsen in 2003 as a way to describe irrelevant, redundant, unsolicited, and low-value information.

7. For an interesting and accessible account on this matter, see Howard and Bradshaw (2018).

8. For a comprehensive explanation of zero rating schemes and their implications, see Coldewey (2017).

9. 'For social scientists, network analysis employs "concepts of location, or nodes, and the relations among these positions—termed ties, connections, or links—to argue that the pattern of relationships shapes the behavior of the occupant of a post, as well as influences others"' (Kahler 2009, 4).

Select References

Amado, G. 2020. 'Mudança na lei de acesso à informação é mais uma janela que se abre para corrupcão por coronavirus'. *Epoca*, 24 March. Available at https://oglobo.globo.com/epoca/guilherme-amado/mudanca-na-lei-de-acesso-informacao-mais-uma-janela-que-se-abre-para-corrupcao-por-coronavirus-1-24325219 (accessed February 2025).

AOS Fatos. 2020. 'Base bolsonarista no Twitter impulsiona desinformação, mas perde espaço na rede', 7 April. Available at https://www.aosfatos.org/noticias/base-bolsonarista-no-twitter-impulsiona-desinformacao-mas-perde-espaco-na-rede/ (accessed February 2025).

AP Exata. 2020. 'Sobre Nós'. Available at www.agenciaexata.com/ (accessed October 2024).

Arnaudo, D. 2017. 'Computational Propaganda in Brazil: Social Bots during Elections'. Working Paper 8, 1–39, Oxford University Research Archive. Oxford, UK: Computational Propaganda Research Project.

Artigo 19. 'Atualizando a censura: Violência contra jornalistas e veículos de communicação', September. Available at artigo19.org/wp-content/blogs.dir/24/files/2020/09/AnaliseViolacoesJornalistas_set2020.pdf (accessed October 2024).

Bandeira, L., D. Barojan, R. Braga, J. L. Peñarredonda, and M. F. Pérez Argüello. 2019. 'Disinformation in Democracies: Strengthening Digital Resilience in Latin America'. *Atlantic Council*, 28 March. Available at https://www.atlanticcouncil.org/in-depth-research-reports/report/disinformation-democracies-strengthening-digital-resilience-latin-america/ (accessed October 2024).

Barry, J. 2016. 'Social Movements in the Digital Age'. In M. Monshipouri (ed.), *Information Politics, Protests, and Human Rights in the Digital Age*, 23–49. Cambridge, UK: Cambridge University Press.

Brazil Federal Senate. n.d. 'Atividade Legislativa', Government of Brazil. Available at legis.senado.leg.br/comissoes/comissao?0&codcol=2292> (accessed October 2024).

Brazil Secretary General. 2020. *Medida Provisória No. 928*, 23 March. Available at https://www.planalto.gov.br/ccivil_03/_ato2019-2022/2020/mpv/mpv928.htm (accessed February 2025).

Carr, P., S. L. Cuervo Sanchez, and M. Aparecida Daros. 2020. 'Citizen Engagement in the Contemporary Era of Fake News: Hegemonic Distraction or Control of the Social Media Context?' *Postdigital Science & Education* 2 (12 July), 39–60. Available at link.springer.com/article/10.1007/s42438-019-00052-z (accessed October 2024).

Castells, M. 2012. 'Changing the World in the Network Society', in M. Castells (ed.), *Networks of Outrage and Hope: Social Movements in the Internet Age*, 218–244. Cambridge, UK: Polity Press.

Coldewey, D. 2017. 'WTF is Zero Rating?' *Tech Crunch*, 16 April. Available at techcrunch.com/2017/04/16/wtf-is-zero-rating/ (accessed October 2024).

Committee to Protect Journalists. 2020. 'Brazil restricts access to government information amid COVID-19 emergency'. *CPJ*, 26 March. Available at cpj.org/2020/03/brazil-restricts-access-to-government-information-.php (accessed October 2024).

Coppins, M. 2020. 'The Billion-Dollar Disinformation Campaign to Reelect the President'. *The Atlantic*, 10 February. Available at www.theatlantic.com/magazine/archive/2020/03/the-2020-disinformation-war/605530/ (accessed October 2024).

D'Silva, M. U., and A. Atay (eds). 2019. *Intercultural Communication, Identity, and Social Movements in the Digital Age*. London: Routledge.

Da Empoli, G. 2019. *Os Engenheiros do Caos*. São Paulo, BR: Vestígio.

De Goiás, D. 2020. 'Moraes Suspende Alteração nas Regras da Lei de Acesso à Informação'. *Diáro de Goiás*, 26 March. Available at https://diariodegoias.com.br/moraes-suspende-alteracao-nas-regras-da-lei-de-acesso-a-informacao/156803/ (accessed February 2025).

Elswah, M., and P. Howard. 2020. 'The Challenges of Monitoring Social Media in the Arab World: The Case of the 2019 Tunisian Elections', Memo, Vol. 1. Oxford, UK: Oxford Internet Institute.

Estado de Minas. 2020. 'Piora desempenho de Bolsonaro nas redes sociais'. *Estado de Minas*, 11 February. Available at https://www.em.com.br/app/noticia/politica/2020/02/11/interna_politica,1121025/piora-desempenho-de-bolsonaro-nas-redes.shtml (accessed October 2024).

Fridman, U. 2020. 'The Coronavirus-Denial Movement Now Has a Leader'. *The Atlantic*, 27 March. Available at www.theatlantic.com/politics/archive/2020/03/bolsonaro-coronavirus-denial-brazil-trump/608926/ (accessed October 2024).

Fórum de Direito de Acesso a Informações Públicas. 2020. 'Alterações no atendimento a pedidos de informação e a MP 928', 4 May. Available at https://informacaopublica.org.br/leia/pandemia-foi-usada-para-negar-atendimento-a-pedidos-de-informacao-mesmo-apos-suspensao-da-mp-928/ (accessed October 2024).

Fundacao Getulio Vargas, DAPP. 2018. 'Impacto das redes sociais e da desinformação nas eleições é tema de debate em think tank dos EUA'. *FGV ECMI*. Available at https://portal.fgv.br/noticias/impacto-redes-sociais-e-desinformacao-eleicoes-e-tema-debate-think-tank-eua (accessed February 2025).

Gold, H. 2020. 'WhatsApp tightens limit on message forwarding to counter coronavirus misinformation'. *CNN Business*, 7 April. Available at https://www.cnn.com/2020/04/07/tech/whatsapp-misinformation-forward-limit/index.html (accessed February 2025).

Government of Brazil. n.d. *Painel Coronavírus*. Available at covid.saude.gov.br/ (accessed October 2024).

Habermas, J. 2006. 'Political Communication in Media Society: Does Democracy Still Enjoy an Epistemic Dimension? The Impact of Normative Theory on Empirical Research'. *Communication Theory* 16, 411. Available at www.worldcat.org/title/political-communication-in-media-society-does-democracy-still-enjoy-an-epistemic-dimension-the-impact-of-normative-theory-on-empirical-research/oclc/5156534851&referer=brief_results (accessed October 2024).

Horwitz, J., and D. Seetharaman. 2020. 'Facebook Executives Shut Down Efforts to Make the Site Less Divisive'. *The Wall Street Journal*, 26 May. Available at www.wsj.com/articles/facebook-knows-it-encourages-division-top-executives-nixed-solutions-11590507499 (accessed October 2024).

Howard, P., and S. Bradshaw. 2018. 'Three reasons junk news spreads so quickly across social media'. *Oxford Internet Institute*, 26 March. Available at www.oii.ox.ac.uk/blog/three-reasons-junk-news-spreads-so-quickly-across-social-media/ (accessed October 2024).

Kahler, M. (ed.). 2009. *Networked Politics: Agency, Power, and Governance*. Ithaca, NY: Cornell University Press.

Legislative Radar. n.d. 'Projetos de Lei'. *Radar Legislativo*. Available at radarlegislativo.org/ (accessed October 2024).

Mandl, C., and A. Caverni. 2020. 'Brazil president takes selfies, cheers demonstrators despite virus warnings'. *Reuters*, 15 March. Available at https://www.reuters.com/article/world/brazil-president-takes-selfies-cheers-demonstrators-despite-virus-warnings-idUSKBN21215X/ (accessed February 2025).

Mello, P. C. 2020. 'Brazil's Troll Army Moves into the Streets'. *New York Times*, 4 August. Available at www.nytimes.com/2020/08/04/opinion/bolsonaro-office-of-hate-brazil.html (accessed October 2024).

Meta. 2018. 'Mais ações para proteger a eleição no Brasil'. *Meta*, 20 September. Available at about.fb.com/br/news/2018/09/mais-acoes-para-proteger-a-eleicao-no-brasil/ (accessed October 2024).

Monshipouri, M. 2016. 'Introduction: Protests and Human Rights in Context', in M. Monshipouri (ed.), *Information Politics, Protests, and Human Rights in the Digital Age*, 1–20. Cambridge, UK: Cambridge University Press.

Neudert, L.-M., B. Kollanyi, and P. N. Howard. 2017. 'Junk News and Bots during the German Parliamentary Election: What are German Voters Sharing over Twitter?' Memo, Vol. 7, 19 September. Oxford, UK: Oxford Internet Institute Data Memo.

Newton, C. 2020. 'How WhatsApp is making it more expensive to spread misinformation'. *The Verge*, 8 April. Available at www.theverge.com/interface/2020/4/8/21212110/whatsapp-forward-limit-encryption-apple-imessage-signal (accessed October 2024).

News Wires. 2020. 'Bolsonaro questions number of Brazil coronavirus deaths'. *France 24*, 28 March Available at www.france24.com/en/20200328-brazil-s-bolsonaro-questions-coronavirus-statistics-says-sorry-some-will-die (accessed October 2024).

Observer Editorial. 2020. 'The Observer view on Donald Trump's coronavirus infection'. *The Guardian*, 3 October. Available at www.theguardian.com/commentisfree/2020/oct/03/the-observer-view-on-donald-trumps-coronavirus-infection (accessed October 2024).

Paixão, M. 2020. 'CIDH realiza audiencia sobre violações à liberdade de expressão e de imprensa no Brasil'. *Abraji*, 31 January. Available at www.abraji.org.br/noticias/cidh-realiza-audiencia-sobre-violacoes-a-liberdade-de-expressao-e-de-imprensa-no-brasil (accessed October 2024).

Política. 2020a. 'ABI envia pedido de impeachment de Bolsonaro à Câmara', 6 May. Available at www.em.com.br/app/noticia/politica/2020/05/06/interna_politica,1145052/abi-envia-pedido-de-impeachment-de-bolsonaro-a-camara.shtml?mc_cid=f0188b56be&mc_eid=027405d16b (accessed October 2024).

_____. 2020b. 'Entidades criticam mudanças na LAI: "Só venceremos com transparência"', 24 March. Available at noticias.uol.com.br/politica/ultimas-noticias/2020/03/24/entidades-criticam-mudanca-na-lai-so-venceremos-com-transparencia.html (accessed October 2024).

_____. 2020c. 'Bolsonaro Endossa Noticia Falsa Para Dizer que Estados Inflam Mortes por Coronavirus', 31 March. Available at https://valor.globo.com/politica/noticia/2020/03/31/bolsonaro-endossa-noticia-falsa-para-dizer-que-estados-inflam-mortes-por-coronavirus.ghtml (accessed October 2024).

Popper, K. 1957. *The Open Society and Its Enemies*. London, UK: Routledge, 3rd edn.

Redação RBA. 2020. 'Unicamp: Notícias falsas divulgadas por Bolsonaro são risco ao cidadão'. *Rede Brasil Atual*, 6 April. Available at www.redebrasilatual.com.br/cidadania/2020/04/pesquisadores-unicamp-noticias-falsas-familia-bolsonaro/ (accessed October 2024).

Reporters without Borders. 2020a. 'Brazil'. Available at rsf.org/en/brazil (accessed October 2024).

_____. 2020b. 'Brazil quarterly analysis. President Bolsonaro's systematic attempts to reduce the media to silence', 16 April. Available at rsf.org/en/news/brazil-quarterly-analysis-president-bolsonaros-systematic-attempts-reduce-media-silence (accessed October 2024).

Ricard, J., and J. Medeiros. 2020. 'Using Misinformation as a Political Weapon: COVID-19 and Bolsonaro in Brazil'. *Harvard Kennedy School Misinformation Rev* 1 (2), 1.

Rudnitzki E., L. Scofield, R. Ribeiro, and N. Viana. 2020. 'A rede de Fake News que derrbubou Mandetta'. *Publica*, 17 April. Available at apublica.org/2020/04/a-rede-de-fake-news-que-derrubou-mandetta/ (accessed October 2024).

Smith, A. E. 2020. 'Covid vs. Democracy: Brazil's Populist Playbook'. *Journal of Democracy* 31 (4), 76–90. Available at https://www.journalofdemocracy.org/articles/covid-vs-democracy-brazils-populist-playbook/ (accessed February 2025).

Supremo Tribunal Federal. 2020. 'Notícias STF', 30 April.

Transparency International. 2020. 'Contrataciones Públicas en Estados de Emergencias'. Available at https://images.transparencycdn.org/images/COVID_19_Public_procurement_Latin_America_ES_PT.pdf (accessed February 2025).

Trevisani, P. 2020. 'Brazil's President Hits the Street, Railing Against the Media'. *The Wall Street Journal*, 11 February. Available at www.wsj.com/articles/brazils-president-hits-the-street-railing-against-the-media-11581435661 (accessed October 2024).

TV Senado. 2019. 'CPMI Fake News: Depoimento da deputada federal Joice Hasselmann'. *YouTube*, 12 April. Available at www.youtube.com/watch?v=YzUyXGRZ9Xc&feature=emb_title (accessed October 2024).

Uberti, D. 2016. 'The real history of fake news'. *Columbia Journalism Review*, 15 December. Available at www.cjr.org/special_report/fake_news_history.php (accessed October 2024).

Vaidhyanathan, S. 2018. *Antisocial Media: How Facebook Disconnects Us and Undermines Democracy*. Oxford, UK: Oxford University Press.

Valfré, V. 2020. 'Conheça Todos Os Pedidos de Impeachment Contra Bolsonaro'. *Estadão*, 20 June. Available at www.estadao.com.br/infograficos/politica,conheca-todos-os-pedidos-de-impeachment-contra-bolsonaro,1101544 (accessed October 2024).

Wardle, C., and H. Derakhshan. 2017. *Information Disorder: Toward an Interdisciplinary Framework for Research and Policymaking*. Strasbourg, FR: Council of Europe.

Westrup, A. C. 2020. 'Desinformação como estratégia de governo'. *Diplomatique*, 1 April. Available at diplomatique.org.br/desinformacao-como-estrategia-de-governo/ (accessed October 2024).

Democracy Upended
Lessons from Afghanistan

Pearl Eliadis and Lucile Martin

Introduction

Although democracy's promise of just governance has never matched its ability to deliver on that promise, the gap between them has widened in recent years. The 'Unpacking Participatory Democracy' initiative spearheaded by Aruna Roy, in collaboration with the Institute for the Study of International Development (ISID), offers critical lenses through which to assess participatory democracy. These perspectives include compliance with constitutional requirements and international law, transparency, accountability, and a special focus on participation in democratic processes that engage with poor and other marginalised people (Pande 2018). The rise of authoritarianism, power imbalances, and official resistance to citizen participation have combined to diminish institutional transparency and political and bureaucratic accountability (ibid.). By linking the theoretical insights of scholars with experiential knowledge of civil society, 'Unpacking Participatory Democracy' illustrates the importance of placing people at the centre of democratic governance. It also illustrates the implications in a country like Afghanistan, where the failure over many years to place people at the centre of democratic initiatives and to engage at local levels contributed to the collapse of democratic institutions.

If the global governance gap was already marked in 2018, it widened in 2020 when COVID-19 struck, with devastating consequences for countries that were already plagued by war, conflict, and inequality. Drastic emergency measures were introduced to fight the virus, thus suddenly and narrowly redefining fundamental rights, especially the rights to life, liberty, and security of the person. These rights were subjugated or reframed in relation to the right to health, which in turn was narrowly framed in relation to avoiding infection by the COVID-19 virus. Meanwhile, other rights, including other social and economic, as well as environmental concerns, were relegated to the background. Nations either declared states of emergency or simply deployed existing emergency legislation without constitutional modifications. There was minimal legislative oversight and accountability mechanisms were suspended. In countries where authoritarian rule has prevailed, governance gaps widened into chasms.

This chapter applies the lessons from 'Unpacking Participatory Democracy' and from the work of the Afghanistan Public Policy Research Organization (APPRO) to the fragile Afghan context. It focuses on the additional social stresses created by the public health threat of the COVID-19 pandemic and the corresponding reduction of citizen-based and people-centred mechanisms to address these threats. Pre-existing factors included longstanding failures to achieve sustained democratic and participatory processes that were capable of engaging meaningfully with people's lives at the local level, and which created conditions that made authentic participatory processes unable to thrive.

We argue that human rights-based perspectives or approaches, coupled with an enabling environment, would have been fundamental to understanding and addressing democratic deficits. These approaches remain relevant in the post-pandemic future of Afghanistan. The importance of human rights-based approaches is underscored by reports about the impacts of the pandemic, showing that blanket emergency measures are often insensitive to — and indeed, worsened by — the health and security of certain marginalised and vulnerable groups. These include migrants, homeless people, prisoners, and women, who often bear the gendered burden of the pandemic. Civil society organisations have also become even more fragile as the political space for their operation has narrowed.

These phenomena have had especially serious repercussions for participatory democracy in countries that have experienced war and violence. This chapter examines how governance mechanisms in Afghanistan, already weakened by conflict and instability, were affected by COVID-19.[1] It proposes sustainable strategies to strengthen the role of civil society as a fundamental mechanism for improving participatory democracy in countries experiencing conflict and instability by examining:

- The human rights implications of the measures taken by the Government of Afghanistan to address the pandemic.[2]
- The extent to which the pandemic has affected the separation of powers among the executive, legislative, and judicial branches of government.
- New challenges to civil society's role as a central actor in promoting participatory democracy and upholding and defending rights using a human rights-based approach.
- Prospective methods for sustaining demands for accountability and transparency from the authorities and ensuring participatory approaches to governance during times of emergency and beyond.

We argue that Afghanistan's unique context provides valuable lessons for countries experiencing conflict and political instability. There is a pressing need for the international community to support Afghan civil society organisations, including human rights defenders. Amplifying the voices and needs of citizens and strengthening accountability mechanisms can be achieved through civil society as a medium- and long-term strategy to ensure agency and participatory approaches to governance at the community level. We further argue that it is more important that these mechanisms be in place during times when ruling authorities actively restrict an enabling environment for civil society.

This chapter begins with an overview of the Afghanistan context in relation to the strains and stresses on Afghan society that predated the pandemic, and the ways in which the pandemic exacerbated those conditions. It also examines the trend among donors to create, foster, and sustain parallel institutions that never really took root. It then examines the broad features of 'pandemic governance' and its implications for participatory democracy in Afghanistan, followed by an overview of the international and national legal frameworks for public emergencies and the extent to which Afghanistan complied with human rights norms. It then proposes a human rights-based approach to governance grounded in inclusive and participatory accountability and decision-making, which would centre on civil society to re-shape modes of engagement at the community level.

Context

In Afghanistan, the pandemic emerged at the intersection of sanitary, humanitarian, and economic crises on the one hand, and armed conflict on the other. Governance and health infrastructures were already weakened by conflict and rampant corruption, and deteriorated further due to the unprecedented pressures placed upon them by COVID-19. The public sector was ill-equipped and ill-prepared to manage further strain. Widespread poverty, internal displacement, and the return of Afghan migrants from neighbouring Iran and Pakistan, countries that were both heavily affected by COVID-19, contributed to Afghanistan's inclusion among the most vulnerable countries in the world facing the virus (Inter-Cluster Coordination Team 2020).

The pandemic thus added new layers of uncertainty to an already fragile peace process and to weak democratic accountability, creating alarming levels of social and economic vulnerability. Civil society should have been a critical source of local community support, data gathering, and advocacy across all these areas. Instead, the pandemic exposed the existing weaknesses and further diminished civil society's relevance, resulting in the erosion of a key mechanism of participatory democracy.

Social and Economic Conditions

In 2017, an estimated 55 per cent of the Afghan population was already living below the poverty line and almost 45 per cent was considered food insecure (Central Statistics Office 2017). As a result of the pandemic, food insecurity was expected to reach emergency levels in 2020, and the poverty rate to increase up to 72 per cent (World Bank 2020). Shortages in food supplies due to the disruption of trade networks led to a rise in the prices of staples such as rice, flour, oil, pulses, and sugar (World Food Program 2020). By the end of March 2022, almost 20 million Afghans, about half the population, were experiencing acute food insecurity, classified as being in crisis or in emergency (IPC 2022).

Already scarce wage-earning opportunities became scarcer because of containment measures, exacerbating the vulnerability of households which relied on daily wages for subsistence (United Nations Office for the Coordination of Humanitarian Affairs 2020a). The widespread impact of the pandemic also strained kinship-based solidarity mechanisms. In the absence of State support, these mechanisms weakened and became more vulnerable precisely for those who depended on them the most: the elderly, the chronically ill, and persons with disabilities (OCHA 2020b, 2020c). Returnees from Iran and Pakistan, who already faced specific vulnerabilities due to their displacement, were stigmatised as 'importers' of the virus (Mashal and Hayeri 2020).

As a result of the pandemic, pre-existing inequalities and inequities in accessing basic rights by different segments of the population worsened. Vulnerable groups, including the urban poor, internally displaced persons, and returnees living in highly concentrated areas, faced higher risks of contamination, with access to health services limited for most in both rural and urban settings (Global Protection Cluster 2020). Lack of accountability from officials, misappropriation and mishandling of resources, perceptions of officials as serving their own interests or being more concerned about reporting to international donors than serving their constituencies further undermined an already limited confidence in the Government of the Islamic Republic of Afghanistan's legitimacy and ability to address the needs of Afghan citizens (Martin and Parto 2020).

The pandemic also aggravated violations of children's rights at a global level, including the risk of ill-treatment and torture.[3] In Afghanistan, the pandemic has raised concerns about increased risks of malnutrition, neglect, exploitation, and abuse. Child labour, a coping strategy for many households, is on the rise (Save the Children 2022). The country was among those with the highest risk of dropouts from the education system as a result of the pandemic (ibid.; Wagner and Warren 2020). This risk was further heightened by the political and economic crisis that ensued with the Taliban takeover. Schools closed for six months and were then only reopened for boys in the secondary schools in March 2022, with an estimated four million children having dropped out of school, and eight million in need of humanitarian aid (*Reliefweb* 2022).

As in other countries in the Asia and Pacific regions, pre-existing gender inequalities and discriminatory social norms were exacerbated, resulting in an inequitable sharing of the pandemic burden (Gender in Humanitarian Action 2020). Women, as health service providers, workers, homemakers, and caregivers, were particularly affected by the pandemic. Strict social norms for many women and girls commonly translate into forced confinement, domestic and sexual violence, and limited movement outside the home, while further restrictions in access to basic services took place, including information, physical and mental health, and other support mechanisms (Elliott 2019; Kurtzer 2020). The diversion of already limited health resources towards the fight against the pandemic placed additional strain on the resources that were available for pre- and post-natal healthcare and family planning. Protection services for survivors of gender-based violence, whether governmental or non-governmental, were notably impacted by the pandemic (UN Women 2020). After the Taliban takeover, the exclusion of girls from secondary education and the collapse of the health system worsened the circumstances for women, girls, and children. Human Rights Watch (2022) reported that the added burden of the impact of the sanctions has deepened the people's misery, compounded by factors such as the increased stress of the *mahram* (male chaperone) and the collapse of the national economy; at the time of writing, virtually all female-headed households were in an acute state of food insecurity, leading to child marriages in exchange for dowries and an increase in child labour.

The COVID-19 Crisis and the Peace Process

The COVID-19 pandemic emerged during a political crisis while a fragile peace process was underway. Following years of fruitless negotiations, the 'Agreement for Bringing Peace to Afghanistan' (2020) between the Taliban and the United States was signed on 29 February 2020, just as the first virus cases were being confirmed in Herat.[4] The Agreement provided for the cessation of violence between the Taliban and the United States, a phased withdrawal of foreign forces, and the organisation of intra-Afghan peace talks intended to pave the way for peace in Afghanistan. The peace talks were originally planned to start on 10 March 2020, but were delayed following a political standoff over the disputed results of the 2019 presidential election and due to the failure of the conflicting parties to agree on prerequisites for talks until August 2020.[5] Calls for a humanitarian ceasefire in light of COVID-19 by the UN Security Council, the Organization for Islamic States, regional governments including China, Iran, and Russia, and international and local civil society organisations were ignored by the Taliban (Halaimzai and Sidiqi 2020). Intra-Afghan peace talks started in Doha in September 2020. However, amidst concerns over the political manipulation of COVID-19 by parties to the conflict, fighting in the country continued, creating further threats at the intersection of conflict and the pandemic for vulnerable citizens.[6] There was also significant concern in the civil society that democratic institutions and constitutional rights would be further threatened by a potential power sharing agreement with the Taliban as an outcome of ongoing negotiations. With the collapse of the Islamic Republic, the flight of its President, and the surrender of national army troops to the Taliban on 15 August 2021, any hopes of a negotiated agreement were dashed.

The Government of the Islamic Republic of Afghanistan and Separation of Powers

At its most basic level, participatory democracy requires respect for the fundamental constitutional structures that set out the rights of the people and their relationship to the government. In Afghanistan, the executive branch of government has historically held the balance of power, and the pandemic did not significantly alter the relative power relationships among the executive, the legislature, and the judicial branches. At the time of the Islamic Republic and since the adoption of the new Constitution in 2004, the executive had systematically encroached on the legislative powers of Parliament and maintained tight control over the judiciary. While it is not unusual for government power to be concentrated in the executive branch, in Afghanistan, the combined effects of weak parliamentary capacity, nepotism, presidential control over the composition and functioning of the judiciary, along with repeated and successful efforts by the government to pre-empt legislative processes further centralised executive power. Legislative powers were seriously undermined and the judiciary did not assume its role as an independent organ of review and oversight (Hamidi and Jayakodi 2015).

Even prior to the pandemic, the Afghanistan government consistently used emergency legislation under Article 79 of the Afghan Constitution, but failed to comply with constitutional requirements that obligated the government to present legislative decrees to the Parliament within thirty days.[7] The government also regularly invoked Article 121 to request judicial review by the Supreme Court of parliamentary bills.[8] Both these government actions undermined legislative power. According to Hamidi and Jayakodi (2015), the combined effect of the abusive mobilisation of Articles 79 and 121 of the Constitution 'allowed the government to implement the laws it desires, without the approval or disapproval of the Parliament' (ibid., 14). Parliament has also failed to use the oversight mechanisms under Article 89, which provide Parliament with 'the authority to establish a special commission, on the proposal of one third of its members, to review as well as investigate the actions of the Government' (ibid., 12).

In Afghanistan, a state of emergency can be declared under Article 143 of Chapter 9 of the Constitution 'if because of war, threat of war, serious rebellion, natural disasters or similar conditions, protection of independence and national life become impossible through the channels specified in this Constitution'.

Since 2001, the Government of Afghanistan had not invoked Article 143 to declare a formal state of emergency, including during the COVID-19 pandemic. Since 2004 it had, however, consistently made use of emergency legislation through decrees under Article 79, as mentioned previously, which resulted in the passing of laws that arguably violated not only the Constitution but also the International Covenant on Civil and Political Rights (ICCPR),[9] to which Afghanistan is a party.[10] The persistent and repeated use of emergency legislation without declaring a state of emergency or using statutory authorisation for special measures related to health emergencies constitutes a legal violation of Article 4 of the ICCPR, which will be discussed below. This failure to respect basic constitutional provisions has consequences for compliance with the rule of law domestically, as well as with international human rights law. It raises important questions about the extent to which the pandemic has exacerbated the Afghan State's non-compliance with principles of good governance and the rule of law, as well as the ability of independent formal or informal institutions of governance, including civil society, to hold it accountable.

The question of what the current constitutional regime actually is in Afghanistan at the time of writing, under the *de facto* Taliban administration, remains open. Former laws adopted under the Islamic Republic are allegedly still in place, pending a review of their compatibility with the Taliban's interpretation of the Shari'a. In the absence of a consolidated legal framework, the ability of civil society to rely on or to challenge laws is hindered.

STATE-CIVIL SOCIETY RELATIONS UNDER THE ISLAMIC REPUBLIC OF AFGHANISTAN

People's campaigns, social audits, and other processes designed to improve participatory democracy are fundamental components in forging new relationships with power and improving both equality and equity (ISID 2018, 9). Under the Islamic Republic, relations between the State and civil society in Afghanistan were more confrontational than collaborative (Durand 2015; European External Action Service [EEAS] 2019; United States Agency for International Development 2016). Commitments made by the last National Unity Government (2014–2020) to protect the operating space of civil society and include it in legal reform processes and strategic planning were not implemented sufficiently. Repeated concerns have been expressed in recent years about the shrinking of the space available for civil society (EEAS 2019). Legislation on access to information, anti-corruption, and on whistle-blower protection were all adopted following persistent pressure from civil society and donors, but were not implemented in practice (Bjelica 2019; UNAMA 2020). Government representatives, for instance, rarely felt compelled to inform citizens about public decisions, even when information was requested through legal channels (Amnesty International 2020; Holland, et al. 2016). In short, there was a palpable lack of a real cultural change in Afghanistan, according to Sayed Ikram Afzali, Executive Director of Integrity Watch and Chairman of the Oversight

Commission on Access to Information in Afghanistan, who shared first-hand experience with respect to the pre-pandemic Afghan context:

> One of the problems faced was access to information and lack of information. [We] tried to learn from India and adapted the access to information law, fought for it for five to six years and got the law, although it is not as strong as people wanted it to be. There have been no complaints/demands filed in the access to information law. People still don't believe that the law would work and that the mechanism would respond. A lot of work needs to be done in this aspect. (ISID 2018, 150)

In addition to a weak culture of accountability and transparency, civil society in Afghanistan did not succeed in coordinating its actions effectively among its own organisations or in engaging effectively with government representatives. Participation in policy processes was limited mainly to a small group of NGOs based in Kabul, which was well-integrated in government and donor circles. At the sub-national level, civil society organisations often lacked structured networks of coordination and information-sharing mechanisms to make their voices heard during decision-making (EEAS 2019). Some progress had been made in the years immediately before the pandemic, following efforts to structure advocacy and extend networks beyond Kabul. However, a cultural shift would also have been needed to support improved awareness about access to information legislation, rather than the traditional reliance on personal acquaintances and networks in Afghanistan (ISID 2018, 86).

In its later years, the Islamic Republic had intensified its regulatory control over non-government organisations (NGOs). The government felt that its legitimacy was being undermined by NGOs, which were providing the bulk of services to the population. As a result, the government sought to 'rein in' civil society, with the Government of the Islamic Republic inclined to consider NGOs as government instrumentalities rather than independent aid actors, and asserting tighter control over their operations. This phenomenon notably culminated in a decree issued by Vice-President Amrullah Saleh in 2021, strengthening government control over NGO operations, requiring government approval for their projects, and official Memorandums of Understanding (MoUs) to be signed with the relevant line ministry. More broadly, a recurrent characteristic of NGO-government relations has been rivalry, rather than constructive engagement. Pressure, and occasionally threats, levied by local government representatives, and/or their inability to follow up on threats by other non-government elements contributed to increase tensions between civil society organisations and the government (Jelinek 2006).

At the time of the pandemic, then, social and economic conditions were dire, the peace process was unstable, and democratic accountability was severely constrained. These conditions prevailed despite some progress in the legislative framework. Civil society organisations were already weak and relatively ineffective, and lacked the ability to coordinate their efforts. The government was already ignoring or minimising the role of the Constitution. The advent of the pandemic in 2020 underscored, exposed, and exacerbated these structural weaknesses.

After the Taliban takeover in August 2021, the restrictive policies of the past administration were dusted off and reinforced. In this increasingly constrained environment, the extent of the leverage that civil society will be able to exert on the *de facto* Taliban administration and the shape that State-civil society relations will take remain to be seen.

PANDEMIC GOVERNANCE

Emergency responses to COVID-19 on a global scale were unprecedented for at least three reasons: *first*, their underlying rationale was a response to disease rather than to military or terrorist threats; *second*, the responses were implemented on a global scale at more or less the same time; and *third*, the synchronicity offered a real-time window into the assessment of the legitimacy of the various measures that were undertaken.

International human rights law provides a framework for assessing the legitimacy of emergency measures. The ICCPR, for example, helps to determine how (and when) rights can be restricted in times of emergency. Upon declaring a formal state of emergency, for example, State parties to the Convention can limit ('derogate from') certain rights in the ICCPR under Article 4, provided that conditions are met: the situation must 'threaten the life of the nation', meaning that the threat must be actual or imminent rather than speculative or potential (Hartman 1985). It is a general rule as well that States must have 'officially proclaimed' a state of emergency *before* exceptional measures are taken.[11] According to the UN Human Rights Committee, which is responsible for overseeing State members' compliance with the Convention, an official proclamation 'is essential for the maintenance of the principles of legality and rule of law at times when they are most needed' (Joseph, et al. 2013; UN Human Rights Committee 2001, para. 2). Emergency measures must be strictly temporary in scope (see, for example, Hartman 1985; UN 2001). Article 4 also states that these restrictions must be non-discriminatory and meet the requirements of legality, necessity, and proportionality, including the fact that measures should be the least intrusive possible to achieve the stated public health goals and be connected to the exigencies of the situation (ICCPR, Art. 4). States are further required to consider the duration, and geographical and material scope of the state of emergency (UN 2001). When States limit individual rights and freedoms during times of emergency, they bear the burden of proof in justifying derogations under the ICCPR (Landinelli, et al. 1981; Scensson-McCarthy

1998). Returning to normality must be the primary objective of the State during the state of emergency (UN Human Rights Committee 1983, 120).

While certain rights may be limited, others are so fundamental they cannot be derogated from in any circumstance. They include the right to life and prohibition of torture and slavery (ICCPR, Art. 4). The principles of legality and the rule of law also require that the fundamental rights to a fair trial and the presumption of innocence must continue to be respected during a state of emergency (UN Human Rights Committee 2001).

During the pandemic, broad restrictions placed on civil society had an impact on its capacity to respond to the crisis. In many countries, laws, decrees, or orders-in-council limited public gatherings, restricted freedom of expression, and constrained freedom of movement. The global developments prompted the UN Special Rapporteur on Freedom of Association and Peaceful Assembly to urge States to take note of the importance of civil society organisations and to not lose sight of their role as strategic partners, precisely because constitutional guarantees, legislative oversight, and respect for international human rights norms—all of which are essential foundations for any form of participatory governance—are most threatened during periods of emergency. Of course, certain restrictions for public health reasons are justified, subject to standards of necessity, proportionality, and non-discrimination. However, civil society organisations have only 'rarely been consulted in the process of designing or reviewing appropriate measures of response and in several cases the processes through which such laws and regulations have been passed have been questionable' (UN Human Rights Office of the High Commissioner 2020). In his communiqué, the Special Rapporteur set out the following key principles:

1. New legal measures must respect human rights.
2. Public health emergencies should not be used as a pretext for rights infringements.

3. Democracy cannot be indefinitely postponed.
4. Participation should be inclusive.
5. Freedom of association and assembly should be guaranteed online.
6. Workplace rights to freedom of association and assembly should be protected.
7. Freedom of expression should be ensured.
8. The participation of civil society in multilateral institutions should be secured.
9. Recognise that international solidarity is needed more than ever.
10. Consider the future implications of COVID-19 for governance and rights and respond to popular calls for reform. (ibid.)

With these international legal standards and principles in mind, the following section will review the measures taken in Afghanistan and their implications for human rights, civil society, and participatory democracy.

COVID-19 IN AFGHANISTAN: IMPLICATIONS OF MEASURES AND RIGHTS

Fragile States like Afghanistan responded to the pandemic at a time when they were already experiencing conflict, environmental challenges, and multiple simultaneous and pre-existing crises of good governance, economic and social rights, as well as humanitarian emergencies. On 27 March 2020, the Ministry of Public Health estimated that 25 million Afghans, out of an estimated population of 34 million, could eventually be affected by the virus (*Tolo News* 2020). In 2022, the World Health Organization reported estimates of more than 200,000 cumulative cases in Afghanistan (World Health Organization n.d.).

The 2004 Constitution of Afghanistan provided for the declaration of a state of emergency under Chapter 9.[12] As previously noted, no public state of emergency was declared in Afghanistan during the pandemic. The government continued its practice of issuing emergency legislation under Article 79 of the Constitution, with the resulting democratic deficits and non-compliance with the Constitution noted earlier. In mid-March 2020, the Government of Afghanistan began taking measures to address the pandemic. A High-Level Emergency Committee was established to address immediate sanitary and health needs. Border crossings were closed, and schooling was suspended. On 22 March 2020, parliamentary sessions were reduced to once a week. A presidential decree was issued on 26 March to facilitate the release of up to 10,000 prisoners as part of an effort to curb the spread of the virus. The decree provided for the release of prisoners over the age of fifty-five, those who were most vulnerable to infection due to underlying health problems, and prisoners who had not been convicted of crimes against national and international security (see Nikzad 2020; OCHA 2020d).

In late March 2020, a nation-wide 'measured lockdown' was enforced throughout the country, including movement restrictions in affected areas, a ban on inter-city travel, and the closure of non-essential businesses and public spaces. Friday prayer gatherings were cancelled, and an order was issued to not reopen schools until after the winter break.[13] There were reports that the implementation of containment measures was dysfunctional, and that disproportionate use of force was used to deploy them. Humanitarian organisations that were previously provided with pass cards enabling them to continue delivering aid were reported to have been intermittently stopped (OCHA 2020b). Provincial governors appeared to have been given free rein to decide on how to implement measures related to COVID-19. In Kabul, for instance, this included the enforcement of restrictions through arrests, fines, and/or the placement of persons in quarantine (ibid.). The Emergency Committee for the Prevention of COVID-19, established by the government, was accused of mismanagement and corruption in the allocation of aid to fight the pandemic (The Killid Group 2020). These measures reinforced concerns that emerging and new lines of conflict would threaten the potential of democracy and pose a particular threat to poor and marginalised people who are already subject to or targeted by dominant power elites (ISID 2018).

After the takeover, the Taliban announced in September 2021 that parts of the 1964 Constitution would be restored, subject to compliance with Shari'a law, although the 2004 Constitution continues to be displayed on official Afghanistan government websites. As previously noted, the status of the Constitution remains unclear at the time of writing.

The effectiveness of constitutional bodies and the extent to which they can protect fundamental rights are practically constrained by the lack of capacity of marginalised people, who are stigmatised and effectively prevented from accessing resources (ISID 2018). The pandemic exacerbated these power imbalances and also exposed violations of ICCPR norms, notably in relation to the right to be free from arbitrary detention, restrictions on mobility rights for residents, and disproportionate and discriminatory impacts on minority groups and marginalised communities. However, further research on the necessity and proportionality of the Afghan government's measures will be required to properly evaluate their legality under the ICCPR and international human rights law more generally. Changes during the pandemic aggravated the already weak capacity of citizens to access their rights, especially basic social and economic rights. The pandemic also further weakened the ability of civil society to mobilise and coordinate amongst themselves to create conditions for increased accountability, to both monitor the way in which pandemic response measures were being implemented and ensure the inclusion of civil society representatives in broader policy processes, including the peace process.

The impact of the pandemic on all aspects of social and economic life, in parallel with political crises, had direct policy implications. When the bulk of the attention of formal governance stakeholders was focused on addressing immediate threats to public health and safety, there was a growing risk of overlooking government commitments made under national and international policy instruments in the medium and long term. The pandemic also raised questions about the extent to which the crisis affected commitments to participation and inclusiveness as part of the ongoing peace process prior to the Taliban takeover—especially for the rights of minorities, migrants, women, and the youth.

Given the global nature of the pandemic, governments are obliged to treat those within their jurisdictions with dignity and respect, which 'requires an attitude of democratic participation, and a willingness to engage the public with generosity and understanding' (UN 2020b). Recognising the roots of inclusion and exclusion is important for understanding the potential for the renewal of democratic systems and processes, and identifying those initiatives can support the strengthening of participatory democracy in the future. For countries to achieve true democracy, meaningful and sustained participation of minority groups and an inclusion of their concerns need to be pursued (ISID 2018).

As early as 2020, human rights groups had signalled strong concerns about the willingness and ability of the Taliban and the government to uphold basic rights in future peace agreements (Human Rights Watch 2020b). The UN Special Rapporteur on the Promotion and Protection of the Right to Freedom of Opinion and Expression took formal note of the challenges posed by pandemics to freedom of expression and to participatory democratic processes (UN 2020b, para. 62). Many civil society organisations and networks had already been severely affected by COVID-19 and, after the Taliban takeover, were further weakened by the evacuation of senior staff and lack of development funding. A key factor going forward will be the capacity to organise and continue holding the authorities accountable, pointing to the critical importance of creating effective governance networks for civil society organisations, and particularly those that are capable of functioning effectively during times of crisis. Clément Voule, current UN Special Rapporteur on the Rights to Freedom of Peaceful Assembly and of Association, stated: 'Civil society must be regarded as an essential partner of governments in responding to the present [COVID-19] crisis, in terms of helping to frame inclusive policies, disseminating information, building shared and cooperative approaches, and providing social support to vulnerable communities' (UN Human Rights Office of the High Commissioner 2020).

From this perspective, weakening constitutional protections, along with disregard for international human rights and the new layers of vulnerability caused by both the conflict and the pandemic, all pointed to the need for sustainable initiatives that could strengthen civil society organisations and fundamental freedoms through inclusive processes that support participation. Unfortunately, subsequent events and the collapse of peace processes created an extremely challenging environment for civil society organisations.

Civil Society, Good Governance, and Participatory Democracy: New Risks

Good governance requires an enabling environment for open and free engagement between the State and civil society. This in turn requires a citizenry that is aware of the right to engage in policy processes alongside public officials and institutions (ISID 2018). This principle is also reflected in the protections afforded by international human rights instruments.[14] The

State must be responsive to the needs of the people and committed to keeping them informed about, and engaged in, public decision-making, policy orientations, decisions, and implementation.[15] Legal and regulatory environments should be capable of supporting rights-based claims. However, in many regions, governments severely limited the ability of civil society to support an effective response during the past pandemic. These elements were already weak or lacking with respect to the governance in Reconstruction Afghanistan (Parto 2017).

As previously noted, UN Special Rapporteur Voule emphasised the importance of governments partnering with civil society organisations to combat the spread of COVID-19. In another statement, he noted that:

> States should support civil society organizations' participation in the design and implementation of effective public health strategies.... *States must ensure that the ability of such organizations to access the communities they serve is not inappropriately limited.* In addition, the crisis must not be used to prevent civil society organizations, defense lawyers, and journalists from undertaking vital work monitoring the police, prisons, migrant detention centers and other components of State legal processes. (UN 2020b; emphasis added)

In this respect, civil society should have been able to play a stronger and more critical role in ensuring that their work was understood by and appropriate to local levels.

Afghanistan also experienced a significant challenge in implementing Western-inspired models of democracy, which were and are perceived as an imported form of governance imposed on the Afghan people, and as an attempt to change their culture and way of life (ISID 2018, 150). To promote good governance and participatory democracy, efforts were needed to explore the roots and traditions within Afghan culture that promote these values of democracy (ibid.). Going forward, Afghan civil society will need to reinvent itself to assess how it can play a role in facilitating processes of good governance and accountability after the political overhaul caused by the collapse of the Islamic Republic and the Taliban takeover.

The onset of COVID-19 exposed and aggravated weaknesses in governance systems that were directly connected to the role of civil society, particularly in terms of government accountability.[16] The effects of the pandemic are evident on two levels: at the operational level concerning modes of engagement between State and civil society, and at the strategic level concerning the prioritisation of policy objectives under the circumstances of a public health emergency.

At the operational level, the COVID-19 pandemic engendered new, short-term operational, technical, financial, and safety challenges for civil society organisations. Traditional modes of operation for these organisations and for rights defenders, which have usually been based on interpersonal interactions, meetings, and seminars, were disrupted.[17] Some organisations lacked the resources for permanent access to the internet and online tools, and did not possess the skills and know-how to conduct virtual advocacy. A recurrent complaint was also that government representatives used COVID-19 as a pretext to remain unresponsive and ignore requests for information.[18] Heavy reliance on donor funding had also made civil society organisations under the Republic highly vulnerable to shifts in donor funding strategies. Short-term emergency funding left many development, rights-based, and policy-oriented organisations without sufficient resources to continue their work in the medium to long term.[19]

At the strategic level, long- and medium-term policy considerations were overshadowed by immediate health concerns. The risk was that the government and the international donors who supported 75 per cent of the national budget would concentrate, at least in the immediate future, on shorter-term rather than longer-term objectives. These objectives included the Sustainable Development Goals, which were already severely impacted by the pandemic. In the absence of a structured, stable civil society capable of rapidly adapting to changing operational circumstances, the pandemic introduced and worsened the situation, with the government acquiring greater leverage to act without oversight. The resulting economic stress and strain on governance left the government even more vulnerable and weak.

In countries that have experienced occupation and conflict, meaningful public participation requires that civil society work to 'decolonise' democracy. Democracy exists and thrives in the spaces between elections, as well as engaging with new models and experimental approaches (Chatterjee 2018, 27–29). As the space for civil society participation in policy processes was eroded, however, government concessions to civil society vis-à-vis participation and inclusion in the peace process were shelved during the pandemic. Legal orders, directives, and decrees issued by the Administrative Office of the President to address COVID-19 were not publicly available. This left civil society organisations with little to no opportunity to engage with the government and hold it legally responsible for decisions that were incompatible with human rights in the country.

States should counter these trends by providing support to civil society organisations and networks that deliver vital social support, and which monitor and advocate for vulnerable communities. Any effective response to the COVID-19 crisis should have included civil society. As stated by Clément Voule, 'No country or government can solve the crisis alone; civil society organizations should be seen as strategic partners in the fight against the pandemic' (UN Human Rights Office of the High Commissioner 2020). If these partnerships are not encouraged and strengthened, both democracy and human rights will continue to suffer.

While human rights violations took place even before the Taliban takeover, since 2021, human rights have continued to deteriorate in Afghanistan. Human Rights Watch has reported summary executions and enforced disappearances of former Members of the Afghan National Security Forces (Human Rights Watch 2021). The Taliban have not upheld pledges to respect human rights and women's rights and have placed severe restrictions on women's and girls' rights and on the media, along with serious violations like the arbitrary detention and torture of opponents (Human Rights Watch 2022a). The country's national human rights commission was closed. The United Nations has called on the Taliban to enforce a 'massive turnaround', including showing respect for international human rights and humanitarian commitments, the end of reprisals against civil society, and the reinstatement of key institutions like the Afghanistan Independent Human Rights Commission. The UN also called on members of the international community to support ongoing initiatives by Afghan women leaders and civil society groups to design and implement strategies to improve the rights of women and girls (United Nations 2022).

Towards a Renewed Approach to Good Governance

This section provides practical guidance in relation to human rights-based approaches, and the significance of ensuring an enabling environment for civil society.

Human rights-based approaches are broadly relevant to measures that are operationally directed towards promoting and protecting human rights, so that policy frameworks are aligned with human rights norms. Some key elements of human rights-based approaches are:

- *Equality-focused:* Outcomes should be based on substantive equality, which means that policies ought to

consciously consider and prioritise groups experiencing discrimination and marginalisation.
- *People-centred*: States and (sometimes) third parties owe a duty to people, not to programmes or policies, or even to systems. Putting people first requires a shift, so that the rights and perspectives of those most affected, or those likely to need that policy or programme, are taken into consideration from the outset.
- *Progressively realised*: Social, economic, and cultural rights, such as education, health, transit, sanitation, and clean water, and adequate social assistance depend on the principle of progressive realisation, recognising that few States can meet targets in the short term and that significant investments in infrastructure and programmes are needed, to the maximum of available resources.
- *Process-oriented*: Equal importance is given to processes of policy development, and meaningful participation is a key strategy to ensure the input of those most affected. Participatory approaches establish and strengthen choices and opportunities for self-development and self-fulfillment within a sustainable development framework (Eliadis 2021).

An enabling environment for civil society operates to connect human rights-based approaches with the broader context in which civil society and human rights defenders are able to function effectively. Such an environment strengthens elements of good governance, such as accountability, transparency, the rule of law, responsiveness, inclusivity, effectiveness, efficiency, and participation. All these elements were affected by the pandemic. When applied to the case of Afghanistan, the constraints created by the unprecedented circumstances of COVID-19 required governance stakeholders to rethink the modalities and mechanisms of State-civil society engagement in order to support good governance. Key elements of an effective strategy during emergency periods should have included:

1. Ensuring the systematic and accessible publication of all emergency measures. The question of information—who wields it, who has a right to access it, who can deny it—are all fundamentally questions of power (ISID 2018, 32). Challenging power structures to ensure the redistribution of power means that citizens need to be aware of what is happening around them and the decisions being made. Information and education are essential to ensure informed participation.

Information about policies should be adapted and made context-specific to the place where they are being implemented (ISID 2018). This necessitates translating the language used in official information documents into local idioms used in Afghan communities. Civil society can also play a crucial role by sharing information about emergency measures with the citizenry. For example, Afghanistan now has a commission created by the Access to Information Law, which was established to facilitate access to information and monitor implementation (ibid.). Members of the commission include the national head of security and officials from foreign affairs, telecommunications, and information, as well as two civil society representatives. The latter can use this mechanism to disseminate accessible information in plain language about all emergency measures.

Precedents can be found in India in the work leading to the Right to Information Act (2015), which began with inquiries made on behalf of poor workers and farmers and led to widespread pro-people legislative reforms that were highly sensitive to the needs of marginalised and vulnerable communities (Chatterjee 2018).

2. Taking a harm-reduction approach that emphasises precaution based on evidence, but is sensitive to the unintended consequences of sweeping measures for at-risk groups. Quality evidence that includes variables sensitive to

discrimination will be needed to inform both the response to COVID-19 and research that contains disaggregated data on whether and how interventions intended to address the pandemic affect pre-existing conditions and impact structural inequalities and vulnerabilities. Disaggregated data, which can discern the impacts of the pandemic on minority groups and develop effective strategies, is beginning to emerge as a key tool in developing crucial public policy. Civil society has an important role to play in engaging with local communities and serving as a partner in the collection and analysis of this data. Exploring different ways of receiving community feedback, as discussed in the Montreal session of the 'Unpacking Participatory Democracy' workshop, has the potential to encourage citizen participation while also improving local infrastructure (ISID 2018, 35).

3. Redefining and increasing the efficiency of modes of engagement of the citizenry to make more voices heard, beyond the 'usual suspects' that have traditionally dominated civil society in Afghanistan. Drawing on the initiatives discussed in this chapter, formal advisory councils or human rights committees with a strong civil society representation could be established to provide the Afghan government with information and advice about the situation on the ground, especially in relation to vulnerable and marginalised communities. The establishment of human rights oversight committees would also ensure that information about emergency measures is regularly communicated to communities.

Innovative mechanisms that could have been used to develop pilot projects or models would also have facilitated participatory democracy. For instance, in the spring of 2020, more than 300 Canadian organisations, activists, and experts issued a joint statement for the creation of oversight committees to engage with governments at all levels in the context of the pandemic (Amnesty International Canada 2020). This joint statement identified the measures needed to strengthen human rights protection in COVID response strategies, track human rights violations associated with COVID-19 responses, and draw upon community-based human rights monitoring and reporting, in addition to other related mandates.

In contrast, the Islamic Republic of Afghanistan, prior to the pandemic, was often out of touch with the realities of policy implementation 'on the ground'. National governance efforts supported by the donor community were often ineffective at the sub-national level: examples from countries such as Brazil and India, for example, indicate that participatory democracy is most effective at the local, municipal, and village levels, and less so at the national government level (ISID 2018, 36). At the same time, without a strong national leadership that will respect, protect, and fulfil fundamental rights, local practices that may discriminate against marginalised or vulnerable groups continue unchecked and diminish access to justice.

It is equally important to avoid promoting *ad hoc* or short-term forms of participation that reinforce long-term marginalisation. Coalitions of groups comprising the poor and the most marginalised can ensure that these groups are not further ostracised by the perpetuation of profound social inequalities (Chatterjee 2018, 28). Composing these oversight committees strategically has the potential to bring about more long-term structural changes (ISID 2018, 36).

The current context under the Taliban makes many of these changes and initiatives in governance support by the donor community difficult to implement. Nonetheless, the lessons from Afghanistan show, at least in hindsight, that fundamental errors over the long term had seeded instabilities and fragility. The pandemic worsened matters, leaving the previous government unable to sustain its legitimacy and withstand pressure, arguably contributing in part to the collapse of the Islamic Republic, with drastic political, social, and economic consequences.

Conclusion

The emergence of a common threat like the pandemic made the need to define a common good more important than ever. Civil society is a crucial actor in ensuring that action is taken to strengthen solidarity, reduce inequalities, and support good governance. Only through practice and the constant vigilance of all actors can democratic principles be safeguarded (Pande 2018, 40). This approach in turn requires creating and claiming spaces within the system in order to make governments work for all groups in society (ibid.). In a context where pre-pandemic conditions were characterised by a lack of the rule of law, weak governance, and structural inequities and inequalities in accessing rights, the 'return to normality' did not result in a return to pre-COVID-19 conditions. Not only were the existing areas of governance dysfunction not addressed by all stakeholders—government, civil society, and the international community—but there was also little effort to develop new mechanisms and reinforce the social infrastructure of civil society in countries experiencing conflict.

A 'new normal' did not emerge for Afghanistan after the pandemic, at least not one that is consistent with international human rights law. Future international development efforts to support a path to good governance should draw capacity lessons from past and current challenges in the modes of engagement between the State and civil society. New mechanisms are needed in the medium and long term, which can act quickly to give voice to community concerns at the local level and strengthen accountability. Participatory democracy can only be realised when these foundations are in place.

Acknowledgements

The authors gratefully acknowledge the research assistance of Eleanor Dennis, BCL, JD (Faculty of Law, McGill University), Yvette Yakibonge, and Nayantara Melissa Sudhakar (Master of Public Policy, 2021) of the Max Bell School of Public Policy, McGill University, and Hadi Kohi, researcher with Afghanistan Public Policy Research Organization (APPRO).

Notes

1. The data presented here is based on a mix of primary and secondary sources. Primary sources include legal sources such as international instruments and legislation. In terms of social research, these include semi-structured interviews and email exchanges with civil society actors and government representatives based in Afghanistan. Secondary sources include legal commentary and reports from treaty bodies and mandate holders, and reports published by local and international NGOs and agencies engaged in Afghanistan, press releases, and media sources. This chapter was submitted in 2020 and updated in 2022 to reflect subsequent developments in Afghanistan, notably the Taliban takeover in 2021.

2. This section draws on original research conducted by the Afghanistan Public Policy Research Organization (2020).

3. The crisis has exacerbated the risk of torture and ill-treatment for countless children, women, and men in all regions of the world. The UN Committee against Torture, the Subcommittee on the Prevention of Torture, the UN Special Rapporteur on Torture, and the Board of Trustees of the UN Voluntary Fund for Victims of Torture have all warned that the COVID-19 pandemic must not be used to avoid complying with the universally recognised duty of governments to eradicate all forms of torture and other cruel, inhuman, or degrading treatment or punishment (United Nations 2020c).

4. For background on the history of peace negotiations in Afghanistan, see APPRO (2020).

5. The nomination of incumbent President Ashraf Ghani as the winner of the 2019 presidential election in February 2020 raised a political controversy, with his rival Abdullah Abdullah holding a parallel inauguration ceremony on 9 March 2020. The two parties did not reach an agreement until 17 May 2020.

6. On the political manipulation of COVID-19 by the government and the Taliban, see Kazemi and Muzhary (2020).

7. Article 79 of the Constitution states that

> During the recess of the House of Representatives, the Government shall, in case of an immediate need, issue legislative decrees, except in matters related to budget and financial affairs. Legislative decrees, after endorsement by the President, shall acquire the force of law. Legislative decrees shall be presented to the National Assembly within 30 days of convening its first session, and if rejected by the National Assembly, they become void.

8. Under Article 121, the Supreme Court can review the constitutionality of laws and legislative decrees at the request of the government. In the vast majority of cases since 2004, the Court has overwhelmingly sided with the executive and upheld the legislative decrees (Hamidi and Jayakody 2015).

9. On the violation of commitments under the International Covenant on Civil and Political Rights (ICCPR) through emergency legislation, see Human Rights Watch (2015).

10. Afghanistan acceded to the ICCPR on 24 January 1983.

11. States must officially proclaim a state of emergency *before* they can derogate from rights under the ICCPR. If no state of emergency has been declared, states may not invoke ICCPR Article 4 and limit citizens' rights within their jurisdiction. See CCPR General Comment No 29, HRC, 2001, UN Doc CCPR/C/21/REV1/Add1 at para 2 (UN Human Rights Committee 2001).

12. Constitution of Afghanistan, 2004 (Ch. 9, Art. 143). Since 2001, as previously noted, the Government of Afghanistan has not made use of Article 143 to declare a formal state of emergency.

13. The lockdown was extended for three months on 6 June. See OCHA (2020b); Rahimi (2020); and Shaheed (2020).

14. For example, Article 25 of the ICCPR protects the right of political participation, which is closely linked to the right of peaceful assembly and the right of freedom of association. See UN Human Rights Committee (2001).

15. Government transparency and accountability are essential for the promotion and protection of human rights. Freedom of expression is a necessary condition for the realisation of government transparency and accountability, which is guaranteed under ICCPR Article 19. See UN Human Rights Committee (2001, paras 2–3).

16. Ensuring accountability during the COVID-19 pandemic was fundamental to make sure that no State instrumentalised the crisis to advance their political agendas. Clément Voule argued that protecting the dignity and respect that are owed to all individuals entails ensuring accountability for government action, 'such that no State is free to use this public health crisis for unlawful purposes beyond the scope of the health threat' (UN 2020b).

17. Clément Voule stated that during the pandemic, '*The right of civil society actors, including journalists and human rights defenders, to freely seek, receive and impart ideas and information, whether concerning the crisis and its management or other subjects, must be ensured.*' (See UN 2020, April 14; emphasis added).

18. COVID-19 saw censorship measures tighten in certain countries, along with the arbitrary arrest and detention of people critical of their government's response or for simply sharing information or views about the pandemic. The Special Rapporteur on the Promotion and Protection of the Right to Freedom of Opinion and Expression outlined five challenges during pandemics related to civic access to information: (*i*) Access to information held by public authorities; (*ii*) Access to the internet; (*iii*) Protection and promotion of independent media; (*iv*) Public health disinformation; (*v*) Public health surveillance (UN Human Rights Office of the High Commissioner 2020, 7–16).

19. Maina Kiai, the previous UN Special Rapporteur, has also argued that to protect freedom of association, associations should be able to access domestic and foreign funding and resources without prior authorisation. See UN (2020b, para. 99).

SELECT REFERENCES

'Agreement for Bringing Peace to Afghanistan', 29 February 2020. Available at https://www.state.gov/wp-content/uploads/2020/02/Agreement-For-Bringing-Peace-to-Afghanistan-02.29.20.pdf (accessed October 2024).

Afghanistan Public Policy Research Organization (APPRO). 2020a. *COVID-19: Outlook and Approaches*.

———. 2020b, 'Short History of Peace Negotiations with the Taliban', 1 April.

Amnesty International. 2020. 'Afghanistan: Implement Access to Information Law', 5 February. Available at https://www.amnesty.org/en/latest/news/2020/02/afghanistan-implement-access-to-information-law/ (accessed October 2024).

Amnesty International Canada. 2020. 'A call for human rights oversight of government responses to the COVID-19 pandemic'. Available at https://www.amnesty.ca/sites/default/files/COVID%20and%20human%20rights%20oversight%20public%20statement%20FINAL_0.pdf (accessed October 2024).

Bjelica, J. 2019. 'Afghanistan's Anti-Corruption Institutions: Too Many, and With Too Few Results'. Afghanistan Analysts Network (AAN), Kabul, 20 May. Available at https://www.afghanistan-analysts.org/en/reports/economy-development-environment/afghanistan-anti-corruption-institutions-too-many-and-with-too-few-results/ (accessed October 2024).

Central Statistics Office. 2017. *Afghanistan Living Conditions Survey 2016–2017*. Available at https://cso-of-afghanistan.shinyapps.io/ALCS_Dashboard/ (accessed October 2024).

Chatterjee, M. 2018. 'Executive Summary'. In ISID, 'From Theory to Practice: The Montreal Workshop. Unpacking Participatory Democracy: From Theory to Practice and From Practice to Theory', Montreal. Available at https://www.mcgill.ca/isid/channels/news/release-unpacking-participatory-democracy-theory-practice-and-practice-theory-report-two-workshops-291157 (accessed October 2024).

Durand, M. 2015. *Panorama of Civil Society Organizations in Afghanistan from the Perspective of Collaboration*. Kabul: Agency Coordinating Body for Afghan Relief and Development (ACBAR).

Eliadis, P. 2021. 'Mind the gaps: Integrating human rights and sustainable development goals into evaluation practice'. In A. Paulson and M. Palenberg (eds), *The Realpolitik of Evaluation: Why Supply and Demand Rarely Intersect*, 123–325. New York: Routledge.

Elliott, V. 2019. 'Briefing: Why women and children are at greatest risk as Ebola continues to spread in the Congo'. *The New Humanitarian*, 5 September. Available at https://www.thenewhumanitarian.org/news/2019/09/05/Congo-Ebola-epidemic-hits-women-children-hardest (accessed October 2024).

European External Action Service (EEAS). 2019. *Afghanistan: EU Country Roadmap for Engagement with Civil Society 2018–2020*. Kabul: European External Assistance Service (EEAS).

Gender in Humanitarian Action Asia and Pacific. 2020. *The COVID-19 Outbreak and Gender: Key Advocacy Points from Asia and the Pacific*. Available at https://wayback.archive-it.org/21210/20230626152423/https://www.humanitarianresponse.info/ (accessed October 2024).

Global Protection Cluster. 2020. 'Afghanistan COVID-19 Situation Report', 5 May.

Halaimzai, S., and R. Sidiqi. 2020. 'Safeguarding Afghanistan's Vulnerable Millions from Coronavirus Threat'. *Gandhara*, 10 April. Available at https://gandhara.rferl.org/a/safeguarding-afghanistan-s-vulnerable-millions-from-coronavirus-threat/30545863.html (accessed October 2024).

Hamidi, F., and A. Jayakody. 2015. 'Separation of Powers under the Afghan Constitution: A Case Study'. Kabul: Afghanistan Research and Evaluation Unit (AREU). Available at https://www.refworld.org/pdfid/555b270d4.pdf (accessed October 2024).

Hartman, J. F. 1985. 'Working Paper for the Committee of Experts on the Article 4 Derogation Provision'. *Human Rights Quarterly* 7 (1), 89–131.

Holland, D., S. Parto, and K. Siddiqi. 2016. *Access to Information: Right or Privilege?* Kabul: Afghanistan Public Policy Research Organization (APPRO).

Human Rights Watch. 2015. 'Afghanistan: Reject Indefinite Detention Without Trial', 15 November. Available at https://www.hrw.org/news/2015/11/15/afghanistan-reject-indefinite-detention-without-trial (accessed October 2024).

Human Rights Watch. 2020a. 'Human Rights Dimensions of COVID-19', 19 March. Available at https://www.hrw.org/news/2020/03/19/human-rights-dimensions-COVID-19-response (accessed October 2024).

―――. 2020b. 'Afghanistan: Taliban Rights Efforts Fall Far Short. Abuses Persist, Protections Fragile as Peace Talks Begin', 30 June. Available at https://www.hrw.org/news/2020/06/30/afghanistan-taliban-rights-efforts-fall-far-short (accessed October 2024).

―――. 2021. '"No Forgiveness for People Like You": Executions and Enforced Disappearances in Afghanistan under the Taliban', 30 November. Available at https://www.hrw.org/report/2021/11/30/no-forgiveness-people-you/executions-and-enforced-disappearances-afghanistan (accessed October 2024).

―――. 2022a. 'Afghanistan: Taliban's Catastrophic Year of Rule', 11 August. Available at https://www.hrw.org/news/2022/08/11/afghanistan-talibans-catastrophic-year-rule (accessed October 2024).

―――. 2022b. 'Economic Causes of Afghanistan's Humanitarian Crisis: Questions and Answers on Sanctions and Banking Restrictions on the Taliban', 4 August. Available at https://www.hrw.org/news/2022/08/04/economic-causes-afghanistans-humanitarian-crisis (accessed October 2024).

Inter-Cluster Coordination Team. 2020. 'Afghanistan: COVID-19 Multi-Sector Humanitarian Country Plan'. *Reliefweb*, 25 March. Available at https://reliefweb.int/report/afghanistan/afghanistan-COVID-19-multi-sector-humanitarian-country-plan (accessed October 2024).

Integrated Food Security Phase Classification (IPC). 2020. 'Afghanistan: Acute Food Insecurity Situation September–October 2021 and Projection for November 2021–March 2022'. Available at https://www.ipcinfo.org/ipc-country-analysis/details-map/en/c/1155210/ (accessed October 2024).

Islamic Republic of Afghanistan. 2004. *Constitution.* https://www.mfa.gov.af/constitution/chapter-nine-the-state-of-emergency.html

Jelinek, E. 2006. 'A Study of NGO Relations with Government and Communities in Afghanistan'. Agency Coordinating Body for Afghan Relief. *ReliefWeb*, 30 November. Available at https://reliefweb.int/report/afghanistan/study-ngo-relations-government-and-communities-afghanistan (accessed February 2025).

Joseph, S., M. Castan, and J. Schultz. 2013. *The International Covenant on Civil and Political Rights: Cases, Materials and Commentary*. Oxford: Oxford University Press, 3rd edition.

Kazemi, H. R., and F. R. Muzhary. 2020. 'COVID-19 in Afghanistan (4): A precarious interplay between war and epidemic'. Afghanistan Analysts Network (AAN), 19 June. Available at https://www.afghanistan-analysts.org/en/reports/war-and-peace/COVID-19-in-afghanistan-4-a-precarious-interplay-between-war-and-epidemic/ (accessed October 2024).

The Killid Group. 2020. 'Afghan Government's Emergency Committee for the Prevention of COVID-19 Wastes AFG. 5 Million'. *Afghanistan News*, 3 April. Available at https://tkg.af/english/2020/05/03/afghan-governments-emergency-committee-for-prevention-of-covid-19-wastes-afg-5-million-funds/ (accessed October 2024).

Kurtzer, J. 2020. 'The Impact of COVID-19 on Humanitarian Crises'. Center for Strategic and International Studies, 19 March. Available at https://www.csis.org/analysis/impact-COVID-19-humanitarian-crises (accessed October 2024).

Landinelli Silva, J., L. E. Echave Zas, O. Patron Zeballos, N. Fernandez, and R. Guarga. 1981. *Ferro v Uruguay*. Center for Civil and Political Rights. Available at https://ccprcentre.org/decision/16528 (accessed October 2024).

Martin, L., and S. Parto. 2020. 'On Shaky Grounds: COVID-19 and Afghanistan's Social Political and Economic Capacities for Sustainable Peace'. Friedrich Ebert Stiftung, November. Available at https://library.fes.de/pdf-files/bueros/kabul/16839.pdf (accessed October 2024).

Mashal, M., and K. Hayeri. 2020. 'Afghanistan's Next War'. *The New York Times Magazine* 23 April. Available at https://www.nytimes.com/interactive/2020/04/22/magazine/afghanistan-coronavirus.html (accessed October 2024).

Nikzad, K. 2020. 'Govt to Release Inmates Due to COVID-19'. *Tolo News*, 22 March. Available at https://tolonews.com/health/govt-release-inmates-due-COVID-19 (accessed October 2024).

Pande, S. 2018. 'Executive Summary'. 'Unpacking Participatory Democracy: From Practice to Theory', the Thiruvananthapuram workshop. ISID, pp. 40–43. Available at https://www.mcgill.ca/isid/channels/news/release-unpacking-participatory-democracy-theory-practice-and-practice-theory-report-two-workshops-291157 (accessed October 2024).

Parto, S. 2017. *Re-conceptualizing Corruption in Afghanistan: An Institution of Bad Governance*. Kabul: Afghanistan Public Policy Research Organization (APPRO).

Rahimi, Z. 2020. 'MoI Puts Ban on Public Gatherings Over Coronavirus'. *Tolo News*, 18 March. Available at https://tolonews.com/health/moi-puts-ban-public-gatherings-over-coronavirus (accessed October 2024).

Reliefweb. 2020. 'Afghanistan: COVID-19 Multi-Sector Humanitarian Country Plan', 25 March. Available at https://reliefweb.int/report/afghanistan/afghanistan-COVID-19-multi-sector-humanitarian-country-plan (accessed October 2024).

———. 2022. 'Educo warns: Afghan girls do not have access to secondary education and this will impact their future and the future of the country'. *News and Press Release*, 10 August. Available at https://reliefweb.int/report/afghanistan/educo-warns-afghan-girls-do-not-have-access-secondary-education-and-will-impact-their-future-and-future-country (accessed October 2024).

Save The Children. 2020. 'COVID-19: An Additional Three Million Children in Afghanistan Need Help to Survive in Afghanistan'. *Reliefweb*, 11 June. Available at https://reliefweb.int/report/afghanistan/COVID-19-additional-three-million-children-afghanistan-need-help-survive-2020 (accessed October 2024).

———. 2022. 'Afghanistan: A Fifth of Starving Families Sending Children to Work as Incomes Plummet in Past Six Months', 14 February. Available at https://www.savethechildren.net/news/afghanistan-fifth-starving-families-sending-children-work-incomes-plummet-past-six-months (accessed October 2024).

Scensson-McCarthy, A. 1998. *The International Law of Human Rights and States of Exception: With Special Reference to the Travaux Preparatoires and Case-Law of the International Monitoring Organs*. New York: Springer.

Shaheed, A. 2020. 'Ministry of Hajj: Amid COVID-19, Pray Home'. *Tolo News*, 21 March. Available at https://tolonews.com/afghanistan/ministry-hajj-amid-COVID-19-pray-home (accessed October 2024).

Tolo News. 2020. 'Coronavirus Reach 110 in Afghanistan', 28 March. Available at https://tolonews.com/health/coronavirus-cases-reach-110-afghanistan (accessed October 2024).

United Nations. 1976. *International Covenant on Civil and Political Rights*. Office of the United Nations High Commissioner for Human Rights. Available at https://www.ohchr.org/en/professionalinterest/pages/ccpr.aspx (accessed October 2024).

———. 2020a. 'Subcommittee on Prevention of Torture and Other Cruel, Inhuman or Degrading Treatment or Punishment. Advice Provided by the Subcommittee to the National Preventive Mechanism of the United Kingdom of Great Britain and Northern Ireland Regarding Compulsory Quarantine for Coronavirus'. Available at https://www.ohchr.org/Documents/HRBodies/OPCAT/AdviceStatePartiesCoronavirusPandemic2020.pdf (accessed October 2024).

———. 2020b. 'Report of the Special Rapporteur on the Promotion and Protection of the Right to Freedom of Opinion and Expression'. HRC, 44th Session, 23 April, Available at https://documents-dds-ny.un.org/doc/UNDOC/GEN/G20/097/82/PDF/G2009782.pdf?OpenElement (accessed October 2024).

———. 2020c. 'COVID-19 exacerbates the risk of ill-treatment and torture worldwide—UN experts'. Office of the United Nations High Commissioner for Human Rights, 26 June. Available at http://www.ohchr.org/EN/NewsEvents/Pages/int-day-torture.aspx (accessed October 2024).

———. 2022. *Afghanistan: UN Human Rights Experts Warn of Bleak Future without Massive Turnaround*, 12 August. Geneva: United Nations.

United Nations Assistance Mission in Afghanistan. 2020. *Afghanistan's Fight against Corruption: Crucial for Peace and Prosperity*, June. Available at https://unama.unmissions.org/sites/default/files/afghanistans_fight_against_corruption_crucial_for_peace_and_prosperity_english.pdf (accessed October 2024).

United Nations Children's Fund. 2020. 'COVID-19 May Push Millions More Children into Child Labour – ILO and UNICEF', 12 June. Available at https://www.unicef.org/afghanistan/press-releases/COVID-19-may-push-millions-more-children-child-labour-ilo-and-unicef (accessed October 2024).

United Nations Human Rights Committee. 1983. *Report of the Committee on Human Rights*, UNGA, 32nd Session, Supp No40/A/32/44.

———. 2001. *CCPR General Comment No. 29: Article 4: Derogations during a State of Emergency*, 31 August.

United Nations Human Rights Office of the High Commissioner (OHCR). n.d. 'About good governance: OHCHR and good governance'. Available at https://www.ohchr.org/EN/Issues/Development/GoodGovernance/Pages/AboutGoodGovernance.aspx (accessed October 2024).

———. 2020. 'States responses to COVID 19 threat should not halt freedoms of assembly and association – Statement of the Special Rapporteur on the rights to freedoms of peaceful assembly and of association, Mr. Clément Voule'. United Nations, 9 April. Available at https://www.ohchr.org/en/statements/2020/04/states-responses-covid-19-threat-should-not-halt-freedoms-assembly-and (accessed October 2024).

United Nations Office for the Coordination of Humanitarian Affairs (OCHA). 2020a. 'Afghanistan: COVID-19 Multi-Sectoral Response. Operational Situation Report', 3 June. Available at https://reliefweb.int/sites/reliefweb.int/files/resources/Afghanistan%20-%20COVID-19%20Multi-Sectoral%20Response%20Operational%20Situation%20Report%2C%203%20June%202020.pdf (accessed October 2024).

———. 2020b. 'Afghanistan Flash Update: COVID-19: Daily Brief No. 21'. Humanitarian Response, 29 March. Available at https://www.humanitarianresponse.info/en/operations/afghanistan/document/afghanistan-flash-update-COVID-19-daily-brief-no-21-29-mar-2020 (accessed October 2024).

———. 2020c. 'Afghanistan Flash Update: COVID-19: Daily Brief No. 22'. Humanitarian Response, 30 March. Available at https://www.humanitarianresponse.info/sites/www.humanitarianresponse.info/files/documents/files/daily_brief_covid-19_30_march_2020.pdf (accessed October 2024).

United Nations Office for the Coordination of Humanitarian Affairs (OCHA). 2020d. 'Afghanistan Flash Update: COVID-19: Daily Brief No. 28'. Humanitarian Response, 6 April. Available at https://www.humanitarianresponse.info/en/operations/afghanistan/document/afghanistan-flash-update-COVID-19-daily-brief-no-28-06-apr-2020 (accessed October 2024).

UN Women. 2020. *Gender Alert on COVID-19 Afghanistan. Issue II: Ensuring Access to Services for Survivors of Violence Against Women and Girls*.

United States Agency for International Development (USAID). 2016. *The 2015 CSO Sustainability Index for Afghanistan*. Kabul: USAID.

Wagner, E., and H. Warren. 2020. *Save Our Education: Protect Every Child's Rights to Learn in the COVID-19 Response and Recovery*. Save The Children International. Available at https://resourcecentre.savethechildren.net/library/save-our-education-protect-every-childs-right-learn-covid-19-response-and-recovery (accessed October 2024).

World Bank Group. 2020. *Surviving the Storm. Afghanistan Development Update*. Available at https://reliefweb.int/sites/reliefweb.int/files/resources/Afghanistan-Development-Update-Surviving-the-Storm.pdf (accessed October 2024).

World Food Program. 2020. *Afghanistan: Countrywide Weekly Market Price Bulletin, Issue 3. Reliefweb*, 4 June. Available at https://reliefweb.int/report/afghanistan/afghanistan-countrywide-weekly-market-price-bulletin-issue-3-covering-4th-week (accessed October 2024).

World Health Organization (WHO). n.d. 'WHO Coronavirus (Covid-19) Dashboard'. Available at https://covid19.who.int/region/emro/country/af (accessed October 2024).

CAN INFORMATION MAKE THE SUBALTERN SPEAK?

RAJESH VEERARAGHAVAN

In the 'Unpacking Participatory Democracy' workshop, sociologist Patrick Heller posed a crucial question: What constitutes the 'surface area of the State', in relation to the welfare of marginalised populations? Development programmes are often framed as mechanisms to expand the state's capacity to deliver welfare to the poor (Corbridge, et al. 2005). However, as Stuart Corbridge and others have noted, while the state's repressive arm may be all too visible, for many marginalised citizens, development programmes are the only way they encounter it as a provider (ibid.). This means that their relationship with the state is often limited to bureaucratic processes and eligibility criteria, rather than through direct claims-making.

Yet, these interventions do not necessarily translate into meaningful empowerment. James Ferguson argues that development interventions often expand bureaucracy while depoliticising poverty, turning governance into a technical issue—what he calls an 'anti-politics machine' that ultimately fails to serve the poor (Ferguson 1994). If the State is encountered only as a provider of welfare rather than as a responsive institution that can be engaged and contested, how do marginalised citizens claim rights instead of just receiving benefits?

One widely promoted strategy for deepening State accountability is democratising access to information, enabling citizens to 'see the state' beyond its bureaucratic surface and engage it as rights-bearing participants. Mechanisms like social audits attempt to turn transparency into accountability, yet they assume that making State actions more visible is enough to empower marginalised groups—a claim that demands closer scrutiny.

But does making the State more visible necessarily translate into greater political agency for marginalised citizens? Some theorists argue that access to information inherently enables citizens to challenge domination, while others contend that information alone does not lead to action—its impact is shaped by structural power, social context, and political mobilisation. Still others suggest that intermediaries—whether grassroots movements, civil society organisations, or organic intellectuals—play a crucial role in activating information for political contestation.

At the heart of these debates is a fundamental question: Can information make the subaltern[1] 'speak'? The literature offers contradictory evidence on whether openness and access to information yield positive social impacts. Yet it rarely examines the assumptions about information in development (Srinivasan 2022).[2]

This chapter turns to social and political theory to examine the relationship between information and social change. The perspectives I review are not meant to be exhaustive, but they map the range of theoretical possibilities, offering very different imaginations of the subaltern's political agency.[3] Since information as an object does not quite enter the discussion of these political theorists, I had to impute its role within their broader frameworks. By testing these different possibilities through a theoretical lens, this chapter examines the conditions under which information transitions from private knowledge to public action.

One illustrative setting where these theoretical questions can be explored is in India's social audits—public forums where marginalised citizens scrutinise government records and directly confront officials over discrepancies between reported benefits and lived realities. Social audits, designed as participatory mechanisms, challenge the assumption that transparency alone ensures accountability. Instead, they raise deeper questions about power, political mobilisation, and the role of intermediaries in translating information into action.

To ground these theoretical debates, I turn to an illustrative example of information-driven accountability: India's Right to Information law and the participatory mechanism of social audits. Although this chapter does not empirically analyse social audits, they offer a compelling context to interrogate broader theoretical questions about the relationship between transparency and power—do initiatives like these truly empower marginalised citizens, or do deeper structural dynamics shape how information translates into action?

Information and State Accountability

Over the past thirty years, many democratic countries have enacted legislation granting citizens the right to access government information, aiming to empower them to monitor State actions. A significant example is India's Right to Information law, embedded in the National Rural Employment Guarantee Act (NREGA). This law introduced an open public hearing process, allowing citizens to inspect public records (Baviskar 2010). One of the most significant mechanisms emerging from this transparency movement has been the social audit—a participatory process in which citizens collectively verify government records, particularly in welfare programmes like NREGA (Veeraraghavan 2021). Social audits, conducted through public hearings, enable marginalised citizens to challenge discrepancies between official documents and their lived experiences. By turning information into a site of collective deliberation, they aim to transform bureaucratic transparency into meaningful accountability.

The rights-based turn and transparency guarantees embedded in these laws represented a fundamental departure from typical welfare programmes, in which citizens are passive recipients of benefits (Dreze and Sen 2013; Khera 2011). This shift has the potential to fundamentally alter the relationship between the Indian State and its citizens. However, as Jonathan Fox cautions, 'institutional reforms that might look "enabling" on paper need to be unpacked and examined from below to determine their actual coverage, depth, and empowerment impacts in practice' (Fox 2007b, 354). Furthermore, as Partha Chatterjee has argued, many citizens are powerless and not even seen as a part of civil society, that is, as citizens with rights. Instead, they operate within 'political society', relying on electoral power, to make claims on the State (Chatterjee 2004). But electoral power is intermittent and a very limited tool for holding the day-to-day State accountable. Therefore, exploring other means of holding the State accountable to its marginalised citizens is crucial.

The dominant theory of government transparency posits that a significant information asymmetry exists between citizens and the State (Stiglitz 2002). This theory suggests that increasing the availability of information, for example, by making government records more accessible to citizens, will lead to a greater scrutiny of government actions and ultimately contribute to holding the government accountable for its mistakes and injustices. This approach to accountability is premised on the principle of openness. An influential study conducted in Uganda and cited in the 2004 World

Development Report exemplifies this theory of 'information for accountability' (Fox 2007a; Reinikka and Svensson 2004). The study used statistical analysis to examine the impact of an informational campaign to raise parental awareness of block grants for schools and the distribution of funds. It found a correlation between newspaper circulation and the likelihood of funds reaching schools in the areas where the newspapers were distributed (Reinikka and Svensson 2004). This study and others like it suggest that access to information can have a tangible impact on citizens' ability to hold the government accountable.

However, not all research supports this claim. Some studies indicate that transparency efforts do not necessarily lead to improved service provision (Banerjee, et al. 2010; Keefer and Khemani 2012; Lieberman, et al. 2014; Ravallion, et al. 2013). Moreover, information interventions can have unintended consequences. For example, Bangalore's Bhoomi project, which digitised land records to reduce corruption, instead facilitated data exploitation by powerful brokers, exacerbating corruption (Benjamin, et al. 2007).

These mixed outcomes from transparency reforms highlight a fundamental tension: Is information alone sufficient to drive accountability, or are deeper structural factors at play? To unpack this, we must move beyond empirical examples and delve into social and political theory, where diverse frameworks offer contrasting views on the role of information in enabling or constraining social change.

Theoretical Perspectives on Information and Social Change

Information as an Enabler of Change

Amartya Sen's influential argument that no famine has occurred in a functioning democracy illustrates the idea that transparency and public pressure can prevent governance failures of the extreme kind (Sen and Drèze 1999). This perspective assumes that making information publicly available enables citizens to hold governments accountable, leading to better outcomes.

Jürgen Habermas's concept of the public sphere (Habermas 1989) provides further support for this view. According to Habermas, the public sphere refers to an idealised space where social issues are resolved through rational discourse, even in the presence of inherent differences in status and identity. He posits that the public sphere emerges when private individuals come together to form a public, and that the more deliberative the process, the more undistorted the communication and the more likely it is that a consensus will be reached among all involved. Habermas's model aligns with Sen's argument that well-informed citizens can mitigate the impact of major public disasters.

Despite the appeal of these optimistic frameworks, they have been met with significant critique. A central concern is whether these models adequately account for the power imbalances that shape who can truly participate in the public sphere. Craig Calhoun, for instance, questions whether Habermas's idealised public sphere can exist in unequal societies.

One of the primary aims of democracy is to provide equal representation for all. However, a key challenge to Habermas' account of the public sphere—and therefore Sen's use of it—is whether individuals who are dominated by others can genuinely express themselves freely. Calhoun critiques Habermas on this point, arguing that his model does not sufficiently account for the power dynamics, communication networks, and structures of influence that shape who participates in the public sphere (Calhoun 1992).

One way to counter power is by organising workers and examining how information can help demystify their conditions. In the Marxist tradition, one of the critical agents of change is workers organising as a class. Building on this critique of the public sphere, Marxist perspectives offer an alternative lens by focussing on structural domination and false consciousness. Ron Eyerman, for example, traces the concept of false consciousness within Marxist thought and its implications for understanding worker agency, and connects it to the work of Herbert Marcuse (Eyerman 1981). According to Marcuse, false consciousness is 'the distorted perception and beliefs an individual or a social class acquires through their life activities in capitalist society'. False consciousness leads to mystification, which causes people to act against their own economic interests.

Providing workers with access to government records, for example, can serve as a tool to demystify bureaucratic documentation, potentially allowing them to fully recognise their exploitation. However, this raises an empirical question: How do workers respond to such information in different political-economic contexts? Does access to these records prompt them to take action and speak out against State officials in public hearings, or do structural barriers prevent them from doing so? Addressing these questions requires further research to understand how workers reactions vary across different circumstances.

However, not all scholars agree that workers can become aware of their domination simply through the provision of information. Pierre Bourdieu challenges the Marxist notion of 'false consciousness' itself. In his view, domination operates through 'misrecognition', a process deeply ingrained in the bodily 'habitus'.

The habitus refers to the dispositions, categories, and ways of seeing the world that individuals acquire through past social interactions. According to Bourdieu, people act spontaneously—without deliberate strategy or intent— because their actions are shaped by these ingrained social structures. As a result, the habitus is not only deeply embedded, but also largely invisible, resistant to change, and particularly unresponsive to new information. Unlike Marxist theorists who could concede information as a possible tool for demystification, Bourdieu does not believe that merely providing information can alter power dynamics. Instead, he highlights the possibility of 'misfirings'—moments when the habitus clashes with the structures it encounters. However, he does not elaborate on how such misalignments might lead to resistance or change, but it is clear that he does not see the provision of information as a solution.

While Bourdieu highlights the internalisation of social structures, James Scott shifts the focus to the ways in which marginalised groups navigate and resist domination in subtle, everyday forms. His concept of 'hidden transcripts' reveals how subaltern voices critique power from behind the scenes, raising further questions about when and how these critiques become public. According to Scott, they engage in subtle forms of resistance that are often perceived as 'weak', because they account for and are constrained by the potential negative consequences of overt rebellion. He writes,

> Every subordinate group creates, out of its ordeal, a 'hidden' transcript that represents a critique of power spoken behind the back of the dominant. The powerful, for their part, also develop a hidden transcript representing the practices and claims of their rule that cannot be openly avowed. (Scott 1992, xii)

Scott remains sceptical of the role that information can play in addressing power imbalances.[4] For him, the issue is not that the workers lack awareness of their oppression, but that structural inequalities prevent them from speaking truth to power. He argues that workers already recognise their situation, and merely providing them with government records would not fundamentally alter this reality. Moreover, he contends that power inequalities will persist, regardless of increased access to information.

In contrast to Scott's focus on covert resistance, Antonio Gramsci explores how consent to domination is actively produced and maintained, offering insight into how information, mediated by organic intellectuals, can disrupt this consent. Unlike orthodox Marxists, Gramsci argues that workers consent voluntarily to this domination, and that there are three faces of hegemonic domination that shape this consent: ideological hegemony, where the ruling elite frames its interests as the interests of all; material concessions, where practical compromises accommodate a range of social groups to maintain stability; and coercion, where force is simultaneously employed and legitimised to sustain consent (Gramsci and Hoare 1971).

In the Gramscian framework, the State does not impose a rigid, top-down domination. Instead, hegemony involves the organisation of consent through the institutions of civil society. Political parties, academic disciplines, caste- and identity-based groups, trade unions, religious organisations, media, NGOs, and other voluntary associations serve to organise the consent of ordinary people by representing the interests of a ruling elite as the interests of all. These institutions amplify dominant ideologies, embedding them within popular consciousness. The organisation of consent, therefore, requires the elaboration of a robust moral ethos that becomes deeply internalised in the psyche of ordinary citizens.

Marxist sociologist Michael Burawoy, in a summary of Marx's writing, attributes the mystification of domination to different spheres of capitalist society:

> Marx's writings are littered with doubts about the capacity of the working class to see through the mystification produced by capitalism – whether this be the hiding of exploitation in the sphere of production, commodity fetishism in the sphere of exchange, or, moving further afield, the subjection of the working class to the power of ideology. (Burawoy 2008, 1)

For Gramsci, workers have 'good sense' and 'common sense'. He describes common sense as 'a chaotic aggregate of disparate conceptions, and one can find there anything one likes', whereas good sense represents an 'intellectual unity and an ethic in conformity with a conception of reality that has gone beyond common sense and become, if only within narrow limits, a critical conception'.

Gramsci offers a way out of this seeming impasse through his idea of 'contradictory consciousness', in which both 'common sense' and 'good sense' coexist within workers' understanding of the world. For 'common sense' to evolve into 'good sense', which is essential for raising the class consciousness of workers, Gramsci argues that one must begin with

> a philosophy which already enjoys, or could enjoy, a certain diffusion, because it is connected to and implicit in practical life, and elaborating it so that it becomes a renewed common sense possessing the coherence and sinew of individual philosophies. But this can only happen if the demands of cultural contact with the 'simple' are continually felt. (Gramsci and Hoare 1971, 330)

Here, Gramsci higlights the role of 'organic intellectuals' — intellectuals emerging from the working class — who are responsible for shaping and elaborate this 'good sense'. This raises an important question: Can information play a role in transforming 'common sense' into 'good sense'?

John Seely Brown and Paul Duguid argue that information — along with the technologies used to transmit it — is not, by itself, an agent of radical social change (Brown and Duguid 2000). They critique what they call 'endisms' — the tendency to assume a singular, all-encompassing logic for social transformation. In particular, they warn against 'tunnel vision', whereby information enthusiasts attempt to 'hack it alone with only information by their side', neglecting the broader social contexts necessary for meaningful change.

These diverse perspectives present contrasting views on information's role in social change. To synthesise, we can categorise these theories into three broad camps based on their assumptions about information's potential to empower:

1. **Information empowers**: This camp believes that information is inherently active and has transformative power on its own. Jurgen Habermas and Herbert Marcuse fall into this category, as do the original designers of the Right to Information Act, who, at the very least, hoped that access to information would lead to greater accountability.
2. **Information is not relevant**: Scholars in this category argue that the mere provision of information is not the issue. Instead, deeper structural inequalities and power imbalances prevent marginalised groups from acting on information. Key thinkers in this group include Gayatri Spivak, Pierre Bourdieu, and James Scott.
3. **Information is useful only in some cases**: This perspective holds that information can be powerful, but only if people actively use it—often with the assistance of an intermediary. Antonio Gramsci's concept of the *organic intellectual* exemplifies this view, emphasising the role of trusted mediators who help transform *common sense* into *good sense* and channel information into political action.

While these theoretical debates provide valuable insights into how information shapes agency, development practice has grappled with similar questions through participatory approaches. The next section explores how participation has been framed as a mechanism for deepening democracy and empowering marginalised communities. Given these perspectives, a crucial question emerges: Will workers consent to their domination in this context? More specifically, can information—when facilitated by a trusted intermediary, such as an organic intellectual—serve to demystify their understanding of exploitation and provoke them to action?

Information and Deepening Democracy Debate

In development academic literature and practice, the role of *participation* has sparked heated debate. On one side, scholars highlight its transformative potential. Robert Chambers, for instance, emphasises the importance of participation by the poor, who have historically been rendered invisible by the development practitioners (Chambers 1994). For Chambers, participation entails rejecting 'the positivist, reductionist, mechanistic, standardized-package, top-down models and development blueprints are rejected, and in which multiple, local, and individual realities are recognized, accepted, enhanced and celebrated' (Chambers 1997, 188). The central argument is that local buy-in and direct involvement of the poor in decision-making lead to more effective and inclusive development outcomes (Gaventa 2006). Although this effort sounds hegemonic in many ways, the participatory approach has gained acceptance in international development policy circles. For example, a World Bank report asserts that 'as participation increases, vital information not in the public domain becomes available and the voices of interested parties can help make governments more accountable; both in turn enhance performance' (World Bank 1994).

However, not all scholars share this optimistic view. Some argue that participation is not an unequivocal good, but instead functions as 'the new tyranny' (Cooke and Kothar 2001). Bill Cooke and Uma Kothari directly challenge the World Bank's perspective, contending that 'the more participatory, the more its outcome will mask the power structure of the community', therefore reinforcing, rather than dismantling, existing inequalities. Others critique the participatory approach for its naïve view of power, pointing out that seeing the 'local' as the site of empowerment, leading to a 'tendency to essentialize and romanticize the local' by ignoring power and social inequalities (Mohan and Stokke 2000). In this view, even when participatory mechanisms claim to empower marginalised groups, they tend to be 'depoliticized and individualized', ultimately obscuring deeper structural inequalaities (Christens and Speer 2006).

Yet, some critics push back against this sweeping condemnation of participation. Scholars such as Hickey and Mohan argue that the key question is how to shift participation from 'tyranny to transformation' (see Mohan and Stokke 2000). Similarly, Glyn Williams asks, '[D]o participatory practices and discourse necessarily de-politicize?' (Williams 2004). Both call for bringing politics back into participation. Williams, in particular, proposes a 're-politicization of participation' through the development of 'a new political imaginary of empowerment'. Building on these critiques, we can ask: How do claims of participatory development regarding transparency and openness act as a 'pressure point' to push politics to the forefront? And what role does information play in this process? While the deepening democracy debate focusses on inclusion and participation, deliberative democracy emphasises the quality and nature of the discussions that take place. This shift from participation to deliberation offers another lens to assess how information can foster political agency.

INFORMATION AND DELIBERATIVE DEMOCRACY

While the deepening democracy debate interrogates who participates, deliberative democracy shifts focus to how participation unfolds. Beyond mere inclusion, it asks: Are discussions equitable? Are voices heard without distortion? A foundational concept for many theorists in this field is the 'public sphere' as articulated by Habermas. According to Habermas, the public sphere refers to an 'ideal speech' situation where social issues are settled through rational deliberation despite inherent differences in status and identity.

As discussed earlier, Habermas defines the public sphere as the domain of private people who join together to form a 'public', historically exemplified by coffee houses and salons. His framework is built on several assumptions: *First*, he assumes that participants engage in debate with disinterest, meaning that they set aside narrow personal concerns. *Second*, he envisions *discursive equality*, in which all participants have an equal opportunity to speak and be heard. *Finally*, he argues that rational discourse ensures that the 'best' argument—determined by universal logic and grounded in facts—prevails, leading to consensus. The more deliberative the process and the more undistorted the communication, the more likely it is that consensus will be acceptable (Habermas 1989).[5]

Using the Habermasian public sphere as a heuristic, Gianpaolo Baiocchi studied the participatory budgeting assemblies in two poor districts in the city of Porto Alegre, Brazil. His study focused on the public nature of these deliberations (Baiocchi 2003). The participants in Porto Alegre faced significant barriers—they were poor, lacked formal education, and had lived under authoritarian rule for decades. Yet, Baiocchi concludes:

> even holding constant the definition of public sphere, its features are present in two poor districts in Porto Alegre, Brazil—a context that would be considered unlikely, given their citizens' material difficulties, their lack of education, and the lack of a liberal political culture.

Baiocchi extends the Habermasian model by emphasising the role of mediation and State sponsorship—two critical factors that raise important question about the viability of deliberative democracy in marginalised contexts. He argues that these participatory assemblies required active support from the State, functioning as a form of 'affirmative action'[6] for the public sphere—to deliberately build and shape institutions that enable marginalised citizens to engage in meaningful deliberation.

Building on Habermas, political scientists Lloyd I. Rudolph and Susanne H. Rudolph argue for a 'democratization' of the Habermasian public sphere, drawing on Mahatma Gandhi's *ashram* (a place of voluntary communal living) as a model (Rudolph and Rudolph 2006). In this context, democratisation refers to the expansion of the bourgeois public sphere to include the 'plebian world of non-literate villagers'. Gandhi is best known for developing *Satyagraha* (*truth force*), a non-violent form of protest that emphasised both self-discipline and sacrifice. His model of resistance extended beyond direct confrontation, incorporating *ascetic living* within his voluntary ashrams and, most importantly for this discussion, *deliberation* with one's adversary.

The Rudolphs propose that the ashram could replace the coffee house as the central locus of the public sphere, offering a radical alternative for addressing power imbalances in deliberation. They argue that Gandhi's model better aligns with Habermas's goal of attaining consensus, albeit by very different means. Whereas Habermas envisions consensus emerging from rational discourse, Gandhi's approach relies on empathy and sacrifice. In this model, exemplification and performance play an essential role, appealing to both the heart and the mind.[7]

Furthermore, Gandhi's ashram challenged the traditional distinction between the public and the private spheres. Unlike Habermas, who assumes that personal concerns must be excluded from public deliberation for discussions to remain rational and effective, Gandhi deliberately blurred these boundaries. As the Rudolphs note, 'Gandhi's deliberative process involves more than rationality and believes that reason without emotion cannot yield knowledge, truth or the public good. Reason has to be strengthened by suffering, not by force.'

However, while Gandhi's ashram presents a compelling alternative model for participatory democracy, it remains largely utopian when assessed as a practical mechanism for expanding deliberative democracy.

As previously discussed, Scott, with his concerns about power differentials, remains sceptical about the possibility of the poor overcoming power imbalances to deliberate in front of powerful representatives of the government and NGOs. Instead, of formal deliberation, he highlights covert strategies of non-compliance and 'weak' forms of protest, which he terms 'hidden transcripts' or 'infra politics' (Scott 1992). In Scott's view, deliberations are neither rational debates that suppress power differentials nor emotional outbursts on the part of the poor. Rather it is a strategic act, carefully calibrated to avoid retaliation and structured around what marginalised groups can realistically get away with (Scott 1987).[8]

Scott argues that these 'hidden transcripts' can be nurtured before a specific audience and in particular spaces, and that these private interactions provide an opportunity to workers to air their grievances. Under what conditions do these private spaces become the 'right' spaces for making 'hidden transcripts' public? Specifically, do structures like social audits and public hearings provide an effective platform for such disclosures? There are two key mechanisms through which workers' 'hidden transcripts' might become public. *First*, private testimonies can be documented—such as verifying whether reported work was actually completed—before being read aloud at public hearings. *Second*, individuals who have given private testimonies may be encouraged to attend public hearings and present their grievances.

The public hearings within the social audit process is designed to translate these often very emotional outbursts into rational arguments, creating a structured space for debate. In this sense, it resembles a Habermasian model of rational deliberation, where 'speech acts' are employed to discuss public issues. However, participation in these public meetings extends far beyond speech. Workers may engage in non-verbal forms of expression—clapping to show support, remaining silent as a form of dissent, shouting slogans in disagreement, or in some cases resorting to direct action or even violence. These diverse modes of participation challenge the notion that deliberation is purely a matter of rational speech.

Moreover, the impact of an information intervention may not be immediately visible during the public hearing itself. Often, its effects unfold outside the formal setting, requiring translation and amplification by intermediaries. Thus, our understanding of information use must expand beyond the narrow view of *speaking out* as the sole marker of participation in a public meeting. Instead of being confined to a spatially restricted metaphor—where participation is limited to what happens in the public hearing—we should consider a more fluid conception that integrates both public and private spaces. Some *hidden transcripts* first take shape in private, incubating through interactions with intermediaries before being made public. The presence of a *willing third party*— whether an activist, an organisation, or a social movement— is often essential in bringing these private grievances into the broader public sphere, whether in the form of speech or documented text.

If we take Scott's hidden transcripts seriously, it opens up avenues for an empirical research into when and how transcripts transition from private spaces into public exposure. This perspective builds on Baiocchi's observation of the crucial role played by *mobilisation through a third party*, which acts as a mediator between marginalised voices and formal deliberative arenas. Recognising this mediation process makes intermediaries themselves a critical subject of research, particularly in understanding the role of organisations such as the Mazdoor Kisan Shakti Sangathan, which have historically facilitated the articulation of subaltern grievances in public forums.

These explorations of participation and deliberation highlight the complex pathways through which information can or cannot lead to empowerment. The conclusion brings together these theoretical insights, reflecting on the conditions necessary for information to translate into meaningful political action.

Conclusion

This chapter has examined three theoretical frameworks that offer competing perspectives on the relationship between information and political agency. At its simplest level, there is an expectation that providing government records leads to an 'informed' citizenry, aligning with both Chambers' participatory model and the Habermasian deliberative ideal. However, the core problem with this assumption is that it largely ignores power and domination. It assumes that people can resolve their differences—despite inequalities of status—simply through communication and access to information, overlooking the structural conditions that determine who gets to speak and who is heard.

Through an exploration of theories on the political habitus, subaltern agency, and intermediaries, this chapter has argued that information alone is rarely sufficient to catalyse contestation. Instead, the ability of marginalised citizens to move from private frustrations to public demands depends on additional forms of agency—often facilitated by intermediaries, social movements, or deliberative spaces. My position falls between Gramsci and Scott; marginalised citizens do not simply consent to domination. Rather, they often express their frustrations in private. The challenge, then, is that moving these frustrations into the public sphere and formal deliberative spaces requires additional agency—often through the involvement of intermediaries.

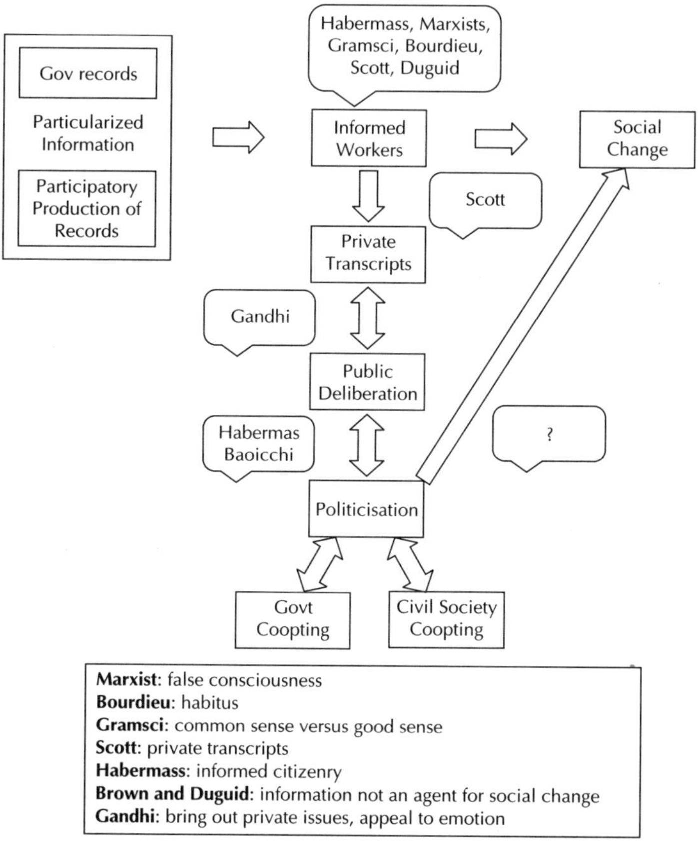

FIGURE 6.1: Framework for Theorising Information and its Link to Social Change

Source: Author.

Intermediaries and the Rhetoric of Specificity

A central argument emerging from this discussion is that intermediaries do not simply act as conduits of information but actively shape the way grievances are framed and articulated.

I argue that information plays a crucial role in fostering a rhetoric of specificity—transforming vague, dispersed frustrations into concrete, actionable claims. Whether through social audits, workers' movements, or deliberative spaces, intermediaries help to translate scattered injustices into specific demands that can be contested in public arenas.

Scott would argue that so-called 'informed' citizens generate more 'private transcripts', but these rarely make their way into the public sphere on their own. Habermas' model of the public sphere suggests a possible pathway bringing these grievances into the open. However, Baoicchi extends this analysis, emphasising that a deliberative space created by the government—combined with the presence of a third-party intermediary (distinct from the government and the workers)—is needed to facilitate this transition. This process, however, is neither automatic nor guaranteed. Please refer to Veeraraghavan (2021), where I have empirically examined these possibilities.

There are three possible trajectories once grievances enter the public sphere:

1. Politicisation: Speaking out catalyses social change, transforming grievances into collective demands that reshape policy and governance.
2. Retaliation or Repression: Speaking out provokes backlash, worsening conditions for those who contest the status quo.
3. Co-optation: Speech is absorbed without challenging power, reinforcing existing structures rather than disrupting them.

Many theorists emphasise politicisation (or re-politicisation) as the most effective pathway for social change (Ferguson 1994; Li 2007; Williams 2004). Politicisation occurs when marginalised groups are able to frame their claims as legitimate political issues, forcing governing institutions to respond. If speaking out successfully politicises an issue, governing institutions must contend with new political realities at the last mile. This raises the question: Can participatory processes, particularly designed from the outside, meaningfully engage in local political struggles?

Yet, politicisation is not the only possible outcome. Speaking out can carry risks, especially in politically charged environments, where State and local elite interests push back against contestation. When intermediaries—civil society organisations, NGOs, or third-party actors—attempt to navigate these tensions, they face a difficult choice: How should they respond? If they seek to avoid political confrontation by *depoliticising* their engagement, do these participatory processes risk becoming empty rituals devoid of substantive impact?

If they fully engage in confrontation, do they risk alienation, repression, or co-optation?

Finally, the role of intermediaries introduces its own set of challenges and contradictions. These intermediaries often have their own interests, which may not fully align with the needs of marginalised citizens. Additionally, governments can strategically use participatory mechanisms as a means of *performative transparency*—appearing to engage with citizens while deflecting deeper scrutiny of corruption and accountability issues. By simply making information available, the government may claim to have fulfilled its duty of transparency while avoiding substantive action.

This underscores a crucial limitation of simplistic 'information-empowers' narratives. Information, by itself, does not inherently challenge power. The real question is: *Under what conditions does information become politically meaningful?*[9]

This chapter has argued that the answer lies not just in access to information, but in how it is mobilised, contested, and mediated. Rather than treating information as a neutral good, we must examine the political structures, power dynamics, and intermediary actors that determine whether information translates into meaningful political action.

In short, information alone does not make the subaltern speak. It is only when mediated through intermediaries, contextualised within social movements, and politicised within public arenas that information becomes a tool of contestation and change.

Notes

1. My use of the word 'subaltern' employs a variant of the original Gramscian sense to indicate groups that are outside the established structures of political representation.

2. Janaki Srinivasan's *The Political Lives of Information* (2022) offers an important critique of the reification of information in development contexts, emphasising how information is not neutral, but shaped by social, political, and institutional forces. Her work, particularly on the MKSS and right-to-information movements, highlights the ways information acquires meaning and political force through its circulation and contestation. While I build on her insights about the politicisation of information, this chapter focusses on the theoretical dimensions of how information transitions into political contestation, drawing from social and political theory to map the conditions under which 'information' can enable marginalised citizens to challenge domination.

3. Gayatri Chakravorty Spivak, in her essay 'Can the subaltern speak?', warns us of the futility of asking this question (Spivak 1988). She argues that the subaltern is usually defined as somebody who cannot speak —*ergo* unable by definition — and as soon as they can speak, they are no longer the subaltern. She also argues that even if the subaltern speaks, the powerful are not willing to hear them. So, for Spivak, particularistic information gets bracketed off and plays no role in getting the subaltern to speak. The problem for her stays at the level of discourse, and it is the discourse about the subalterns that has to change. However, assumptions about information pervade academic and policy interventions, and so it helps us to take it seriously.

4. Scott does hold out the remote possibility of these private transcripts getting out under certain conditions.

5. Criticisms of the Habermasian public sphere span questions about the historical existence of the sphere to the narrowness of his concept, specifically 'bracketing off' gender, identity, and idealising aspects of rationality to settle differences (Calhoun 1992).

6. Thanks to Patrick Heller for suggesting this phrase.

7. The land redistribution movement was started when Vinoba Bhave, a Gandhian, appealed to the landholders to voluntarily return the land.

8. See Scott's *Weapons of the Weak* for the different 'weak' forms of protest (Scott 1987).

9. See Srinivasan (2022) for a pathbreaking empirical work on the role of information in development.

SELECT REFERENCES

Banerjee, A. V., R. Banerji, E. Duflo, R. Glennerster, and S. Khemani. 2010. 'Pitfalls of Participatory Programs: Evidence from a Randomized Evaluation in Education in India'. *American Economic Journal*, Economic Policy 2 (1), 1–30.

Baviskar, A. 2010. 'Winning the Right to Information in India: Is Knowledge Power?', in J. Gaventa and R. McGhee (eds), *Citizen Action and National Policy Reform*. London: Zed Books.

Benjamin, S., R. Bhuvaneswari, and P. Rajan. 2007. 'Bhoomi: "E–Governance", or, an Anti-Politics Machine Necessary to Globalize Bangalore?' CASUM-m Working Paper, 1–53.

Baiocchi, G. 2003. 'Emergent Public Spheres: Talking Politics in Participatory Governance'. *American Sociological Review* 68 (1), 52–74.

Bourdieu, P. 2000. *Pascalian Meditations*. Stanford, California: Stanford University Press.

Brown, J. S., and P. Duguid. 2000. *The Social Life of Information*. Boston: Harvard Business Press.

Burawoy, Michael. 2008. 'Can the Working Class Know Itself?' Lecture III, 'Does the Working Class Exist? Burawoy Meets Bourdieu', 28 March. Available at http://burawoy.berkeley.edu/Bourdieu/Lecture%203.pdf (accessed October 2024).

Calhoun, C. (ed.). 1992. *Habermas and the Public Sphere*. Cambridge: MIT Press.

Chambers, R. 1994. 'The Origins and Practice of Participatory Rural Appraisal'. *World Development* 22, 953–969.

———. 1997. *Whose Reality Counts?: Putting the First Last*. UK: Intermediate Technology Publications.

Chatterjee, P. 2004. *The Politics of the Governed: Reflections on Popular Politics in Most of the World*. New York: Columbia University Press.

Christens, B., and P. W. Speer. 2006. 'Tyranny/Transformation: Power and Paradox in Participatory Development'. *Forum: Qualitative Social Research 7*.

Cooke, B., and U. Kothar (eds). 2001. *Participation: The New Tyranny?* New York: Zed Books.

Corbridge, S., G. Williams, M. Srivastava, and R. Véron. 2005. *Seeing the State: Governance and Governmentality in India*, Contemporary South Asia, Vol. 10. Cambridge: Cambridge University Press.

Drèze, J, and A. Sen. 2013. *An Uncertain Glory: India and its Contradictions*. Princeton, NJ: Princeton University Press.

Eyerman, R. 1981. 'False Consciousness and Ideology in Marxist Theory'. *Acta Sociologica* 24 (1/2), 43–56.

Ferguson, J. 1994. *The Anti-politics Machine: Development, Depoliticization, and Bureaucratic Power in Lesotho*. Minneapolis: University of Minnesota Press.

Fox, J. 2007a. 'The Uncertain Relationship between Transparency and Accountability'. *Development in Practice* 17 (4–5), 663–671.

———. 2007b. 'Unpacking Accountability Politics', in *The Politics of Accountability in Mexico*. Oxford University Press.

Gaventa, J. 2006. 'Triumph, Deficit or Contestation? Deepening the "Deepening Democracy" Debate'. IDS Working Paper 264. Brighton, UK: Institute of Development Studies.

Gramsci, A., and Q. Hoare. 1971. *Selections from the Prison Notebooks*. International Publishers Co.

Habermas, J. 1989. *The Structural Transformation of the Public Sphere*. Cambridge, MA: MIT Press.

Jenkins, R., and A. M. Goetz. 1999. 'Accounts and Accountability: Theoretical Implications of the Right-to-information Movement in India'. *Third World Quarterly* 20 (3), 603–622.

Keefer, K., and S. Khemani. 2012. 'Do Informed Citizens Receive More...or Pay More? The Impact of Radio on the Government Distribution of Public Health Benefits', WPS 5952. The World Bank, Policy Research Working Paper.

Khera, R. 2011. *The Battle for Employment Guarantee*. New Delhi: Oxford University Press.

Li, T. M. 2007. *The Will to Improve: Governmentality, Development, and the Practice of Politics*. Durham: Duke University Press.

Lieberman, E. S., N. Daniel, L. Posner, and L. Tsai. 2014. 'Does Information Lead to More Active Citizenship? Evidence from an Education Intervention in Rural Kenya'. *World Development* 60, 69–83.

Mohan, G., and K. Stokke. 2000. 'Participatory Development and Empowerment: The Dangers of Localism'. *Third World Quarterly* 21 (2), 247–268.

Ravallion, M., D. van de Walle, P. Dutta, and R. Murgai. 2013. 'Testing Information Constraints on India's Largest Antipoverty Program'. Policy Research Working Paper, 6598. Washington, DC: The World Bank.

Reinikka, R., and J. Svensson. 2003. *The Power of Information: Evidence from a Newspaper Campaign to Reduce Capture*. Washington, DC: The World Bank.

Rudolph, L., and S. H. Rudolph. 2006. 'The Coffee House and the Ashram Revisited', in *Postmodern Gandhi and Other Essays: Gandhi in the World and at Home*, 140–177. Chicago: University of Chicago Press.

Scott, J. C. 1987. *Weapons of the Weak: Everyday Forms of Peasant Resistance*. New Haven, CT: Yale University Press.

———. 1992. *Domination and the Arts of Resistance: Hidden Transcripts*. New Haven, CT: Yale University Press.

Sen, A., and J. Drèze. 1999. *The Amartya Sen and Jean Drèze Omnibus: Comprising Poverty and Famines, Hunger and Public Action, India: Economic Development and Social Opportunity*. New Delhi: Oxford University Press.

Spivak, Gayatri. 1988. 'Can the Subaltern Speak?' in *Marxism and the Interpretation of Culture*. London: Macmillan.

Srinivasan, J. 2011. 'The Political Life of Information: "Information" and the Practice of Governance in India'. Ph.D. Thesis, University of California, Berkeley.

Stiglitz, J. 2002. 'Transparency in Government. The Right to Tell: The Role of Mass Media in Economic Development'. Washington, DC: The World Bank, 27–44.

Veeraraghavan, R.. 2021. *Patching Development: Information Politics and Social Change in India*. New Delhi: Oxford University Press.

Williams, G. 2004. 'Evaluating Participatory Development: Tyranny, Power and (Re)politicisation'. *Third World Quarterly* 25 (3), 557–578.

World Bank. 1994. *The World Bank and Participation*. Washington, D.C.: World Bank. Available at https://documents1.worldbank.org/curated/en/627501467990056231/pdf/multi-page.pdf (accessed February 2025).

Knowledge Panchayats

Shiv Visvanathan

I

Democracy in the twenty-first century has a way of caricaturing itself. As a piece of scholarship it remains fossilised, mimicking its nineteenth-century model of voice and representation. Democracy becomes a demography of numbers. Yet while scholarship, especially psephology, sticks to the quantitative and representational character of democracy, movements have realised that democracy has become more protean. It has to be read and re-read across many indices. One has to redefine citizenship, participation, and justice, not as abstract concepts but as lived worlds. The formal idea of democracy and the phenomenological sense of democracy, the formal, abstract, and the lived complexity of democracy become different worlds.

Democracy has changed in three ways. *First*, it has to become a contract across three mediums, the oral, the digital, and the textual. These are not three forms of technology, but three epistemic worlds. One needs to rework a new relationship between the three domains. *Second*, democracy paid little attention to knowledge. It created the citizen as a consumer of knowledge, not as a critic or creator. Once we see the citizen as the custodian of a knowledge system, the relation of knowledge to democracy can no longer be treated as black boxes. The citizen as a person of knowledge is not a passive consumer. He is insistent on redefining and debating his world.

Third, in confronting the knowledge revolution and its residue, democracy realises it can no longer be reductionist in terms of bytes of information but has to reflect on knowledge. Knowledge adds an epistemic and cosmological component to information. For example, a right to health is not just access but an engagement with health, the body, and suffering as modes of knowing. Democracy, also like science, realises that there is no one answer. One has to engage with plurality and complexity.

Finally, democracy as a performative exercise has created new expectations. Protest is expected to articulate alternatives, and create the possibility of a thought experiment and alternative institutions. The engagement between movements and scholars showed that democracy has become more demanding and tentative. A mere rhetorical critique, an act of opposition, is not enough. Protest is expected to create institution for the future.

One has to emphasise this as one discovered that democracy grows and becomes more substantive as scholar and activist meet to thicken democracy as an institutional imagination. Such an encounter leads to redefinitions of language, technology, even the very ritual of politics. The above prelude is an addendum to the original chapter as the academic rewrites his experience, often watching activism and protest as real-life stories. Politics then has to be retold thrice, as paradigm, as the hermeneutics of a discourse, and as an act of storytelling, an unfolding of memory. This becomes amply clear as we look at protest movements today.

II

Protest today is a much more manifold exercise. Its very logic demands that it display a pedagogic function. A mere political demonstration is not seen as performative enough. Today society demands that protest go beyond critique and posit a feasible alternative. Protest, in that role, has to be both utopian and pragmatic. Protest and movements of protest have to survive long enough to invent institutions that embody the dream of alternatives. The Right to Information Act (RTI) evolved by the Mazdoor Kisan Shakti Sangathan (MKSS) was a realisation of both a dream and a pedagogy. Democracy became a true leaning experience, enacted across a variety of domains. Yet every protest has to be self-critical and inventive, add new imaginaries to the shop-soiled political imagination. This chapter argues that the Right to Information is now incomplete without the Right to Knowledge, and tries to visualise the idea of the Knowledge Panchayat as a theatre for debating knowledge and its consequences. The chapter is divided into three parts: it describes the impact and role of RTI; argues for the extension of information into knowledge; and elaborates the role of the Knowledge Panchayat in this context.

III

The Right to Information

A sociology of information has to go back to its roots in social theory, to the origins of the social contract. The social contract as a theory is a fictitious agreement between sovereign and citizen, focused more on materiality, equality, and freedom. Abstract ideas like knowledge and information lay inarticulate, part of the tacit assumptions of the social but not yet a constitutionally articulate presence. Citizenship was defined more in terms of access rather than competence or performance. The performative nature of citizenship would have emphasised the need for information. Information cannot be defined purely in terms of access. The metaphor of information mediates between orality and textuality and determines the quality of memory in a society. Information gives agency to citizenship, which often gets reduced to the passivity of a few rituals like voting and consumption.

The RTI struggle in India was not just a struggle to legislate about information, but an attempt to theorise about information both as grammar (*langue*) and as the myriad variations of speech (*parole*). One often forgets that movements do not merely challenge the system, but theorise about it as well. In fact, they emphasise that theorising about a society is part of the practice of citizenship. Such struggles also break the stereotypes regarding information in a society. The first wave of struggles comprised battles to obtain food, clothing, and shelter. Such claims were seen as both immediate and subsistence-based. They were material demands on the State. Information was at first distant to such narratives of struggle. They valorised storytelling, but not information. Information was seen as esoteric, abstract, an expert's prerogative rather than a layman's right, as symbolic, and as a luxury. When the MKSS began its struggles, one of the first stereotypes it had to face was why a subsistence society needed information, and in particular the question of whether the claim of the margins for information was an act of arrogance and an aspirational piety. Such stereotypes challenged the credibility of the movement, seeking to expand its impetus beyond the contours of *roti, kapda, aur makan* (food, clothing, and shelter). The demand for information did not seem compatible within the older framework of struggle as political economy. A right to information appeared as an act of snobbery, especially when demanded by a marginal group.

In breaking stereotypes, MKSS emphasised three things: *first*, the critical nature of information and its necessity as a part of any substantive contract. *Second*, it revealed that citizenship without the right to information confined democracy to the elites and allowed corruption to become a way of life. *Third*, a right to information added content to the game of equality, making citizenship a more open playing field.

The RTI began with two perspectives, one political and the other pedagogic, one legislating about various aspects of information and the second creating a learning process about the life-giving nature of information. The political economy of food, clothing, and shelter acquired a different nuance when such 'material goods' were read as part of the information polity. The RTI struggle emphasised that democracy possessed its own form of snobbery, which in turn prevented the democratisation of a democracy. Some rights, as a result, pretended to be middle-class prerogatives. As the RTI story itself asked: 'How did a group of illiterate villagers incapable of "thinking or thought" arrive at this politically smart definition of information rights?' The MKSS showed how struggle and reflective struggle become a process challenging a myth of equality, where, in an Orwellian sense, some are more equal than others.

The MKSS as a peasant proletarian movement saw struggle as a part of the drama of democracy. The performative nature of struggle also created a variation and density of meaning. A right to information is a composite of dialects, where information on health, environment, education, and governance adds to a reciprocal richness of citizenship.

The RTI realised that struggle invented new options and opened up new possibilities, leading to a skeletal minimum idea of rights acquiring a richness of meaning. A struggle is a process of constant discovery and consolidation. It acquires a creativity through this constant hermeneutic of reading itself as a text. Even encountering a thesaurus of items around a key word adds to the availability of multiple worlds. Transparency, for instance, also needs access, visibility, and clarity; each synonym adds to the richness of the life world.

Concepts are not just abstract terms in a system; they are lived out as performative acts of citizenship. Consider a basic term like visibility. The MKSS, as part of its increasing repertoire of activities, opened a fair price *kirana* store. Every day, it made a formal announcement of prices, which challenged the marked-up prices of other stores and also showed how information, when used openly, consolidated the world of ethics. Information challenges the misuse of power, and access to records was a means to challenge such misuse. The RTI realised that the ritual of asking for information was an effective method to establish the right to question, the right to equality, and accountability. Lack of information was one form of scarcity that was discriminatory. The system realised that information was power and sensed that the right to information questioned unfettered power. As a result, when the poor ask for information, false cases are imposed on them, as the system realises that sharing information is literally an act of sharing power.

The RTI movement also realised that information as a public good needed a public space for enactment and interrogation. The *jan sunwai* added to the semiotics of a democracy that was accessible and informal, and where the government could not be both the accused and the arbitrator. Rights had many layers, and the right to information had to institutionalise transparency, accountability, audit, and redressal into the weave of governance, inaugurating the idea of an ethical administration. One went beyond the outer layers of democracy, such as participation and representation, to audit, accountability, and transparency. Transparency inaugurated the dismantling of the oppressive misuse of power.

The MKSS, in its ethnography of the RTI, showed that a campaign for information begins with the naiveté of rudimentary demands, but acquires subtlety, nuance, and variety as the protest proceeds, akin to a classic learning process. The struggle for RTI begins with a minimum core of expectations about wages and employment, and expands through dream-time, drama experiment, and storytelling as the struggle evolves. This process, which challenges the assumptions of governance while adding to the folklore of citizenship, is a continuous one of invention and consolidation. A *padayatra* by citizens acquires the power of a policy *yatra* as citizens accumulate stories about misgovernance, which gradually develops into a citizen's discourse, which in turn challenges expert policy.

While confronting the first wave of success, the movement for information also confronts the proliferating need for information in domains like health, governance, disasters, wages, hygiene, agriculture, and natural resources. The Bhopal gas disaster and the anti-dam movement realised that information itself has to open up new metaphors of understanding for citizenship. In confronting this, the RTI realises that information, for all its acquired richness, is still incomplete. A political economy of rights needs a politics of knowledge, an interrogation of epistemologies in which information is embedded. An RTI analyses that a right to knowledge enhances the power of citizenship by treating the citizen not merely as a passive consumer, but also as a processor of governance as knowledge, challenging the power of expertise and the nature of epistemologies that determine the fate of life and livelihood.

An RTI is a law, a piece of legislation which has to be understood within a wider notion of constitutionality and culture. In that sense, an RTI is a rudimentary expression of a deeper political and cultural unconscious. An RTI represents a project with multiple strands, a dream of democracy which embodies a model of knowledge, citizenship, community, and communication. It goes beyond the standard behavioural demands of participation and representation. It reminds one of a story, a vignette in a Harvard seminar one of us was fortunate to participate in. A speaker was asked why movements use the word epistemology when the World Bank president may not understand the meaning of the term. He answered, 'precisely'. One is not accusing the World Bank of illiteracy, but alluding to the fact that it represents merely one view of the world, which is more managerial and technocratic. When the World Bank talks of participation or representation, key words in the democratic glossary today, it assumes a world of discourse and even the terms of negotiation. It asks for a representation of epistemes, worldviews, etc., descriptions of the world which might be difficult to articulate in these discussions. Information here has a more reductive aspect. It is functional and instrumental, it fills a gap, a lack, but does not question a worldview. One can explain such an omission only through stories. The World Bank and development data is often indifferent to storytelling.

One is reminded of an anecdote that Medha Patkar often recounted during the final stages of the Narmada battle. Army jeeps had been called in to evacuate people. A young *jawan* asks an old man why he was refusing to leave when he had been promised an equivalent piece of land. The old man answered, 'How can I leave when my ancestors live here? This is where I belong.' The old man was trying to explain that land is not property. It is also a sacrament of belonging. He was talking of a world where identity is ancestry and genealogy not a commodity. Such notions might be difficult for development experts to understand. They often bowdlerise storytelling in their official annual reports by reducing it to coloured boxes which carry human interest material stripped off its culture and context.

However, it is not merely a question of an anecdote. Storytelling connects us to discourses, epistemes, and theoretical frameworks which validate and legitimise meaningful acts of culture. It adds a different dimension to citizenship. A citizen is not merely one who is a resident of a place or has membership in a community. Citizenship represents claims, entitlements to knowledge. A citizen has to be seen as a person of knowledge, a trustee of epistemes, much of which could be orally articulated. Their idea of democracy is not merely a certification of those in power. It could be a claim asking for a representation of an alternative world. In that sense, a thick description of a right to information involves four other assumptions, *first*, that a right to information is a right to the frameworks of the epistemologies of knowledge within which information is articulated. For example, a society where nature is conceived as a resource visualises economics differently from a way of thinking where nature is part of the sacred. *Second*, a right to knowledge is a recognition of a process of communication where a citizen represents their own myths and epistemes of knowledge. They are not a passive recipient of information but an active interrogator of the knowledge systems within which 'expert information' is transmitted to them. A right to information presupposes a dialogue of epistemes, not a mere submission to a questionnaire. *Third*, citizenship is not a mere demand for access to information, but requires an access to a commons of culture with competing articulations. Doubt, difference, and diversity are part of the access to knowledge that a citizen needs to debate a discussion. *Fourth*, a citizen does not merely assent to a project as a *fait accompli*, but sees democracy as a commons of decision-making, where one articulates alternative worldviews. Information, while life-giving, provides an opening to a rich world of culture and context, without which democracy would be impoverished. *Finally*, an RTI also implicitly seeks to subvert the asymmetry between experts and laymen and invent a more even playing field between different forms of knowledge. In that sense, information without the idea of knowledge and community would be an amputated term.

From Information to Knowledge.

The transition from one frame to another involves a bit of muddling through, experimenting with new ideas of democracy, and contending with ideas of information and citizenship which confuse identity and identification. The very fluidity of the new requirements calls for thought experiments to draw scenarios for the future. The availability of alternatives based on different worldviews and epistemes becomes critical and life-giving in this context. Let me outline seven quick ethnographies and scenarios as thought experiments, to explore the everydayness of knowledge democracies on the ground.

IV

Ethnographies and Scenarios

In 2018, a group of weavers met a group of scholars, historians, and anthropologists of cloth and innovation to discuss the fate of weaving in India. The first situation one confronted was the orality of a culture, where the link between orality, memory, and community was critical. A relation between ethics, tradition, and memory gave one a different language of innovation from that conceptualised in management textbooks. One has to emphasise that one is not confronting an ethnoscience, or knowledge labelled as a lesser form of understanding as a subaltern science. One was confronting a different idea of epistemology and community linked to livelihood. The terms of discourse need a different kind of articulation and dignity as forms of knowledge. They demanded a separate glossary of understanding which needs translation not as a search for equivalence, but as an exploration of an alternate universe of understanding. Words like competence and ownership require a different set of creation myths. The case often cited is the story of Yellappa, one of the last of the master weavers. Yellappa belongs to a separate universe of discourse, with its unique rituals of craft competence. One needs an articulation of his worldview, from cosmology to craft, to capture his sense of competence. One also has to grasp how knowledge survives, and how it is stored and transmitted in an oral society. In fact, seminars such as the above become important because one realises that one needs a new social contract, the articulation of a communication model between different cultures, where the relation between word and world has to be clearer. Knowledge Panchayats modelled on such seminars can be playful exercises to express plural worlds. The power of orality, memory, and the articulation of sensoria as choreographers of the body, rather than the indexicality of instruments, needs to be understood.

Many of these encounters are not always statements of mutuality and reciprocity. They often become battles for survival where one needs to provide a diverse agency for evaluation. The case of the People's Linguistic Survey of India (PLSI) can provide a model for such agency. Usually a survey becomes an act of governmentality where the government, in collecting information, tacitly imposes its categories and classifications on the discourses of a people; a process we dub 'development'. One needs to challenge the biases and stereotypes inherent in such a policy process without letting it become reified into a science. Ganesh Devy, the literary critic who directed the survey, challenges the very definition of language. Language, the government officially proclaims, is part of any form of life that possesses a script to articulate it. Such a definition is either empirical or inclusive. It carries all the biases of what Marshall McLuhan calls the Gutenberg galaxy (McLuhan 1962). In one cavalier sweep, the government officially eliminated almost 2,000 oral languages, imposing silence upon the tribal. One needs Knowledge Panchayats to challenge such acts of linguicide as models of governmentality. Citizens and civil society need to appropriate and domesticate social science tools like the survey to create the availability of alternative memory. Devy counterposes to the monumentality and officialdom of the Linguistic Survey of India, a people's survey examining the survival of oral languages and grammars. It is an attempt to map a commons of competence through the agency of civil society, which the government is indifferent to in its instrumental search for an allegedly more stable and efficient monolingual world. A people's survey of languages, rivers, and crafts can be an extension of the Knowledge Panchayat, adding to the competence, rather than accentuating the vulnerability of, marginal groups. Knowledge Panchayats are needed to show that the diversity of languages, cultures, or knowledge cannot be evaluated through a monolingualism of efficiency, as economists employ it.

The Knowledge Panchayat is an affirmation that a citizen is not merely a passive consumer of knowledge, but is also a critical commentator, evaluator, and generator of that knowledge. A Knowledge Panchayat asserts a citizen's right to produce knowledge and evaluate decisions according to his preferred categories of knowledge. Knowledge Panchayats, in that sense, become exercises in the comparative anthropology of knowledge. This assessment is done pluralistically, avoiding hierarchies and hegemonies of knowledge. Science is no longer read as monopolistic or hegemonic, nor are other knowledges viewed tolerantly as 'ethnoscience', children of a lesser god of knowledge.

The *third* model one thinks of centres around the assessment of technological controversies. Misria Ali, in her study of the debates on the nuclear plant in Kudankulam, shows that anxiety is often articulated through local dialects and responses from the sensorium (Ali 2009). The language is not that of a scientific formula, but a home science mix of hunches, smells, and signs read by wise people. Such an anxiety cannot be dismissed as imaginary, a layman's construct, lacking the accuracy of measure that scientific instruments provide. Ali argues that Cartesian and housewife anxieties are of different kinds, speaking dialects and presenting morels of evidence from distinctly separate worlds. But to dismiss the latter, claiming that the world of expertise has no place for them, would be unfair. They represent claims to knowledge which need to be translated with its sense of epistemic plurality recognising the need for 'epistemic brokerage'. One can cite as an example of this the work of the environmentalist Nityanand Jayaraman (2001). Studying a factory that was involved in polluting the environment, Jayaraman recounts a scenario where local people complained of smells in terms of local dialects and metaphors. The experts investigating the complaints dismissed these descriptions as unscientific. In his paper, Jayaraman catalogues the language of anxieties and complaints in terms of the sensoria and establishes their empirical validity by showing that science, by appealing to a univocal universalism, might be behaving more provincially than one expects. A Knowledge Panchayat, in that sense, becomes a mediator, an epistemic broker, a translator between different dialects of knowledge.

A *fourth* major source of angst has been the debates around biotechnology. One senses in retrospect that one is mediating two sets of debates, the first between people arguing for traditional crops and relating food security to diversity against corporate scientists offering quick fixes in the form of BT cotton and genetic engineering in general. There is also a debate now articulated between the world of science and its dissenting imaginations. In that sense, the GMO controversy has to be read twice, as a debate within science and as a debate of the wider consumers of science. The idea of risk haunts science and the structural uncertainty of science demands an ethics, an innovative sense of law that goes beyond the precautionary principle. The battle is also one between lobbyists, corporate scientists, parts of the World Trade Organization (WTO), and social movements convinced that local or traditional agriculture has its own innovative solutions to offer. One also senses that questions about food security, genetic risk, and escalating costs in terms of new inputs have not been fully or convincingly answered by science. The science academies in India blustered and eventually ended up reproducing company reports, which reflected the corporate biases of firms. The millennial answer offered by some scientists—that genetic engineering is a final and ultimate choice to world hunger—was also unconvincing. The world of experts gets bracketed and, for now, the world of expertise has lost its sense of conviction. One also discovered that experts, instead of conducting independent, autonomous investigations, were relying on company reports. There was a realisation that the best lacked conviction and the centre could no longer hold because it had been invaded by interest groups representing pesticides and polluting fertilisers, who were indifferent to the robust power of the traditional seed industry. At a time when science academies can no longer claim objectivity and are uncertain about the future, one needs a new structure of knowledge mediation where the entire spectrum of the industry, from the marginal farmer, the traditional seed grower, the NGO worried about the fate of traditional diversity, to the representatives of the patent system, the social movements attempting to create a new commons for agriculture, the academies, the industry, and the consumer as citizen, can all find a voice in a public forum that is also sensitive to the rights of the future.

Democracy today has to invent new institutions which are epistemically more representative and responsive, and which can adjudicate between the long run and the short run, advocates of the commons and the WTO, and between productivity and diversity. The Knowledge Panchayat is a forum whose time has come. It has to be a chain of being that represents science not only as interest group articulation but also as a way of life, where stakeholder rather than shareholder participation is emphasised. One has to realise that the Knowledge Panchayat is not merely an attempt to rescue the marginal farmer. It is equally an attempt to restore the integrity of a risk-oriented science contaminated by corporate interests dedicated to profit.

A *fifth* example that one is almost forced to invent is the necessity of a Knowledge Panchayat for the Anthropocene. The Anthropocene is a planetary issue involving planetary considerations often reread parochially in terms of nationalist ideologies. A serendipitous term coined by the Swedish scientist Paul Crutzen, it is an attempt to look at global space and evolutionary time by exploring human inventions in nature, by recognising that these have proved damaging on a planetary scale. A Knowledge Panchayat has to first help define the problem, understanding that it is a social construct. Second, while validating the critique of activists from the developing world who demand that the industrial West bear maximum responsibility for such damage, the Panchayat has to mobilise a new planetary consciousness, an ethics that recognises that large areas in the developing world are vulnerable. One needs a science that is sensitive to such problems and reads the problematic of the Anthropocene as a challenge to the relation between knowledge and democracy on a global scale.

Finally, Knowledge Panchayats are not merely institutions for firefighting. They also need to invent the problematic of the future. This issue emerges in a crucial manner when we confront violence, peace, and war. In this sense, a Knowledge Panchayat is also a Peace Panchayat, exploring non-violent forms of knowledge and creating new ethical startups where peace is no longer a prerogative of security experts and the State. In a profound sense, the Knowledge Panchayat becomes an ashram for a satyagraha of knowledge, linking knowledge, consumption, violence, and waste into a new epistemics of peace, mimicking, if necessary, a dialogue among religious cosmologies. A Knowledge Panchayat thus becomes a curator and trustee of knowledges and an inventor of the institutions and ethics required for it.

V

In considering the panchayat, one realises that one is confronting one of the oldest and most democratic of institutions, an embodiment of village politics and an expression of a civilisational worldview. It is almost primordial in its sense of polity, and one is harnessing it to play a modern role in enacting and examining the politics of knowledge. The panchayat, in that sense, is not a formal organisation. It also evokes a sense of community. One must see it more as a public space where the psychodramas of modern life, especially around knowledge, are enacted. The fears, the anxieties, the hopes, and the possibilities in our society, as reflected in knowledge, technology, nature, and change, need to be rendered both articulate and visible before one can adjudicate or even broker competing views. The essential encounter is between the linearity and rigidity of managerial innovation chains, with their catechisms of progress, and the protean community we call the panchayat.

The orality of the panchayat, its sense of folklore, sets the background for the debates around technology. One wants the formal language of cost benefit, of efficiency, to rub shoulders with the traditional language of wisdom, such that technology runs the gauntlet of parables and proverbs while articulating the power of the contemporary. Language and the varieties of dialect become critical because what the Knowledge Panchayat provides is an enactment of the fear, anxieties, and expectations of a community, articulated both as a trial of a forthcoming technology and seminar, a running discourse like a *katha* on the possibilities and limits of a new innovation. The visibility and articulation of origins and benefits constitute a blending of pedagogy and democracy around the fate of knowledge and technology.

Such a psychodrama cannot be a mainstream middle-class text. The margins, the minorities, the dissenters, and the defeated need a voice and democracy must invent a script that represents their worldview and the fate of their world as knowledge, science, and technology alters the world at large. Knowledge and technology invoked Prometheus and Proteus. The panchayat provides local myths and dialects to read the technology. One needs representation of technology as a chain of being and a sense of a dialogue of difference, where local and global, macro and micro sociologies can map out their connectivities. A Knowledge Panchayat is different from a *jan sunvai*. The latter is more informal; it consumes information and reacts to it. The Knowledge Panchayat is akin to a focus group where experts, NGOs, and academics articulate their views on a knowledge system, commenting on everything from productivity to diversity. It is the decoding of a technology, both formally and informally, and one hopes that hyphenation gives it an interpretive power where technology assessment, philosophical speculation, and old-fashioned ethics, the everydayness of conscience, can meet on one forum instead of appearing to be part of parallel worlds. Such an encounter needs both storytellers to capture these moments and epistemic brokers who can translate the claims and counter-claims. One must emphasise the presence of the storyteller as a trustee of memory because in technological controversies, marginal groups are erased before the story even ends. The fate of these groups must enter the popular consciousness. In a pedagogic sense, a Knowledge Panchayat links the ethics of memory to the ethics of innovation, and becomes a trustee of both.

As one looks reflectively at the institution that one is inventing, one realises that language is a critical metaphor. Questions of interpretation, translation, epistemic brokerage, and mediation become central, and technology and knowledge are almost read like literary texts where one transforms technology, which is viewed in a linear fashion, into a literary text sensitive to paradox and irony. As a pedagogic exercise, the Knowledge Panchayat sensitises one to the unhindered consequences of epistemes and technologies. One also realises that the felicific calculus of the greatest good of the greatest number leads to crude majoritarianism. Knowledge Panchayats seek to articulate and represent diversities, providing thereby a pluralistic rather than a majoritarian view of technology. In an old-fashioned sense, it allows for a free play of ethics and dissent, for conscience to be given a public space. Ethical choices and ethical experiments are provided with a public audience. One is reminded of two examples in this context. Ravi Subramaniam, an astronomer deeply interested in the fate of food, argued in a discussion that technology needs not only self-reliance but also self-control. He observed that with technology, every 'can' becomes an 'ought'. If something is technologically possible, one feels a compulsive need to realise it. He claimed that against the alleged progressivism of technology, one needs a sense of primitivism, a deliberate simplicity rather than simplification, as an ethics and aesthetic of lifestyle and livelihood. The scientific infiltration into food might create adulterations, monstrosities that lay people may not be aware of. One needs an ethical and epistemic asceticism to challenge the linear bias of technology.

There is also a need for *communitas*, a sense of sharing between people. A poignant example comes from a dialogue among tribal people at a hearing of the Asian Women's conference. A tribal woman was appalled to hear that tribes in Bihar starved for over 120 days a year as a result of drought. Drought led to starvation for thirty days a year in her locality. She recounted the story and, as an act of solidarity, decided to starve for sixty days a year.

This same spirit of human solidarity and community is captured in the art critic Ananda Coomaraswamy's story of a woman who discovered that a washing machine had been invented. She refused to use it, asking 'what will become of my washerman'. A sense of reciprocity, of sharing access provides the very metaphor of the commons, even as an unconscious metaphor can create filters against technologies that move towards enclosures or panopticons. A sense of the commons of technology can create what the scientist C. V. Seshadri called a shared holism. He suggested that tea be drunk in mud pots (*kullar*s) rather than paper or plastic cups to help sustain the livelihood of the potter.

In this context, a Knowledge Panchayat becomes a device for creating both technological literacy and wisdom, a site where folk wisdom can challenge the introgeny of the expert. As a cultural critic observed, the Knowledge Panchayat has to possess the playfulness of an *adda*, where the passion we bring to discussing a film, a manifesto, or a novel is extended to the nuances of technology. The argumentative Indian must now extend their imagination to the travails of technology. A Knowledge Panchayat is a ritual of conversation that challenges the linearity of the narrative around technology. For example, discussions on technology create a narrative which mimics the innovation chain, chapterising itself into invention, innovation and diffusion. There is a typecasting here that we must mention: Left and Marxist groups focus on the diffusion stage, as they are concerned more with the distributive effects of technology.

Gandhian groups, however, are more prone to discussing issues of scale and the use of local materials. Groups focusing on an epistemic critique might open the black box of invention and examine science as a mode of thought. The discourse here fits into standard boxes. In a philosophical sense, innovation gets caught in the language of systems, while Knowledge Panchayats can add a life-world perspective. A conversation can act at right angles to the discourse and the discussants may also speak about coping, *jugaad*, improvisation, and 'make dos' as part of the repertoire of technology. Emic and etic views can mirror each other to widen perspectives. In this sense, innovation is disembedded from a corporate managerial technocratic discourse and read as part of the everydayness of technology or knowledge systems.

The Knowledge Panchayat is a thought experiment which, when institutionalised, has to convey to people the message that they can decide and debate about technologies using different cultural perspectives. In that sense it is a community, a commons of learning, and a philosophical debate which discusses not only the cost-benefit but also the language of suffering. Second, the notion of community includes a representation of ancestors and the unborn. It represents all stakeholders of a technology and gives voice and weightage to the vulnerable and to what Gandhi called 'the last man'. As a communication model, it allows for debate, an anarchy of views, and can even employ the storyteller and street theatre to create scenarios of understanding and argument. It has to create a sense of alternative wagers and side bets, instead of treating technology as a linear juggernaut. It has to provide for the specialised roles of translation and brokerage, inviting a wider articulation of the technological project. In that sense, it has to literally invent a language of empowerment where technology and science have created acts of fait accompli.

Democracy has to invent a theatre, a pedagogy which examines the hubris of expertise and the tragi-comedy of technology more visibly and pluralistically. It has to invent a language to analyse—even psychoanalyse—the creation myths of technology, explore publicly the unconscious of a technology using formal audits, folklore, proverbs, and riddles, add to the life-worlds of a technology, combining aesthetics and politics, and economics and ethics within local frames that embody both *swadesi* and *Swaraj*, a sense of the neighbourhood and a caring for the planet.

Knowledge and technology in that sense acquire a carnivalesque role, where the standard hierarchies of expertise are subverted. One is surprised as one moves across villages with the frequent use of the word climate. They often sense its symptoms, but add wryly that climate change becomes a public term when the government washes its hands off a disaster or a technology it cannot control.

VI

As we move towards a more concrete sense of the Knowledge Panchayat, we need to ask what STS as a discipline has to offer in terms of insight and advice. One essay in particular comes to mind. It is by a chemist, Isabelle Stengers, who was a close collaborator of Illya Prigogene and the author of a classic study of Alfred North Whitehead (see Stengers 2014, 2015). The second is by the Dutch scholar Wiebe Bijker and the third is by Bruno Latour, on the relation between knowledge and politics as it unravels in a democracy (Bijker 2017; Latour 2004).

Stengers, in her book *In Catastrophic Times* (2015), has a brilliant essay on the genetically modified organism (GMO) controversy. Stengers begins by locating a distance from science and its role in the GMO debate. She remarks that it is futile to engage in a head-on critique; one must begin by immersing oneself in the 'experience of perplexity'. The controversy is a crucial learning experience, marking a historical divide in her engagement with and understanding of science. She realises that the invasion of GMOs had reacted an epidemic level with their promise to produce biomass fuels, and adds that while the presence of GMOs was overwhelming, the argument in its favour from responsible quarters was less than convincing. What one witnessed was the enacting of a relation between science and innovation.

On 12 February 1997, there occurred a dramatic moment for French science. The prime minister repudiated the recommendations of a Commission for Bimolecular Engineering by refusing to launch three varieties of genetically modified coral. It was a stunning event, as if 'the French government had betrayed science, giving way to irrational fears' (European Commission 1997). It had stumbled over an affair usually restricted to experts.

But the politicians had correctly sensed which way the wind was blowing. They realised that the scientists themselves were seriously divided over the question. In fact, in the aftermath of the mad cow crisis, trust in science was low, and a militant movement against science had begun. What they did not anticipate was that a minor eruption would transform into a major crisis, a situation which, despite pressure from the WTO, lobbyists, the industry, and other European governments, refused to subside. Groups that had been distinct in their critique of GMOs now found a common constituency.

Stengers emphasises the need for intelligibility and the importance of an open mind. Yet, what appalled her was the arrogance of scientific colleagues who claimed that this was a scientific response to world hunger. They proclaimed its inevitability rather than its feasibility in the name of 'scientific progress', a rhetorical claim rather than an argument. Doubts which had surfaced during earlier nuclear controversies bubbled up again. She admitted her naiveté and her shock when she discovered that independent expertise was serving as a blatant mouthpiece for the industry. Requests for further information would be dismissed on grounds of secrecy. The world of science as public knowledge was behaving peculiarly.

She also discovered that scientists were erasing evidence by destroying the experimental fields where GMO crops were being studied. In addition, Monsanto was organising a private militia to suppress anyone who was farming seeds it owned.

The controversy moves towards a more complex gradient—from technically specialised questions to the very fate of agriculture caught in the claws of a rapacious fertiliser and pesticide industry. The distinction between public and private researcher breaks down as the knowledge economy becomes a source of pollution, contaminating public funding. What one witnesses is the appropriation of agriculture through the patent, which serves as the pretext, and the ambivalence of the State and science. What is distressing is the silence of researchers watching this trend. Given the decline in trust, the public 'seeks to renew practices of production that modernization had once condemned (the slow food movement, networks for traditional seeds, permaculture)' (Stengers 2015, 39).

The corporation and science masquerading as the custodians of truth strike back, imputing anxiety, irrationality, and superstition, while ignoring the more urgent task of reconciling the public and science. What one witnessed was not expert science but open citizenship as citizens took over the role of asking good questions, questions which left experts mute and stuttering. These citizens' conferences in their rudimentary form represent the Knowledge Panchayats in a more constructive relation between the public and science. The emphasis is no longer on the lone conscience keeper, but on institutional mechanisms to keep trust open.

Yet Stengers does not jump to problem-solving. She is more interested in unfolding the problematic. She does not demand a court of justice which a Knowledge Panchayat is not. She seeks not to find fault, but to deepen responsibility for the earth and all the species we are dragging into the catastrophe. She suggests a period of reflection before one moves to problem-solving. One has to frame the problem not like a kangaroo court, but as the remaking of a cosmological myth, where one moves towards a different allegory of responsibility. Knee-jerk solutions 'hypothecate' us to the problem as much as the culprits we wish to challenge. One has to grasp the fact that man has to understand nature in different ways. Responsibility is also acknowledging the limits of an answer.

VII

The Knowledge Panchayat was invented twice; once as a theoretical project and once as the recreation of a venerable institution, the adda. An adda is a playful celebration of a community in conversation. An adda is open-ended; it is not a focus group or an encounter between experts speaking the language of policy and cost-benefit analysis. The panchayat as adda takes on a fluid, flexible, even anarchic form. Let us create an ethnography around a particular issue. Imagine a debate around biotechnology. Science policy debates would follow the logic of a restricted code of expertise; here, one needs a generalised language of discussion. The plurality of membership becomes obvious. The participants range beyond standard interest groups to also include human rights activists, alternative agriculture experts, reporters, homemakers, consumers, and consumer associations. The panchayat is both a community and a chain of being, allowing anyone with an interest to claim a voice and a hearing. It has to be conducted in ordinary language, but it has to allow for translators and epistemic brokers.

The role of the latter as the mediator of knowledge is to explain differing theories and translate their consequences. A religious theory of suffering and a cost-benefit analysis can both be scrutinised for insight without one being seen as superior to the other. The logic of the debate as a philosophical script goes beyond standard concepts like efficiency and productivity towards questions of obsolescence and loss of diversity. A Knowledge Panchayat as a democratic device virtually creates a new glossary of pain and suffering, and of competence. The margins are not erased by a majoritarian juggernaut. The finality of expertise does not foreclose the debate. In fact, one creates a script for doubt, alternatives, side bets, uncertainty, and the different metaphors in which they are articulated. Everyday problems can be inserted into the formal discourse of expertise.

The Knowledge Panchayat as a community is also conscious of its limits. It realises that technology creates margins and forces them into obsolescence. It is therefore sensitive to alternative ways of solving their problem. Justice and diversity weigh more heavily than words like efficiency, speed, and productivity. Dialogue is essential and cannot be hurried.

In fact, as the Knowledge Panchayat develops, a tradition of storytelling and kathas of the earliest panchayats are foregrounded. Memory becomes critical and, as science becomes a part of folklore, new epics are born and retold.

As a result of these efforts, nature becomes represented as persons. Each ecosystem or occupational group acquires a systematic representation. The resolution is not through majoritarianism, but through plurality and panarchy. Panarchy is a modernist term which shows that different levels of scale require different kinds of understanding and resolution. As a result, the hierarchical models of decision-making are no longer the standard.

There is always a separate debate where a decision is evaluated across the four grids of epistemology, ethics, aesthetics, and politics. One needs a model of dialogue and not an analytical one to create a moral vision. The panchayat is that groundbreaking idea. It is philosophical as it exposes tacit knowledges; it is ethical as it demands a resolution in terms of indigenous categories; it is therapeutic, not only because it allows conversation but because it takes flaws and doubts seriously. It is democracy's antidote to technocracy and majoritarianism, a literacy which indicates that any form of life can turn ironic. The panchayat re-reads democracy to create life-giving forms and institutions. One wishes it had been employed during the recent farmers' protests in Delhi. Modern technocracy needs a hearing aid, and a Knowledge Panchayat is one way to bring dialogue, debate, and drama into current democratic life.

Movements like the MKSS realise that governments and bureaucracies love to subvert ground-level innovations and experiments in democracy, and such subversion has to be challenged through everyday experiments and debates. It is but logical that the epic Right to Information combined with the right to epistemology in a Knowledge Panchayat.

It shows that everydayness and plurality are still the domain of an inventive citizenship. The MKSS, in reinventing itself, reinvents the imagination of democracy.

SELECT REFERENCES

Ali, Misria. 2019. '"Solving" Nuclear Fear'. *Seminar* 719 (July).

Bijker, Weibe. 2017. 'Constructing Worlds: Reflections on Science, Technology, and Democracy (and a Plea for Bold Modesty)'. *Engaging Science, Technology, and Society* 3, 315–331.

European Commission. 1997. 'Commission Recommendations of 29 July'. European Union: Publications Office of the European Union. Available at https://op.europa.eu/en/publication-detail/-/publication/5b156bd7-d3d8-4c49-8756-9712787709b1 (accessed February 2025).

Jayaraman, Nityanand. 2001. 'Unilever's Mercury Fever'. *CorpWatch*, 4 October.

Latour. Bruno. 2004. *Politics of Nature: How to Bring The Sciences into Democracy*. Boston, MA: Harvard University Press.

McLuhan, Marshall. 1962. *The Gutenberg Galaxy: The Making of the Typographic Man*. Toronto: University of Toronto Press.

Stenger, Isabelle. 2014. *Thinking With Whitehead. A Free and Wild Creation of Concepts*. Boston, MA: Harvard University Press.

———. 2015. *In Catastrophic Times: Resisting the Coming Barbarism*, Andrew Goffey (trans.). Open Humanities Press.

The Fiscal Dimension of Justice

From Inequality, the Consequences of COVID, and Systemic Racism

Vivek Ramkumar

The unprecedented economic and health effects of the COVID-19 pandemic dominated media coverage since the beginning of 2020. But 2019 was also a turbulent year, as people in many countries took to the streets to protest against the public policies that imposed undue hardships on them. And even as the coronavirus pandemic swept across the globe, public protests continued and, in some countries, intensified. Many protests were explicitly focused on overthrowing institutionalised racism and its many consequences — including those that worsened the effects of the coronavirus pandemic on communities of colour.

The one thing that the coronavirus pandemic and the recent protest efforts made clear is how critical government budgets are to determining how society will respond to such issues. Decisions on the collection, allocation, and expenditure of public funds through government budgets impact everyone.

Yet for large sections of the population in many countries—especially those who are socially and economically vulnerable and suffer the consequences of various forms of injustice—budgets remain remote and complicated processes that are neither clearly explained nor open to their participation.

In this chapter, I discuss the fiscal dimensions of the calls for justice against the backdrop of the COVID-19 pandemic. I propose that the antidote to injustice is the expansion of democratic engagement in the public budgeting arena. I will discuss the many challenges that too often stand in the way of the implementation of meaningful and inclusive mechanisms of public participation in budgeting. I will also discuss how these barriers can be overcome to ensure that public participation policies and opportunities begin to keep pace with the theories of public participation. The chapter also draws on the discussions held at a workshop, 'Unpacking Participatory Democracy: From Theory to Practice', that I attended in November 2016 in Montreal, Canada.

Protests, a Pandemic, and More Protests

In 2019, tens of thousands of protesters mobilised in many countries around the world, including France, Iraq, Chile, Lebanon, Haiti, and Ecuador. In Chile, one million people took to the streets to protest a subway fare increase, while in Haiti, increases in fuel prices caused mass disaffection in the population. In Lebanon, the public that was already angered by a patronage political system was moved to protest by a tax levied on the use of WhatsApp, while in France protesters who came to be symbolised by yellow vests demonstrated against tax burdens on the working class. In Ecuador, economic austerity measures provoked widespread unrest, while in Iraq, anti-corruption demonstrators highlighted their displeasure with the government.

In isolation, the policy measures that provoked these public protests may appear fairly routine and exemplify the typical technical trade-offs that characterise the routine decisions made by governments every year. Yet, many of these protests sought to address underlying issues of economic hardship, inequality, and the corruption of political elites. People vented their frustrations at economic systems that appear rigged and benefit only a chosen few. Most of the protests in 2019 were manifestations of the helplessness many segments of widely varying national populations feel at not having a voice in decisions that impact their lives.

Throughout 2020, the COVID-19 pandemic devastated national economies and, in some countries, the devastation continued to worsen. In January 2020 (before COVID-19 became a household name), the International Monetary Fund (IMF) projected a global growth rate for 2020 of more than 3 per cent (IMF 2020a). By April, the IMF was projecting a decline of 3 per cent. And in June 2020, the IMF revised its projection again to forecast a decline of 5 per cent. In many countries, growth projections have fluctuated even more drastically. In its October 2020 World Economic Outlook, the IMF stated that the pandemic had caused a severe setback to the projected improvement in average living standards across all country groups, which would not only reverse the progress made since the 1990s in reducing global poverty, but would also increase inequality (IMF 2020b).

Many governments have responded to the multifaceted public health and economic consequences of the COVID-19 pandemic by committing large sums toward relief and recovery. But poorly designed emergency measures in turn created new opportunities for corruption in public spending and contracting, and may only exacerbate the underlying inequities in many societies.

Moreover, if recent trends in public spending hold, governments are likely to underperform on the promises that they have made—particularly as their revenue projections worsen. The International Budget Partnership (IBP) examined data collected by the World Bank from thirty-five countries and found that these governments *underspent* their overall budgets by 10 per cent on average over an eight to ten-year period (de Renzio, et al. 2019). To put this in perspective: The degree of underspending is equivalent to what would be needed for an entire health or education budget in many of the countries analysed. At a time when the public is more reliant than ever on essential government services, it will be catastrophic if governments reduce their spending levels, especially for essential services such as health, education, and social safety net services.

Broken promises on budgets will undoubtedly further erode public trust in government, especially if governments do not take their populations into confidence and explain their budgets, justify modifications to their budgets, and institute strong accountability measures on the implementation of budgets.

Further, and of particular relevance given the growing demands for reductions in and even elimination of police budgets, in every region of the world for which data were available, IBP found that police budgets are either significantly overspent or are underspent by much less than the level of underspending identified in overall national budgets (Ramkumar 2020). IBP's analysis suggests that police budgets in many countries tend to be protected from in-year reductions—even as other government functions and investments suffer from under-execution. For example, Uganda overspent its police budget by 16 per cent between 2010 and 2016, but failed to spend one out of every four budgeted dollars. Shockingly, Uganda underspent its immunisation budget by more than 75 per cent, even as the government declared vaccine shortages on five occasions. In Mexico, the budget for police services was overspent by $2.3 billion between 2009 and 2016.

The State of Open Budgets

Ultimately, the central mechanism to address and eliminate racism from public institutions and reduce inequality is fiscal justice, and fiscal justice requires the participation of impacted communities in budget decisions. People must be empowered with information on government budgets and they must have access to formal mechanisms through which to engage with governments during budget decision-making.

In fact, there is a growing body of evidence that shows that the best way to manage public funds efficiently and effectively is through budget systems that are transparent, open to public engagement and scrutiny, and that have robust oversight institutions and mechanisms. This framework has been codified into widely accepted international norms and standards on open budgeting.

IBP's Open Budget Survey (OBS) is one of the most authoritative sources of information on how countries perform on open budgets. The survey is typically published every two years. The design of the survey is based on the premise that efficient, effective, and accountable budget systems rest on the three pillars of budget transparency, public participation in the budget process, and oversight by formal government institutions. The absence of any one of these three pillars weakens the entire system. Results from the OBS 2019 (the latest survey was published by the IBP on 29 May 2024) revealed that very few countries are solid across all three pillars.

The Survey uses 140 indicators to calculate scores for countries, which range from a minimum of 0 to a maximum of 100. IBP considers scores of more than 60 to be adequate. The global average score on transparency is 45, while the combined average global score for the role of legislatures and audit agencies in providing budget oversight is 53. However, the average global score on public participation is just 14 out of 100. What this tells us is that while we have a long way to go to achieve all elements of accountability, the area in which most countries are weakest is the provision of mechanisms for public participation.

In some ways, these findings are easy to explain. While transparency and formal oversight have gained much legitimacy in both academic and policy circles as important components of democratic systems, the same cannot be said about public participation. Here, policy has not kept pace with theory. Norms on transparency and on the constitutional role played by formal oversight institutions such as legislatures are well-developed and are widely known and accepted by academia and practitioners. This is not the case with public participation. Over the past two decades, institutions like the IMF, the Organization for Economic Cooperation and Development (OECD), the Inter-Parliamentary Union (IPU), and the International Organization of Supreme Audit Institutions (INTOSAI) have created standards on budget transparency and oversight. However, it was only six years ago that the IMF revised its fiscal transparency code and introduced a standard recommending public participation in budgeting.

Challenges to Instituting Public Participation

Two of the best examples of public participation in budgeting are from Brazil and India.

In Brazil, a participatory budgeting model has been created at the municipal level to enable citizens to directly inform budget allocations. The model has now spread to many other cities around the world. Studies have shown that the participatory budgeting model is associated with improved socioeconomic outcomes for residents who live in jurisdictions that follow such systems. It has also been shown to contribute to improved tax collections.

In India, the social audit model pioneered by the Mazdoor Kisan Shakti Sangathan (MKSS) has enabled hundreds of thousands of citizens to provide evidence on whether they actually received entitlement monies meant for them. Testimonies provided by local communities that are the intended beneficiaries of public programmes during public hearings held as part of social audits have enabled millions of dollars of stolen funds to be recovered and returned to the rightful beneficiaries.

While the cases of public participation in Brazil and India are inspiring, they are among a handful of good practices that exist in the public budgeting arena. There are three basic challenges that are holding back the expansion in public participation.

The *first* challenge to advancing public participation from theory to practice is to identify practical mechanisms through which millions of citizens can realistically participate in complex public policy decisions in a timely manner — particularly given that such decisions are typically made by a small number of central authorities.

A *second* challenge to public participation is determining how mechanisms meant to enable public participation will interact with existing representative structures. Most Constitutions place the power of the purse with the representatives of the public. We know that, in practice, the executive is usually able to find many ways to undermine legislatures. Some have argued that public participation mechanisms may provide a backdoor route for the executive to further undermine formal oversight institutions. Others, especially in well-functioning democracies, question the need for public participation in budgeting, particularly if they believe that elected representatives in their countries respond effectively to constituents and address their concerns through their formal oversight powers.

A *third* challenge is ensuring that formal mechanisms for public participation do not result in the creation of tokenistic structures that do not empower the public, or that are captured by special interests to advance narrow agendas. Public hearings in legislatures, town hall meetings organised by executive agencies, or fraud hotlines set up by audit agencies are common mechanisms currently being used to foster public inputs on budget and public policy issues. But these mechanisms may lack accountability, that is, the public may not be told how their inputs are used to formulate the final decisions. This is why many civil society advocacy groups, including those that focus on topics of poverty alleviation, often invest significant resources in privately lobbying decision-makers rather than on using formal mechanisms for participation to make their cases.

These challenges to public participation could also be viewed within a broader frame of democratic challenges that countries are confronting, including the impact of colonisation. My fellow panellist at the Montreal workshop, Ellen Gabriel, suggested the need to review the colonisation of democratic theory and practice. She stated that indigenous forms of democracy based on deliberation and decision-making existed long before the Europeans arrived in North America, and were based on the active participation of both the clan and women. These practices have been supplanted by newer forms of democratic practices that have undermined genuine participation from the population.

Towards Solutions

Promoting public participation in the current environment is not an easy task. The rise of populist leaders with authoritarian tendencies around the world makes it much harder to advance inclusive systems for public engagement in government now than it was a decade or two ago. Today, in such countries as Brazil, Hungary, India, the Philippines, Russia, South Africa, Turkey, and even in the United States, democratic systems have enabled the rise of leaders whose policies and practices flout democratic norms.

However, some governments are experimenting with innovative ways to bridge the gap between the state and citizens (IBP 2020). In one example, the Mexican government established a 'social comptrollers' system in which social programmes that primarily benefit disadvantaged communities are directly monitored by committees composed of beneficiaries of the programmes. Both South Korea and Portugal recently launched participatory budgeting at the national government level. In Sierra Leone, the government is consulting with the public on its draft budget through policy hearings. And in New Zealand in 2019, the government widely consulted with the public to develop its first 'Wellbeing Budget', and provided feedback to the public on how their views were used in the final budget.

Proponents of popular participation can leverage the steps being taken by these countries to describe how public engagement can occur in practice and to inform demands for further innovations. Just as transparency got a big boost from new technologies that helped eliminate technical barriers and expand the availability of budget data, public participation needs similar innovations. Proponents for public participation can also create strong and clear narratives explaining the need for public participation and why public engagement within democratic frameworks needs to go beyond election day.

It is not essential that every citizen be involved in every government decision. What is important is that governments change the way they view how decisions are made and ensure that diverse voices are included at appropriate venues during the decision-making process. In this way, they can better ensure that decisions are made that reflect the priorities and meet the needs of citizens. It is critically important that people who believe in the benefits of participation think through these issues and develop the mechanisms that can make it possible and the narratives that will explain the mechanisms and build support for them.

If there is one silver lining in the COVID-19 crisis, it is that governments and international financial institutions have committed significant sums of monies to support response and recovery efforts. Concurrently, there has been a call for greater accountability in public spending. In fact, the IMF's approach, which is encapsulated in the phrase 'do whatever it takes but keep your receipts', provided governments with the flexibility that they needed to implement emergency fiscal measures during the crisis, while also emphasising the need for a judicious use of these funds and for accountability (Fouad, et al. 2020). The fears that unscrupulous officials and contractors might take advantage of emergency spending measures to usurp public funds makes transparency and public engagement in budgeting very topical.

Conclusion

In this chapter, I have described the essential fiscal dimension to addressing the coronavirus pandemic, whose devastating effects have been worsened in many communities by systemic racism. Ultimately, fiscal justice cannot be achieved without the participation of the impacted communities in budget decisions. Governments need to change the way they function so there is a better way for them to find out about the public's demands than through mass demonstrations, and for this to happen, the public needs to have access to good information about budgets, as well as an input into decision-making regarding them.

Opaque and unaccountable systems of budgeting can, and must, change. They must change not only because people are demanding it, but also because open budgets benefit everyone, and they offer a pathway to justice!

Select References

de Renzio, Paolo, Lakin Jason, and Chloe Cho. 2019. *Budget Credibility Across Countries: How Deviations are Affecting Spending on Social Priorities*. Washington, D.C.: International Budget Partnership. Available at https://www.internationalbudget.org/wp-content/uploads/Budget-Credibility-Across-Countries.pdf (accessed November 2024).

Fouad, Manal, Gerd Schwartz, and Claud Wendling. 2020. *Do Whatever it Takes but Keep the Receipts: The Public Financial Management Challenges*, IMF Public Finance Management blog, 22 April. Available at https://blog-pfm.imf.org/pfmblog/2020/04/-do-whatever-it-takes-but-keep-the-receiptsthe-public-financial-management-challenges-html (accessed November 2024).

International Budget Partnership. 2020. *Open Budget Survey 2019*. Washington, D.C.: Available at https://www.internationalbudget.org/sites/default/files/2020-04/2019_Report_EN.pdf (accessed November 2024).

International Monetary Fund. 2020a. *World Economic Outlook 2020, January 2020: Tentative Stabilization, Sluggish Recovery?* Washington, D.C.,: IMF. Available at https://www.imf.org/en/Publications/WEO/Issues/2020/01/20/weo-update-january2020 (accessed November 2024).

_____. 2020b. *World Economic Outlook 2020, October 2020: A Long and Difficult Ascent*. Washington, D.C.: IMF. Available at https://www.imf.org/en/Publications/WEO/Issues/2020/09/30/world-economic-outlook-october-2020 (accessed November 2024).

Ramkumar, Vivek. 2020. *Police Reforms Require Budget Reforms*. Washington, D.C.: International Budget Partnership, 23 June, Available at https://www.internationalbudget.org/2020/06/police-reforms/ (accessed November 2024).

9

Do Indians have a Right to Know their Foreign Donors?

Inayat Sabhikhi

Introduction

There have been several recent changes to laws that govern foreign funding to political parties and non-profits. When the Indian National Congress (INC) and the Bharatiya Janata Party (BJP) were found by the Delhi High Court to be violating the law by accepting donations from Vedanta, they used their legislative powers to retrospectively amend the law, and make their illegal actions legal. This happened through a series of obscure amendments to the Foreign Contributions Regulation Act (FCRA) law tacked onto the budget bill, that is, the Finance Bill of 2016 and 2018. In 2020, the FCRA law was directly amended to further regulate philanthropic contributions into the country. This chapter will lay out some of the details of these legal changes and their implications for participatory democracy. These are the growing role of unaccountable big money in elections and the use of institutional design to disadvantage opposition parties and evade public scrutiny.

Recent Changes to Political Party-Funding Architecture

The financial architecture of funding for political parties has always had loopholes that prevent transparency and accountability. The recent changes have widened these loopholes and opened up direct foreign contributions to political parties. With the opening up of funding by which foreign companies can contribute to parties, the diaspora that facilitates and tightens these links also becomes deeply relevant.

Under the rules as they existed until a few years ago, only individuals and domestic for-profit companies could contribute to political parties via cash, cheque, or demand drafts. Political parties were required to file an annual income statement, listing both sources of income and expenditures, with the Election Commission (EC) acting as a constitutional oversight body. Contributions below Rs 20,000 ($280) could be anonymous. Political parties traditionally exploited this loophole to avoid a disclosure of donors.

Over the past few years, there have been several changes to campaign finance. The most significant has been the replacement of cash donations with a new mechanism for political donations, the so-called 'electoral bonds'. Under this system, private parties can now make anonymous donations via a bond with the State Bank of India (a public-sector bank) in fixed denominations ranging from Rs 1,000 ($15) to Rs 1 crore ($1.5 million), during allotted windows. These donations remain anonymous not only to the general public, but also to the recipient political party and opposition parties.

The stated objective of these reforms is to use the transparency of the banking system to target the practice of money laundering in campaign finance, that is, using 'black money' earned through illegal activities for untraceable cash donations. In fact, the overall package of campaign finance reforms has decreased rather than increased the overall transparency. The total share of income from unknown sources through electoral bonds has been steadily increasing for all six major political parties. In the returns filed for 2017–2018, income from unknown sources was over half (51.38 per cent) of these parties' collective income (ADR 2019).

But the problem is much worse when one considers the other 'reforms' that accompanied the introduction of the electoral bond scheme. Recent amendments to the Foreign Contribution Regulation Act now allow foreign-owned companies to contribute to political parties, and an earlier cap on contributions from domestic companies has also been removed. Further, the requirement that corporations reveal political donations in their annual profit and loss statements has also been relaxed.

So now theoretically, donations to political parties can be not only 100 per cent anonymous, but also 100 per cent by foreign companies or loss-making companies. Taking all this together, it has enabled large-scale anonymous donations via shell companies in tax havens set up explicitly for this purpose.

The story of how this regression in transparency vis-à-vis electoral funding came about is equally important. It is through publicly accessible documents that the Association for Democratic Reforms (ADR) filed and won a case in the Delhi High Court, showing donations from the Vedanta group to the BJP and the INC—which was squarely illegal under Indian law at that time. This led to a series of shrewd and quick moves by both parties, which used their legislative powers to retrospectively amend the law to legalise their actions. There were strong objections put up against this by the Reserve Bank of India (RBI) and the EC, as the RTIs of communication between these institutions showed, which amounted to nought in the end (Sethi 2019).

Recent Changes to Non-Profit Architecture

Meanwhile, the architecture governing funds to the non-profit sector has also seen a package of reforms. In 2020, the FCRA, which governs foreign contributions to non-profits, was amended without consultation to bring in stricter provisions of regulation. These included reducing the percentage of funds that can be spent on administrative expenses (from 50 per cent to 20 per cent) and stopping subcontracting grants to smaller organisations (Bhatnagar 2020). Investment in human resources and subcontracting to smaller outfits have been key to doing effective grassroots work in the past.

Soon after the change in law, about 50 per cent of the total registered non-profits had their licences cancelled on regulatory grounds, such as not filing Income Tax returns (Press Trust of India 2021). At present, 22,274 out of 49,678 non-profits have active licences, as per the Ministry of Home Affairs.[1]

The other significant change was the setting up of the PM CARES fund to channel philanthropic dollars for COVID-19 relief. It was both exempt from FCRA regulations, that is, anyone from anywhere could contribute to it, and removed from the RTI, away from public scrutiny. As per estimates, this fund raised over 1.27 billion dollars (Bhuyan and Salve 2020). Guha (*The Hindu* 2020) called it an 'unhealthy precedent', that is 'basically encouraging sycophancy, chamchagiri and loyalty to the Prime Minister'. Non-profit leaders said that between the squeezing of foreign funds via the FCRA and the channelling of domestic funds to PM CARES, non-profits in India will be forced to close shop (Bhatnagar 2020).

The New Foreign Funding Architecture

Taken together, at present foreign funds can be donated to non-profits only via tedious and closely scrutinised FCRA, regulated by the Home Ministry. This scrutiny likely works to the advantage of organisations affiliated with the ruling party, which continue to function and grow (US Department of State 2017). Domestically, given the success of the fundraising for PM CARES, similar initiatives are likely to be launched to channel scarce domestic philanthropic funds into opaque and centrally controlled government funds.

These changes in the foreign funding architecture thus enable the following (see Table 9.1):

1. Theoretically, India's political parties can be 100 per cent funded by Amazon India, or any other subsidiary of a foreign company, domestic company, or a loss-making shell company set up by any foreign government.
2. The ruling government, via the State Bank of India, has a full account of *all* donations being made via electoral bonds, to itself and to opposition parties. None of the opposition parties have this information.
3. Philanthropic foreign money is scrutinised at the discretion of the Ministry of Home Affairs. Licences can be cancelled with little redress.
4. Philanthropic domestic money can be continuously diverted to funds like the PM CARES and others like it, which can be set up by executive order from time to time.
5. Legislative scrutiny has reduced, since opposition parties do not have access to donations to the ruling party or to other opposition parties. Public scrutiny has reduced as well, since companies are not required to disclose donations in the annual profit and loss statements.

TABLE 9.1: Summary of changes in foreign funding architecture

		Previous System	Recent Changes
1.	Anonymous contributions	Only below Rs 20,000 in cash	Any amount via electoral bonds
2.	Foreign companies	Not allowed	Allowed via Indian subsidiaries of any company meeting foreign direct investment (FDI) limits
3.	Domestic companies	Only profit-making companies	Removed, any domestic company
4.	Spending cap	Up to 7.5% of 3 years' average net profit	Removed, no spending cap via amendment to Companies Act 2013 via Finance Bill 2017
5.	Disclosure documents	Via annual profit and loss statement of company	Requirement removed via amendment to Representation of the People Act, 1951 via Finance Bill 2017
6.	Foreign philanthropy	Via FCRA	FCRA made stricter
7.	Domestic philanthropy	Via corporate philanthropy	Options to now channel directly to ruling party via funds like PM-CARES
8.	Legislative scrutiny	Limited	Reduced, since electoral bonds are only visible to the ruling government
9.	Public scrutiny	Limited	Reduced, since electoral bonds + FCRA are only visible to ruling government + No disclosure via profit and loss statements

CHANGE IN INCENTIVES

This creates a new set of incentives for foreign donors—both institutional and individual.

For the traditional international non-government organisations, say a Bill and Melinda Gates Foundation, it becomes harder to provide resources to India with the tightening of restrictions and cancellations based on technicalities. Like for any capital, this creates an incentive for foreign philanthropists to move resources to places where they have fewer barriers to entry and better returns (however defined) for their investment.

Conversely, the rules governing donations by foreign companies to political parties have been made much simpler. Not only is anonymity afforded and reporting requirements reduced, but the number of companies that qualify as 'foreign' has also been widely expanded to mean any company investing in India that meets the limits of foreign direct investment. These create incentives for increased donations to political parties by a wider range of companies. However, the incentives are not meant for all political parties, but give the ruling party an advantage for reasons listed earlier and below.

Parallely, this elevates the role of individual donors from the diaspora. Taking the United States for illustrative purposes, the general impression and average statistics of the Indian-American within America is one of high education and income levels, making them coveted donors to American political parties (Badrinathan, et al. 2020). The polling of Indian-American voters shows that their voting patterns are determined by kitchen table issues such as education and healthcare, and that US–India relations is not a major concern (ibid.). However, even as US–India relations are not a high priority while Indian-Americans vote in the United States, they are active in their communities and contribute to a series of non-profits affiliated to the ruling party in India, which are registered in the US and operate in India (Kumar and Hussain 2020).

This incentivises the ruling party to further appeal to the diaspora. This cultivation is likely to favour certain themes in discourse—such as nationalism, pride, and nostalgia (Jaffrelot and Therwath 2007). It is also likely to imply investments in marketing and media agencies that generate content that will appeal to a distant diaspora and distract from domestic problems (Bansal, et al. 2019).

Implications for Participatory Democracy

The implications of these changes in legal architecture and the incentives created do not bode well for participatory democracy. They affect two core aspects of participatory democracy: increased unaccountable big money in elections dilutes universal franchise, and the changes in institutional design disadvantage public scrutiny.

Diluting the Vote, Moving towards Plutocracy

With big money playing a greater role in elections and fundraising from the diaspora, the value of the vote gets diluted. If funds are being raised from foreign companies and the diaspora, neither of whom have voting rights but have significant interests in shaping the elections, the Indians who do vote for governments or their policy proposals are being shortchanged.

Inequality in wealth and income, along with election expenditures, have been on the rise. India's 2019 national elections were the most expensive elections ever held anywhere in the world, with an estimated expenditure of Rs 55,000 crore ($7.74 billion) (Bhattacharya 2019), much of which was financed through private donations. As per recent estimates, nearly all total donations to the BJP, and 93 per cent of the electoral bonds purchased, were in the highest two denominations, indicating high net donors (Dubbudu 2018).

The future of this path from countries like the USA, which have allowed big money in politics, is clear. When big donors play a large role in politics, it has a disproportionate effect on policymaking, and dilutes the mandate which the ruling government wins through votes (Lessig 2019). For example, a *New York Times* investigation of the 2016 US presidential election found that just 158 families, along with the companies they own or control, contributed $176 million in the first phase of the campaign, that is, over half the money raised (Confessore, et al. 2015).

Unlike the United States, which had incremental constitutional law expansions on the right to vote and the right to stand for public office, India has always had absolute universal franchise and expansive criteria to stand for political office. This will be undone if wealthy individuals and companies are given more room to influence political funding. The levers of reform then shift to caps on contributions, on expenditures, on time periods for campaigning—none of which have been found to be effective in curbing this institutionalised corruption (Lessig 2019).

Fewer Checks and Balances

There is a clear advantage to the ruling party when it comes to receiving funds, particularly from companies interested in doing and maintaining business. Investigative work by *Scroll.in* shows that the prime minister, as the star campaigner for the BJP, combines official work with BJP events, without much clarity on the share of costs between Indian taxpayers and the party, thus possibly using taxpayer resources to subsidise fundraising for the party (Lalwani and Subramanian 2019).

This has been borne out through information obtained so far on the sale and redemption of bonds, with the ruling party being by far the biggest beneficiary of donations via electoral bonds (amassing 94.5 per cent of the share of total donations through electoral bonds) (Vishnoi 2018).

An important caveat to this proposed anonymity is that the confidentiality of donor information is subject to an exception for when the information is 'demanded by a competent court or upon registration of a criminal case by any law enforcement agency'. This ambiguous framing grants sweeping powers and discretion to law enforcement agencies, which have a troubling history of being politicised by ruling parties (Sethi 2019). This too works in favour of the ruling party. It also compromises the institutional integrity of the State Bank of India (SBI).

While theoretically any opposition party can use this architecture to their advantage as well, the ruling party has a considerable advantage in the form of State power and resources, that is, control over law enforcement agencies and over the SBI, which channels all electoral bonds and donations to the FCRA. The ruling party can also create executive order funds like PM CARES, which are exempt from the FCRA, to directly obtain philanthropic US dollars.

This combination of electoral bonds which offer a permanent advantage to the ruling party, the lack of power of the opposition parties, and the reduced philanthropic resources for social development and civic capacity point to a reduction in the system of checks and balances.

Alternatives

An alternative worldview, rooted in the people's movement for the Right to Information and the Bhilwara Principles of Social Accountability, could offer a new way of thinking about the required accountability framework around political funding to retain and strengthen participatory democracy.

Theory and practice show us that transparency is a necessary, but not a sufficient, step for accountability. With funding for political parties, there has been a loss in transparency, as well as a cynical use of the legislative privilege by political parties to avoid institutional scrutiny from courts and the Central Information Commission, the legally constituted body under India's Right to Information law.

How can ordinary Indians ever challenge this? The Bhilwara Principles offer a constructive framing with which to arrive at what *should* be the case, given their origins, practical use, and growing institutionalised acceptance (Swamy, 2019). These principles were first framed by Dalit activists in the face of the severe atrocities they faced, and which were then adopted and developed further by activists and social movements. It has also been adopted by India's Supreme Audit Institution, the Comptroller and Auditor General (CAG), to develop a set of minimum standards for social audits (ibid.).

To really get a handle on how political funding should be reformed, the Right to Information and the Bhilwara Principles, rooted in people's movements, can offer a way to radically reimagine the relationships between political parties themselves, between voters and the ruling government, and between voters and opposition parties to uphold the value of one vote per person. The Bhilwara Principles are: *jankari* (information), *bhagidari* (participation), *karwahi* (redress), *suraksha* (protection), *sunwai* (hearing), and *jan manch* (collective platforms).

For illustrative purposes, consider the first principle, information on foreign donations. In political funding, two key transparency documents have been lost—disclosure by companies in their annual profit and loss statements, and disclosure of donations by electoral bonds. The primary tools of transparency that remain are the Income Tax filing on incomes and expenditure by political parties with the Election Commission, and Right to Information applications with the SBI, which is currently governing electoral bonds.

The Right to Information Act is clear about proactive disclosures on all matters that affect the public. The spirit of this law is unequivocal—that a voter should have information on political funding to determine allegiances, conflict of interest, the value of their vote, and determination of policy. Not only would it benefit voters, but it would also strengthen opposition parties, thus providing an essential checks and balance function. The limited information on the quantum of effects of changes to the political party funding architecture can only be ascertained through the RTI at present, that is, the aggregate statistics on bonds redeemed, and to which party.

In the interest of strengthening democratic practice, political parties, regular donors, and foreign and domestic companies can demonstrate moral leadership and continue to disclose their contributions, even though they are not legally bound to.

Conclusion

The question of whether Indians have a right to know their foreign donors is currently mired in double standards. The spectre of an all-invasive foreign hand is repeatedly used by political parties to discredit people's movements. On the other hand, legal and policy pathways have been created for our political parties to be completely funded by a foreign company—whether with *bona fide* interest in doing business or *malafide* intentions of interference. In an increasingly connected world, with growing ease of financial transfers, it is well worth reconsidering where and how national interests should be prioritised. Enabling political party funding is a clear case of putting the party over the country. The loser is the common person dealing with relentless election campaigns funded by vast amounts of unaccountable money, while the struggle for social and economic dignity remains distant.

Note

1. Last accessed in the year 2020.

Select References

Amnesty India. 2020. 'Amnesty International India Halts its Work on Upholding Human Rights in India due to Reprisal from Government of India'. Available at https://x.com/AIIndia/status/1310806154939766544?s=20 (accessed November 2024).

Association for Democratic Reform. 2014. 'Political Party Watch'. New Delhi: ADR. Available at https://www.adrindia.org/research-and-report/political-party-watch (accessed November 2024).

_____. 2019. 'Analysis of Sources of Funding of National Parties of India, FY 2017–18'. New Delhi: Association for Democratic Reform. Available at https://www.adrindia.org/research-and-report/political-party-watch (accessed November 2024).

Badrinathan, S., D. Kapur, and M. Vaishnav. 2020. 'How Will Indian Americans Vote? Results From the 2020 Indian American Attitudes Survey'. Carnegie Endowment for International Peace, 14 October. Available at https://carnegieendowment.org/research/2020/10/how-will-indian-americans-vote-results-from-the-2020-indian-american-attitudes-survey?lang=en (accessed November 2024).

Bansal, S., G. Sathe, R. Khaira, and A. Sethi. 2019. 'How Modi, Shah Turned a Women's NGO into a Secret Election Propaganda Machine'. *HuffPost*, 4 April. Available at https://www.huffpost.com/archive/in/entry/how-modi-shah-turned-a-women-s-rights-ngo-into-a-secret-election-propaganda-machine_in_5ca5962ce4b05acba4dc1819?ncid=other_twitter_cooo9wqtham (accessed November 2024).

Bhatia, G. 2019. 'The electoral bonds scheme is a threat to democracy'. *Hindustan Times*, 18 March. Available at https://www.hindustantimes.com/analysis/the-electoral-bonds-scheme-is-a-threat-to-democracy/story-PpSiDdUjIw5WNBUzDsSzxI.html (accessed November 2024).

Bhatnagar, G. V. 2020. 'Leading NGOs Believe FCRA Changes Will "Kill" Voluntary Sector'. *The Wire*, 22 September. Available at https://thewire.in/rights/fcra-amendment-ngo-sector-impact-grassroots-activism (accessed November 2024).

Bhattacharya, A. 2019. 'India's $7 Billion Election'. *Foreign Policy*, 23 April. Available at https://foreignpolicy.com/2019/04/23/indias-7-billion-election/ (accessed November 2024).

Bhuyan, A., and P. Salve. 2020. 'PM CARES Received At Least $1.27 Bn In Donations—Enough To Fund Over 21.5 Mn COVID-19 Tests'. *India Spend*, 20 May. Available at https://www.indiaspend.com/pm-cares-received-at-least-1-27-bn-in-donations-enough-to-fund-over-21-5-mn-covid-19-tests/ (accessed November 2024).

Confessore, N., S. Cohen, and K. Yourish. 2015. 'Buying Power'. *The New York Times*, 10 October. Available at https://www.nytimes.com/interactive/2015/10/11/us/politics/2016-presidential-election-super-pac-donors.html (accessed November 2024).

Dubbudu, R. 2018. 'It's official: 95% of the Electoral Bonds purchased in 2017–18 went to the BJP'. *Factly.in*, 30 November. Available at https://factly.in/its-official-95-of-the-electoral-bonds-purchased-in-2017-18-went-to-the-bjp/ (accessed November 2024).

The Hindu. 2020. 'Coronavirus outbreak: Ramachandra Guha slams creation of PM CARES Fund', 30 March. Available at https://www.thehindu.com/news/national/coronavirus-outbreak-ramachandra-guha-slams-creation-of-pm-cares-fund/article31211597.ece (accessed November 2024).

Jaffrelot, C., and I. Therwath. 2007. 'The Sangh Parivar and the Hindu Diaspora in the West: What Kind of "Long-Distance Nationalism"?' *International Political Sociology* 1 (3), 278–295.

Janta Parliament. 2019. 'Policy Proposals: Peoples Policy for Post COVID-19 Times'. Available at https://jantaparliament.wordpress.com/policy-proposals/ (accessed November 2024).

Kapur, D. 2019. 'The Indian prime minister and Trump addressed a Houston rally. Who was signaling what?' *Washington Post*, 29 September. Available at https://www.washingtonpost.com/politics/2019/09/29/prime-minister-modi-india-donald-trump-addressed-huge-houston-rally-who-was-signaling-what/ (accessed November 2024).

Kumar, R. 2019. 'The Network of Hindu Nationalists Behind Modi's "Diaspora Diplomacy" in the U.S.'. *The Intercept*, 25 September. Available at https://theintercept.com/2019/09/25/howdy-modi-trump-hindu-nationalism/ (accessed November 2024).

Kumar, R., and M. Hussain. 2020. 'How Sri Preston Kulkarni's Run for Congress Got Tangled Up in Indian Politics'. *The Intercept*, 29 October. Available at https://theintercept.com/2020/10/29/sri-kulkarni-congress-indian-politics/ (accessed November 2024).

Lalwani, V., and N. Subramanian. 2019. 'Modi keeps combining official travel with BJP events, but who is paying the bills?' *Scroll.in*, 12 February. Available at https://scroll.in/article/912885/modi-keeps-combining-official-travel-with-bjp-events-but-who-is-paying-the-bills (accessed November 2024).

Lessig, L. 2019. *They Don't Represent Us*. New York: Dey Street Books.

Mathew, B., and V. Prashad. 2000. 'The Protean Forms of Yankee Hindutva'. *Ethnic and Racial Studies* 23 (3), 516–534.

Meghwanshi, B. 2020. *I Could Not Be a Hindu*, N. Menon (trans.). New Delhi. Navayana.

Misra, S., and T. Patel. 2021. 'The Inequality Virus—India Supplement 2021'. Oxfam India, 22 January. Available at https://www.oxfamindia.org/knowledgehub/workingpaper/inequality-virus-india-supplement-2021#:~:text=The%20Coronavirus%20pandemic%20has%20been,Great%20Depression%20of%20the%201930s (accessed November 2024).

Osnos, E. 2014. 'Embrace the Irony'. *The New Yorker*, 6 October. Available at https://www.newyorker.com/magazine/2014/10/13/embrace-irony (accessed November 2024).

Prashad, V. 2002. 'Countering Yankee Hindutva'. *Frontline*, 20 December. Available at https://frontline.thehindu.com/the-nation/article30246989.ece# (accessed November 2024).

Press Trust of India. 2021. 'Govt cancelled FCRA licence of over 20,600 NGOs in 10 years'. *The Economic Times*, 9 February. Available at https://economictimes.indiatimes.com/news/politics-and-nation/govt-cancelled-fcra-licence-of-over-20600-ngos-in-10-years/articleshow/80772291.cms?utm_source=contentofinterest&utm_medium=text&utm_campaign=cppst (accessed November 2024).

Sabhikhi, I. 2020. 'India's New Electoral Bond Scheme Won't Reduce Electoral Corruption. It Will Make the Problem Worse'. Cambridge, MA: The Global Anticorruption Blog, Harvard Law School, 20 January. Available at https://globalanticorruptionblog.com/2020/01/20/indias-new-electoral-bond-scheme-wont-reduce-electoral-corruption-it-will-make-the-problem-worse/ (accessed November 2024).

Scroll.in. 2019. 'Explainer: What we now know about the BJP's secretive electoral bonds scheme after a week of exposes', 22 November. Available at https://scroll.in/article/944518/explainer-what-we-now-know-about-the-bjps-secretive-electoral-bonds-scheme-after-a-week-of-exposes (accessed November 2024).

Sethi, N. 2019. 'Electoral Bonds Are Traceable: Documents Nail Govt Lies On Anonymity'. *Huffpost*, 20 November. Available at https://www.huffpost.com/archive/in/entry/bjp-anonymous-donors-electoral-bonds-state-bank-of-india-narendra-modi-arun-jaitley_in_5dcf7239e4b01f982f022b85?utm_hp_ref=in-paisapolitics (accessed November 2024).

Srivas, A. 2018. 'Finance Bill Amends FCRA Again to Condone Illegal Donations to BJP, Congress from Foreign Companies'. *The Wire*, 1 February. Available at https://thewire.in/business/finance-bill-seeks-amend-fcra-condone-illegal-donations-bjp-congress-received-foreign-companies (accessed November 2024).

Swamy, R. 2019. 'Explorations in the Concept of Social Accountability'. New Delhi: Centre for Budget, Governance and Accountability. Available at https://www.cbgaindia.org/working-paper/4734/ (accessed November 2024).

———. 2020. *From Peoples Struggles to Public Policy: The Institutionalization of the Bhilwara Framework of Social Accountability in India*. Washington, D.C.: Accountability Research Center. Available at https://accountabilityresearch.org/publication/from-peoples-struggles-to-public-policy-the-institutionalization-of-the-bhilwara-framework-of-social-accountability-in-india/ (accessed November 2024).

US Department of State. 2017. *2017 Report on International Religious Freedom: India*. Available at https://www.state.gov/reports/2017-report-on-international-religious-freedom/india/ (accessed November 2024).

Vaishnav, M. 2019. 'Electoral Bonds: The Safeguards of Indian Democracy Are Crumbling'. *HuffPost India*, 25 November. Available at https://carnegieendowment.org/posts/2019/11/electoral-bonds-the-safeguards-of-indian-democracy-are-crumbling?lang=en (accessed November 2024).

Vaishnav, M., and J. Chokkar. 2019. 'Have Electoral Bonds Made a Bad System Worse?' *The Hindu*, 6 December. Available at https://carnegieendowment.org/posts/2019/12/have-electoral-bonds-made-a-bad-system-worse?lang=en (accessed November 2024).

Various. 2002. 'The Foreign Exchange of Hate: IDRF and the American Funding of Hindutva'. Mumbai: Sabrang Communications & Publishing Pvt. Ltd, and The South Asia Citizens Web, France.

Vishnoi, A. 2018. 'Electoral Bonds: Ruling BJP bags 95% of funds'. *The Economic Times*, 29 November. Available at https://economictimes.indiatimes.com/news/politics-and-nation/electoral-bonds-ruling-bjp-bags-95-of-funds/articleshow/66858037.cms (accessed November 2024).

The Wire. 2019. 'Centre's Access to Information on Electoral Bonds' Donors is Unfair: Opposition', 12 December. Available at https://thewire.in/politics/bjp-electoral-bonds-donor (accessed November 2024).

Speak for Us
Democracy, Digital Media, and the Politics of Voice

Sohini Sengupta

In modern democracies, citizens and leaders increasingly claim to speak in the voice of a people. This form of public discourse could suggest the stability or strength of political order or the increasing depth of democratisation. The proliferation of images, views, opinions, and information, especially through a user-mediated internet, adds to this sense of informed participation underpinned by a digital democracy. But can such abundance also indicate a new production of silence when diverse voices get streamlined into predetermined narratives? The nature and status of collective voice in the context of postcolonial democracies like India is the subject of this short commentary. More specifically, the chapter is concerned with the production, generation, and distribution of social information and its representation as people's voice on user-mediated internet and its effects on informed deliberations in democracies. This chapter argues that beyond citizen disillusionment with political representatives and formal institutions that the scholarship associated with post-democracy indicates, it is important to understand how user-mediated internet can be used as an instrument for disruption through the production, consumption, and dissemination of curated content that claims to stand for the popular voice. The inability of users to distinguish between concerns voiced by citizens who use social media and political actors who have a new tool for communication and for disrupting the signals of political rivals (Bradshaw and Howard 2018, 30) is at the heart of this illusion.[1]

Behavioural advertising, micro-targeting of communities, campaigns of persuasion, and a deluge of misinformation, surveillance, and manipulation are well-established aspects of the new age of information and communication. More than aware citizens taking their political representatives to task around public policy promises, political actors with resources use social media extensively and systematically to herd voters during election cycles through a deluge of popular narratives, rhetoric, and troll attacks that sweep through critical issues, from crime and gender, to environment, development, and poverty, and in recent years, the COVID-19 pandemic. It may be argued that the information generated through computer-mediated communication is a reflection of the popular voice and indicates a more direct form of democratic participation. For the proponents of direct democracy, citizens are becoming political communicators through making and disseminating online content around issues that can shape the public agenda (Kneuer 2016). But as the philosopher Douglas Walton (1989, 89) argues, the fallacy of popular argument creates two main errors of judgement: *first*, by making a weak argument appear compelling, and *second*, by diverting our attention from more important issues. Not only is popular truth a 'weak form of knowledge', but what appears as a deluge of popular voice on social media is also often professional actors managing the emotions and attention of constituents rather than fostering substantive debates on public policy (Harsin 2018).

Speaking not just to 'the people' but assuming the voice of the people is enabled by the use of viral marketing on social media platforms. What this chapter highlights are the accountability problems that emerge from the difficulties of attribution in the context of widespread 'viral' content on social media, generated and managed by human or non-human actors through the use of 'organic posts' or sticky content. Thus, on a particular day an Indian X handle with the profile of a young urban person with a common upper-caste surname can post on the health benefits of 'Washington Apples' and emote outrage on the conduct of a political party during state elections on multiple, separate threads. This dedicated tweeter could be a health conscious and politically engaged person or a professional influencer from a media-marketing firm. The distorted informational context that is created by thousands of posts that echo or repeat such content across multiple social media platforms serves to disrupt informed debate. Such modes of communication originate from the field of modern internet advertising, which is used not only to manage and shape consumer behaviour seamlessly, but to also aid, as Manuel Castells (2011) argues, 'subliminal campaigns of political promotion' that have a destabilising effect on democracies.

The world over, representative democracies are facing a crisis of legitimacy as growing inequalities fuel discontent among citizens, who express their dissatisfaction with the rule of experts, elites, and elected leaders (Castells 2018). The 'democratic paradox' is described as the rising expectations of citizens and the failing power of democratic institutions (Ulbricht 2020). In this context, populist governments everywhere are feeling the need to manage discontent (Landemore 2017, 53–54). An important characteristic of all populist regimes is their claim to speak in the name of *'the people'* and *'against various elites'*, and thus harness democratic energies for anti-democratic practices (Brubaker 2017, 358). The crisis of democracy predates the current surge in populist politics. This has been attributed to two factors: *first*, the competition between different groups of political elites and, *second*, the rising need for leaders to obtain direct access to the masses (Kohli 1991). The erosion of freedom, in terms of speech, religion, and association, beyond elections has invited scrutiny (Varshney 2015, p.919). A critical lacuna in Indian democracy is the compromised ability of excluded population groups to exercise their rights as citizens (Heller 2000). The concerns around voice acquire added significance in this context.

Effective democracy through the participation of all citizens requires an expansion of freedom, reduction of inequalities, and improvement in living conditions. On social media, popular voices that claim to protect a people tend to transact in spectacular narratives that appropriate events and episodes of social crisis for reasons and interests that depart from rational conversations around expanding justice and fairness in social policy. The management of perceptions around risks and threats, including directing attention to newer interpretations of existing uncertainties, not only create symbolic and economic value for the participants, such as users and platform owners, but also enable populists to claim that they were available to protect the people from such dangers (Brubaker 2017). Dangers in social media are framed as existential harm that may occur through the violations of bodily integrity, breakdown of community boundaries or permeability of national borders, through the maleficent actions of intruders such as pollutants, germs, weeds, foreigners, immigrants, minorities, and the poor. Bauman (2006) describes this condition as fear derived from a state of endemic uncertainty, nourished by the feeling that people were vulnerable to unknown threats, whose causes could not be determined and whose consequences will not be addressed.

Thus, while many have viewed the digitalisation of society as a solution to the crisis of legitimation, the growing use of social media as an instrument of persuasion and manipulation amplifies multiple disaffections only to produce the illusion of participation while sowing distrust in the mediating role of institutions. Voices representing the 'people' on social media follow a well-known pattern, defined in opposition to, *first*, the economic, political, and cultural elite, and *second*, to the dangerous 'others' who are presented as 'undeserving of benefits and unworthy of respect' (ibid., 363). Divisive threat-protection narratives tend to dominate social media discussions of public policy like a targeted marketing operation.

The transformed space of communication, so influential for the political process, does not bode well for democracies precisely because it is built on 'the commercialization of our demons' (Castells 2018). The accountability for this state of affairs rests not only on governments but also on the business model of monopolistic firms that extract and control large amounts of data (Srnicek 2017) through which citizens, and not governing regimes, are rendered transparent in the cyberspace. There is some reason to believe that distorted informational contexts affect democracies. A Pew research report published in 2020 highlights how the use of digital technologies to manipulate facts can affect the way people think about the effectiveness of democratic processes and institutions (Anderson and Rainie 2020). In a recent report of the Oxford Internet Institute, empirical evidence is cited to show how manipulated public opinion on social media is threatening democracies worldwide (Bradshaw, et al. 2020). The next section discusses the pattern and logic of speech on a platform such as X, which tends to be used more frequently for political and policy discussions. The concluding section will explore whether such speech acts expand or diminish dimensions of democracy such as civil and political rights, the rule of law, procedural decision-making, and effective governance.

Surplus, Excess, and Misleading: The Disinformation Crisis

Don't miss what's happening. People on twitter are the first to know.

(Twitter tagline)

Part of the reason why political messages on Twitter (now known as X) evoke strong emotions is because they are meant to do so. This has very little to do with the intention, allegiance, or affiliation of the user, who composes and posts 140-character messages that aim to bring disrepute to or celebrate the achievements of individuals and dramatic events. As X researchers have found, simple negative posts about opponents tend to become more popular and go viral on social media rather than issues facing a country, and are used extensively in political campaigns. Such posts are meant to create a 'high arousal negative outcome' like anger among the voting public towards a targeted other (Pancer and Poole 2016). The proliferation of such sentiments on X, though, is not necessarily reflective of the spontaneous voice of the people or of vibrant public debate, but is often an outcome of a well-designed strategy meant to stir and churn public emotions for political or commercial gains.

There are nearly 700 million internet users in India and the numbers are set to rise. Till 2019, individuals using the internet constituted only 34 per cent of the population.[2] Secure internet servers per million people were 479.9 in 2020 (compared to, say, 7,494.4 in Malaysia).[3] Facebook was used by 324 million people, Instagram by 80.59 million, and WhatsApp had 400–500 million active users. More than 70 per cent of users of all three platforms were men in the age group of 18–34 years.[4] Social media users in India are predominantly young and male. X is the place where policymakers, politicians, Heads of State, and journalists can air their views. As of April 2024, the 25.45 million X users in India made up the third highest in the world, after USA and Japan.⁵ Conversations on X can be humorous, playful, or abusive and are used to influence opinions on a continuous basis in order to shift the emphasis on issues of public concern. A brief look at the 24-hour X trend suggests that followers are expected to trend particular issues and reach the top of the rankings based on the maximum number of posts. Through hashtags, which are user-generated descriptions, interested people are gathered around issues of critical public concern and encouraged to engage with and respond to news in high speed and in real time. Often, the critical event is produced through such practices by constructing widespread adversarial responses.

Let me take as example a viral hashtag on Twitter (as it was then called) that had emerged in response to an innocuous post from an Indian film personality, whose message spoke about using a religious occasion to help the needy instead of circulating digital greetings (*Hindustan Times* 2021). This trending hashtag was supported by 83,000 posts by the end of the day. I manually analysed seventy-seven posts by a single user profile on this hashtag, posted within a 12-hour period on 11 March 2021, which incited followers to trend the hastag.⁶ Of these posts, 60 per cent were targeted hate. This was directed not only towards the actor, but also included direct abuse aimed at leaders of opposition parties in election-bound states, while 23.4 per cent was targeted praise of leaders of the ruling political party, and 17 per cent was amplification of the majority religion. All used language that was abusive towards minority religions and gender. Gender-based hate played out in two ways in a quarter of the targeted abuse posts: veiled threats were made towards women political leaders by calling them liars and demons from popular epics.⁷ The information circulated promoted and encouraged trolling and misogynistic attacks, and advocated violence towards defined others. Images from the trending hashtag played out in multiple online platforms, Facebook, YouTube, and online news sites. A divisive message was created by using the supposed voices of an aggrieved and outraged public that piggybacked on the celebrity actor's innocuous statement.

In another instance, a series of posts targeting Muslim refugees was circulated on X as part of an election campaign in eastern India.[8] The posts that were part of an X campaign for the upcoming elections carried a sepia-toned image of a group of men and women walking with bundles on their heads and holding the hands of their children, and came with the following copy in Hindi: 'Rohingyas and unlawful Bangladeshis were encouraged to settle here during ... rule. This put the honour of the sisters and daughters of ... at risk! Governments who support such people will never be chosen by the people of....'[9]

This particular image and message was posted thirty-four times over three hours from different accounts and handles.[10] At 5:00 pm on 24 March, the hastag on X that carried this message was trending at number three. This is an example not only of a sustained targeting of a vulnerable community, but also of using the momentum to turn public discourse away from an assessment of the performance of the incumbent government towards fictitious issues, patriarchal sloganeering, and reputational damage, and thus corralling the public and opposition parties within a framework of inconsequential exchanges (Goel 2019). Rohingyas emerged as a pan-Asian scapegoat for political parties seeking to retain control over, and the allegiance of, disaffected populations facing economic uncertainties and widespread unemployment following the pandemic lockdowns.[11] The message also subtly sowed distrust in mobile population groups, especially migrant workers, whose plight was extensively reported in the print media following the first COVID-19 lockdown in India, and which resulted in debates about State responsibility and human suffering. Trend dependence of user-mediated internet like Facebook and X can promote xenophobic outbursts against vulnerable population groups (Latif 2020).

If the foundation of a reasonable dialogue is the free choice of participants to decide whether to support or oppose a conclusion, the threat of force closes the 'possibilities of free dialogue' (Walton 1989, 94).

X is used to influence opinions on a continuous basis to shift emphasis on issues of public concern. Take the case of the periodic controversies over forest fires in India in recent years. X posts on the issue of forest fires routinely circulate images of fire-devastated landscapes and dead wildlife from the internet to highlight the incapacity of state governments and bureaucracies (see Suresh 2019), and to amplify the need for strong Central or armed forces interventions. Technology is celebrated and rural or tribal populations and unnamed elites are criticised to strengthen themes of national pride.[12] See, for instance, two posts from a popular thread on forest fires in an eastern Indian forest reserve on 4 March 2021, which had little to say about the forest or its wildlife. The first undermined the state government's public distribution programme,[13] advising the government to 'spend less on one rupee rice and spend more on a properly equipped fire fighting force to tackle forest fires'. Some posts appealed to national pride by describing how elite environmentalists' worry about bush fires in Australia and the Amazon did not extend to India's biosphere. Others criticised the traditional media for paying greater attention to 'Muslim' film personalities rather than to issues of national significance. What can be observed here are the subliminal ways of influencing public discourse about the legitimacy of welfare programmes and state administrations. There is also a constant refrain about making choices or choosing sides. In this choice environment, citizens are being 'nudged' into comparing incommensurable entities, such as a public distribution system empowered by the National Food Security Act, 2013 versus 'fire fighting' equipment powered by military helicopters. What is achieved is the fragmentation and corralling of public discourse against vertical elites (bureaucracy and the traditional news media) and undeserving others (impoverished rural or tribal people) (see Brubaker 2017). The celebrity whose innocuous comment evoked outrage, the image of a scapegoated mobile group, and the burning forests provide dramatic opportunities to reinforce dominant political messages.

Social media platforms are more than intermediaries that create a bridge between narrators and listeners as they also make content accessible in particular forms (Gillespie 2018). Should platforms bear transparency obligations and legal liability for factually incorrect and misleading content? In an altercation between the Indian government and X over posts related to the farmers' protests, the platform emerged at first as the 'champion of free speech'. The point that was highlighted by observers was not just whose authority counts, but also whether X could afford to alienate a large market like India in order to uphold 'freedom of expression'. Eventually, X blocked many accounts as ordered by the Government of India, since these were viewed as 'incitements' (Siddiqui and Ghoshal 2021). According to international law, incitement is a 'dangerous form of speech' (United Nations 2019). What is significant for the present discussion is whether questions of accountability can be limited to the much too narrow confines of content moderation or compliance with national law or government directives. A great deal of popular content on X borders on 'hate speech',[14] and tends to be divisive and factually misleading. There is a case for using universal human rights standards to broaden both platform and state policies and the involvement of third party observers, especially actors from civil society and the press, public authorities and courts.

Conclusion: Attribution and Accountability

The discussion about democratic crisis and social media communication looked at X posts in order to illustrate how voice is created and supported by political interests through fallacious arguments. Attributing cyber incidents, however, is a complex phenomenon. Insurance policy writers discussing the risk from incidents of cyber attack have remarked on the problems of attribution, which varies contextually and is dependent on how the facts about such incidents are obtained and received by decision-makers (Bateman 2020). While a concern about securing against the risks to assets and resources (from bank accounts to the personal details of citizens, as well as national assets) posed by cyber crime drives the insurance market, protection of the freedom of speech and human rights collides with emerging policies aimed at regulating expression on social media platforms. Any national or international legal framework would have to address multiple contradictions. A key question remains: Should the regulation of social media content be protective or punitive? Whether this can improve the attribution of cyber incidents will be an important concern for accountability. How can citizen and civil society oversight be created in what would otherwise become an opaque bureaucratic process of command and control through regulation? Who should judge or evaluate what content should be removed from online platforms? Who has the right to censor 'free speech' in the public interest: elected governments, constitutional authorities, or technology companies? Without democratic deliberation on these issues, the power to set and enforce the boundaries of public speech will remain captive to the priorities of private companies (Gillespie 2018).

Recent concerns with *infodemic*—an excess of information, whose accuracy is suspect and which requires constant, diligent verification—point to the difficulties that people face in locating trustworthy information. The involvement of users and the co-production of information disrupt conventional ways of attributing responsibility and seeking accountability. As some experts have observed, the use of information technology may undermine democracy without leaving any evidence or trace. Transparency activism must include calls for the declaration of resources used in political campaigns through social and digital media, and the role of professional political actors. Citizens should know the sources of content that vilify individuals and social groups, damage reputations, and lead to polarisation. Social media platforms must comply with fairness laws that apply to the traditional news media and publishers, and content moderators must adhere to the principles of human rights. Freedom of speech, the foundation of civil and political rights, requires continuous protection under national and international legal statutes, but the inability to discern the qualitative difference between speech and commercial campaigns, enabled by the blurring boundaries between human and automated speech, anonymity, and the unprecedented speed of exchange on social media platforms, may undermine the same rights. Ethical and informed use of social media platforms by political actors and protection for vulnerable groups, rather than punitive regulation, should underpin digital voices to realise the dream of net-utopians who believed that 'smart mobs' (Rheingold 2002) would work to strengthen and not compromise the expansion of democratic freedoms. Claiming to be the voice of the people is a dangerous game for democracy, and one in which there are very few participants.

Notes

1. The recent report by Oxford Internet Institute, titled 'Industrialized Disinformation: 2020 Global Inventory of Organized Social Media Manipulation', finds that eighty-one countries used social media to spread computational propaganda and disinformation about politics that are disrupting democracies, elections, and human rights.

2. See https://data.worldbank.org/indicator/IT.NET.USER.ZS?locations=IN (accessed November 2024).

3. See http://wdi.worldbank.org/table/5.12 (accessed November 2024).

4. See https://napoleoncat.com/stats/facebook-users-in-india/2020/01 (accessed November 2024).

5. See https://www.statista.com/statistics/242606/number-of-active-twitter-users-in-selected-countries/ (accessed November 2024).

6. The exact content of the posts will not be discussed because of the risk of inadvertent amplification of negative and malicious speech.

7. Trending at No. 3, #WhoTheHellAreUSonuSood, with 83,000 posts at 9:00 pm, 11 March 2021. At 10:00 pm, this hashtag was no longer trending. But the material was available in the timeline of the user quoted here on 12 March as well.

8. The consistent online scapegoating of the Rohingya community has been well-documented by the national and international media. See Dahiya (2020).

9. See https://twitter.com/hashtag/AssamWantsBJPAgain?src=hashtag_click, https://twitter.com/Tagorenaveen0 (accessed November 2024).

10. For the widely documented role played by Facebook in escalating the Rohingya crisis in Myanmar in 2017, see Safi (2018).

11. See, for instance, the situation in Malaysia (Cheong 2020).

12. See the on-loop circulation of the image of military helicopters dousing forest fires in Manipur (Choudhury and Tiwari 2021).

13. See https://twitter.com/KumarManash002 (accessed November 2024).

14. See https://www.un.org/en/genocideprevention/documents/advising-and-mobilizing/Action_plan_on_hate_speech_EN.pdf (accessed February 2025).

Select References

Anderson, J., and L. Rainie. 2020. 'Concerns about Democracy in the Digital Age'. Pew Research Center, 23 February. Available at https://www.pewresearch.org/internet/2020/02/21/concerns-about-democracy-in-the-digital-age/ (accessed November 2024).

Bateman, J. 2020. 'War, Terrorism and Catastrophe in Cyber Insurance: Understanding and Reforming Exclusions'. Carnegie Endowment for International Peace, 5 October. Available at October, 5. https://carnegieendowment.org/2020/10/05/war-terrorism-and-catastrophe-in-cyber-insurance-understanding-and-reforming-exclusions-pub-82819 (accessed November 2024).

Bauman, Z. 2006. *Liquid Fear*. UK: Polity Press.

Bradshaw, S., H. Bailey, and P. N. Howard. 2021. 'Industrialized Disinformation: 2020 Global Inventory of Organised Social Media Manipulation'. Working Paper 2021, 1. Oxford, UK: Project on Computational Propaganda.

Bradshaw, S., and P. Howard. 2018. 'The Global Organization of Social Media Disinformation Campaigns'. *Journal of International Affairs* 71 (1.5), 23–32.

Brubaker, R. 2017. 'Why Populism?' *Theory and Society* 46 (5), 357–385.

Castells, M. 2011. 'Democracy in the Age of the Internet'. *Transfer: Journal of Contemporary Culture* 6, 96–103.

———. 2018. *Rupture: The Crisis of Liberal Democracy*. Cambridge: Polity Press.

Cheong, H. T. 2020. 'In Malaysia, why has solidarity turned to hostility for Rohingya refugees?' *Globe*, 11 December. Available at https://southeastasiaglobe.com/rohingya-xenophobia-malaysia/ (accessed November 2020).

Choudhury, R., with V. Tiwari. 2021. 'On Camera, Air Force Chopper Lifts Water to Fight Wildfire in Manipur'. *NDTV*, 3 January. Available at https://www.ndtv.com/india-news/on-camera-indian-air-force-chopper-lifts-water-to-fight-wildfire-in-manipur-2347193 (accessed November 2024).

Dahiya, H. 2020. 'Why Rohingya Refugees Are an Easy Target for the Fake News Factory'. *The Quint*, 20 June. Available at https://www.thequint.com/news/webqoof/rohingya-crisis-how-misinfomation-rests-at-the-heart-of-the-issue (accessed November 2024).

Gillespie, T. 2018. 'How Social Networks set the Limits of What we can say Online'. *Wired*, 26 June. Available at https://www.wired.com/story/how-social-networks-set-the-limits-of-what-we-can-say-online/ (accessed November 2024).

Goel, V. 2019. 'When Rohingya Refugees Fled to India, Hate on Facebook Followed'. *The New York Times*, 14 June. Available at https://www.nytimes.com/2019/06/14/technology/facebook-hate-speech-rohingya-india.html (accessed November 2024).

Harsin, J. 2018. 'Post Truth and Critical Communication Studies'. In 'Communication', *Oxford Research Encyclopaedia*, 20 December. Available at https://oxfordre.com/communication/display/10.1093/acrefore/9780190228613.001.0001/acrefore-9780190228613-e-757 (accessed November 2024).

Heller, P. 2000. 'Degrees of Democracy: Some Comparative Lessons from India'. *World Politics* 52 (4), 484–519.

Hindustan Times. 2021. 'Sonu Sood says people should celebrate Maha Shivratri by helping someone rather than "forwarding Lord Shiva's photos"', 11 March. Available at https://www.hindustantimes.com/entertainment/bollywood/sonu-sood-s-says-people-should-celebrate-maha-shivratri-by-helping-someone-rather-than-forwarding-lord-shiva-s-photos-101615439543876.html (accessed November 2024).

Kneuer, M. 2016. 'E-democracy: A New Challenge for Measuring Democracy'. *International Political Science Review / Revue Internationale De Science Politique* 37 (5), 666–678.

Kohli, A. 1991. *Democracy and Discontent: India's Growing Crisis of Governability*. Cambridge: Cambridge University Press.

Landemore, H. 2017. 'Deliberative Democracy as Open, Not (Just) Representative Democracy'. *Daedalus* 146 (3), 51–63.

Latif, R. 2020. 'Malaysia can't take anymore Rohingya refugees, PM says'. *Reuters*, 26 June. Available at https://www.reuters.com/article/us-myanmar-rohingya-malaysia-idUSKBN23X19Y (accessed November 2024).

Pancer, E., and Poole, M. 2016. 'The popularity and virality of political social media: Hashtags, mentions, and links predict likes and retweets of 2016 U.S. presidential nominees' tweets'. *Social Influence* 11 (4), 259–270.

Rheingold, H. 2002. 'Transforming Cultures and Communities in the Age of Instant Access', in *Smart Mobs: The Next Social Revolution*. New York: Basic Books.

Safi, Michael. 2018. 'Revealed: Facebook hate speech exploded in Myanmar during Rohingya crisis'. *The Guardian*, 3 April.

Available at https://www.theguardian.com/world/2018/apr/03/revealed-facebook-hate-speech-exploded-in-myanmar-during-rohingya-crisis (accessed November 2024).

Siddiqui, Z., and D. Ghoshal. 2021. 'Twitter blocks dozens of accounts on India's demands amid farm protests: Sources'. *Reuters*, 1 February. Available at https://www.reuters.com/article/us-india-farms-protests-twitter-idUSKBN2A12J9 (accessed November 2024).

Suresh, H. 2019. 'Fact Check: Images of Burnt Animals supposedly from Bandipur Fire are Fake'. *The News Minute*, 25 February. Available at https://www.thenewsminute.com/article/fact-check-images-burnt-animals-supposedly-bandipur-fire-are-fake-97314 (accessed November 2024).

Srnicek, Nick. 2017. 'The challenges of platform capitalism: Understanding the logic of a new business model'. *Juncture* 23, 254–257.

Ulbricht, L. 2020. 'Scraping the Demos: Digitalization, Web Scraping and the Democratic Project'. *Democratization* 27 (3), 426–442.

United Nations. 2019. *Strategy and Plan of Action on Hate Speech*. New York: United Nations. Available at https://www.un.org/en/genocideprevention/documents/UN%20Strategy%20and%20Plan%20of%20Action%20on%20Hate%20Speech%2018%20June%20SYNOPSIS.pdf (accessed November 2024).

Varshney, A. 2015. 'Asian Democracy through an Indian Prism'. *The Journal of Asian Studies* 74 (4), 917–926.

Walton, D. 1980. 'Why is the 'ad Populum' a Fallacy?' *Philosophy and Rhetoric* 13 (4), 264–278.

———. 1989. *Informal Logic: A Handbook for Critical Argument*. Cambridge: Cambridge University Press.

Safeguarding Democracy from Organised Information Manipulations
Paid News, Fake News, and Hate Speech in India

Vipul Mudgal

Paid news, hate speech, and fake news as organised disinformation are old political devices with overlapping features. They have acquired a new salience in our lives today as all three have bounced back in new and more virulent forms, mostly on, but not confined to, digital media platforms. In this chapter, the terms are understood in their broad perspectives, that is, 'paid news' is news which can be favourably written and presented in popular news outlets for commercial considerations in cash or kind; 'fake news' is organised and deliberate disinformation, motivated half-truths, or political hoaxes; and 'hate speech' is xenophobic, racist, or intolerant utterances, or identity-based slurs and prejudices, created and disseminated to achieve political outcomes such as winning elections.

In India, all three have been around for decades. Political parties and candidates have always used paid or unpaid forms of lies, leaks, rumours, or distorted information to discredit rivals, particularly during elections. There is nothing new in politicians, corporate lobbyists, and vested interests using the power of money to influence media coverage. The same can be said of the presence of hate speech in inventive forms, in the name of free speech. But the range, or speed, of the lie machines available today is simply breathtaking. Technology can cloud the public sphere really fast. It is not necessary to be factually correct to be heard or liked. We seem to be drowning in a constant demand for and supply of deceit. There is also evidence to show that manipulated information undermines democracy by polarising societies and denying ordinary voters the right to make informed choices. It also restricts the powers of the Parliament, judiciary, and other democratic institutions to bring to account those spreading false and motivated information for political gains.

The agenda-setting functions of the media and its role in steering public opinion is well-known. But what has changed the consumption and distribution of information forever is the emergence of computational propaganda and its proliferation on social media. It has also led to manipulated information becoming a real threat to democracy and social harmony. Samantha Bradshaw and Phil Howard (2019), who monitored the manipulation of social media by governments and political parties, have termed this the 'global disinformation disorder'. They collated evidence of organised social media manipulations in seventy countries in 2019, up from forty-eight countries in 2018 and twenty-eight countries in 2017 (ibid., 5). This marks an increase of 150 per cent in three years. In India, the new disorder has polarised the public along sectarian lines and weakened democratic institutions. A case in point is the country's once-powerful Election Commission (EC), whose statutory power to enforce candidates' campaign expenditure ceiling and clamp down on hate speech has been directly affected by the opacity of global digital platforms.

Bradshaw and Howard (2019) have also found that as a tool of 'information control', the computational propaganda is being used around the world to suppress fundamental human rights and 'drown out' political dissent. This phenomenon has contributed to the rise of populism and autocracies in almost all parts of the world. Having come to power by winning elections, these autocrats have used a combination of propaganda and subversion of democratic institutions to stifle free expression. Cas Mudde and Cristobal Kaltwasser (2017, 4) associate populism with the emergence of a strong and charismatic figure who claims to have a direct connection with the masses. What matters is not the evidence or truth, but the leader's ability to overwhelm people with fabricated information at will. People are simply 'numb and disoriented, struggling to discern what is real in a sea of slant, fake and fact', as Sabrina Tavernise and Aldan Gardiner (2019) argue in a *New York Times* article on the coverage of US President Trump's impeachment hearing.

In India, scholars and practitioners of democracy have of late acknowledged the role of social media and digital platforms in the spread of paid news, fake news, and hate speech, particularly during the elections. The extent of its impact, however, is still unfolding. In real practice on the ground, the new information disorder polarises opinions, queers the pitch for free and fair elections, and vitiates the atmosphere for free speech. In all three, there is the presence of illegality, manipulation, and subversion of democratic systems. All three exist independently, but they converge on digital media, where the boundaries between them are blurred and where they are mostly transacted in slush money or surrogate forms of payment, often in unaccounted-for cash. Some of this will be elaborated upon in the following sections but first, let us examine the main aspects of the three features of manipulated information being discussed here.

Paid News: The Best Coverage Money Can Buy

The essence of India's widespread practice of selling editorial space for hyped-up and compromised news stories is not always captured in routine content analyses of text and footage. Paid news is difficult to detect, partly because the practice is 'underground' and the compromised news stories are camouflaged as routine coverage without any disclosure to the readers. In normal practice, media houses are not answerable to anyone for allocating space to competing parties, candidates, or issues. Their omissions and commissions are accepted as matters of editorial discretion. India's top English and Hindi dailies devote only around 2 per cent of their total coverage to the issues of rural India, and even less to matters of hunger, poverty, and suicides (Mudgal 2011). In any case, every single social, political, or business event cannot be covered on a given day. So an unsuspecting reader assumes that what is presented in the news columns is professionally curated by skilled journalists.

Journalists' professional prerogative allows media companies to camouflage sponsored stories as routine news coverage without the need for disclosures. However, paid news is not to be confused with the paid-up 'advertorials' that most media outlets carry, and where the content may have been written by the clients themselves or by the PR agencies hired by them. These go with tags such as 'focus' or 'spotlight' or 'media-net' or 'marketing/impact feature', etc. While an undiscerning reader cannot make out the difference, an advertorial is still a legal way to get around sponsored content. A former Chief Election Commissioner of India, N. Gopalaswami, believes that such a practice must be termed as paid news, especially when the newspapers carried 'advt' in small letters at the end of a sponsored news items (see Press Council of India n.d.).

Another brazen form of paid news, called 'private treaties', was started in India by one of its richest and most profitable media firms, the Bennett, Coleman and Company Ltd or BCCL, more commonly known as the Times Group. A privately held company, BCCL also has many allied companies which form India's largest media conglomerate, dwarfing rivals by earning several times more profits (*The Hoot* 2017). The owners of the BCCL were the pioneers in offering sponsored features that were questionable, but legal. But under the 'private treaties', companies were offered positive publicity for prices negotiated in shares or stock options. Such companies were assured a profusion of positive news in the BCCL group's outlets after the deal was struck through private treaties, and it was understood that negative features on them might also be minimised. This allowed fledgling entities going for a fresh stock market listing to create a positive buzz about themselves, at great cost to shareholder democracy and denying a level playing field to other, similar companies. The biggest losers are the readers, who do their due diligence through their news outlets before investing their life's savings in a stock.

The Times model, replicated by other media companies, also applies to candidates and parties during elections. Today, it is common knowledge that media organisations maintain secret rate cards for selling positive publicity, paid for in cash or kind. Candidates and parties are approached by advertising agents, and sometimes even journalists from mainstream news outlets, with 'solutions' and PR deals. Superior packages can be bought to deny their rivals their (normally) rightful coverage. For a higher consideration, their rivals can also be singularly criticised, over and above this denial of coverage! *Cobrapost*, an investigative news portal, carried out a sting operation in 2018 which showed media owners and top managers, among them Indian media's Who's Who, candidly agreeing to promote the right-wing Hindu agenda for a price. About two dozen media bigwigs readily agreed to carry out 'malicious media campaigns' which could lead to 'communal polarization for electoral gains, and to defame political rivals' in the run-up to the 2019 national elections (*Cobrapost* 2018). The sting tapes show the Times Group agreeing to carry out the 'Hindutva' agenda for Rs 500 crore (about $6.8 million) (ibid.).

Dragging a media organisation to court is an unrealistic option for victims such as the rival parties preparing for elections or private companies gearing up for stock listings. This is because their rivals' informal deals with media companies are difficult to prove. Besides, legal battles consume an enormous amount of time, energy, and resources. Victims opting for the legal option may also invite greater hostility and vilification campaigns. However, they can avert a news blackout and unpleasantness in the midst of a crucial battle if they strike their own deals and play by the rules of the game. In any case, buying peace is not an unviable option for most, considering that a staggering 88 per cent of winning candidates in the 2019 parliamentary elections were millionaires (with a net worth in crores or over 10 million INR; see ADR [2019]), roughly around 100 times India's per capita income for that year. This applies to all political parties; over 30 per cent of winners had a net worth above INR 5 crore (or 50 million) (ibid., 16).

The big picture shows that paid news takes only a fraction of the money spent on direct 'vote-buying' or on public meetings with movie stars and hired crowds. It is an open secret in India that candidates for the Lok Sabha and Assembly elections spend much more money than is legally permitted. Many powerful candidates have publicly stated that the statutory expenditure limit is ridiculously low and unrealistic. It came as a shock to no one when BJP leader Gopinath Munde admitted to having spent Rs 8 crore on his 2009 parliamentary election, which was more than thirty times the permissible expenditure limit of Rs 25 lakh at the time (*The Times of India* 2013). Munde received notices from the Election Commission and the Income Tax Department, but managed to save himself by asserting that his was merely a figurative expression! Wealthy candidates are present in almost all political parties. The clandestine nature of the paid news deals blends perfectly in such a murky scheme of affairs. However, payments in kind, rather than cash, are murkier and even more difficult to prove. It is common for political parties to reward media owners by nominating them to Parliament as members of the Rajya Sabha or the Upper House. Some are routinely rewarded with lucrative mining licenses and government contracts.

Paid news was first reported nationally in *The Hindu* by journalist P. Sainath in the 2009 parliamentary elections, even though the practice was more than a decade old by then. Known for his groundbreaking coverage of farmers' suicides and stories on rural poverty in India, the 2007 Ramon Magsaysay Award winner Sainath blew the whistle on the practice of paid news being indulged in by the local Marathi-language publications, media owners, and politicians. It was only after his exposés that many leading intellectuals and civil society organisations started to raise the issue in public forums. Sainath took on the most powerful politician of the day in Maharashtra, the state Chief Minister Ashok Chavan of the Congress party, and openly dared him to sue him or to prove him wrong. He cited identical laudatory stories in multiple publications with different bylines, terming them 'fun reading':

> Sometimes, you find a page of mysteriously fixed item sizes, say 125–150 words plus a double-column photo. The 'fixed size' items are curious. News seldom unfolds in such rigid terms. (Advertisements do) Elsewhere, you can see multiple fonts and drop case styles in the same page of a single newspaper. This was so because everything—layouts, fonts, and printouts came from the candidate seeking a slot…. (Sainath 2009)

Much of India's thriving national and regional media ignored the issue, with the exception of a handful of editors and columnists like Ajit Bhattacharjee, Kuldip Nayyar,

B. G. Verghese, and Prabhash Joshi. Many journalist unions, and later the Editors' Guild of India, also raised the issue after the exposé. Among the politicians who spoke out clearly against paid news was the then Vice-President of India, Mohammad Hamid Ansari. Addressing the seventeenth biennial session of the National Union of Journalists (NUJ), Ansari said: '... paid news and the declining role of the editors and their editorial freedom was posing a major threat to the media' (*The Indian Express* 2013).

Paid news first got the publicity it deserved later in 2009 when a report commissioned by the Press Council of India (PCI) and written by K. Sreenivas Reddy and Paranjoy Guha Thakurta was not allowed to be made public[1] by the Council, which was dominated by media barons. In theory, PCI members are nominated by different agencies, but the media barons manage to make up an overwhelming majority over others (Mudgal 2015). This report was blocked for many years, but finally a Right to Information (RTI) adjudication led to its full disclosure on the PCI website (ibid.). It connected the dots between paid news and democracy in India:

> The phenomenon of 'paid news' goes beyond the corruption of individual journalists and media companies. It has become pervasive, structured and highly organized and in the process, is undermining democracy in India. Large sections of society, including political personalities, those working in the media and others, have already expressed their unhappiness and concern about the pernicious influence of such malpractices. (ibid.)

Former Chief Election Commissioner of India, T. K. Krishnamurthy, an avowed opponent of illegal campaign finance, believes that legal cases must be pursued against a few and exemplary punishment meted out, even if one is unable to catch the big fish (Mudgal 2015).

India's Ministry of Information and Broadcasting later acknowledged the practice in its submission to the

Parliamentary Standing Committee on paid news in 2013, calling it '… a treaty between two private parties with mutual consent', which could be a clandestine financial transaction difficult to establish (Parliament of India 2013). However, 'private treaties' started by the Times Group and later followed by most other media groups did not receive as much regulatory attention, despite the fact that it was equally illegal and undemocratic. India's stock market regulator, the Securities and Exchange Board of India (SEBI), also wrote to the PCI with suggestions of mandatory disclosure norms and enforcement of guidelines for the media to safeguard the interests of the investors (Press Council of India n.d., 5). The practice of private treaties still continues under different monikers, even on digital platforms. As a result, paid news and its many avatars continue to undermine elections and democratic institutions in India.

FAKE NEWS AND ORGANISED DISINFORMATION

This term applies to content that masquerades as news, and is deliberately designed and disseminated to deceive readers for political, commercial, or other partisan purposes. The content normally exists either as complete falsehood or in permutations and combinations of fiction, half-truths, or alternative facts. Fake news is often, but not always, unlawful. It is found more abundantly on social media and is targeted at unsuspecting audiences who often feel compelled to forward it further.

As a term, 'fake news' may not be sufficient to capture the entire phenomenon of information deception. It also comes in different packages of disinformation, misinformation, and fiction. A 2018 UNESCO report, titled 'Journalism, Fake News and Disinformation', defines the overlapping phenomena as:

> ... disinformation is generally used to refer to deliberate (often orchestrated) attempts to confuse or manipulate people through delivering dishonest information to them. This is often combined with parallel and intersecting communications strategies and a suite of other tactics like hacking or compromising of persons. Misinformation is generally used to refer to misleading information created or disseminated without manipulative or malicious intent. Both are problems for society, but disinformation is particularly dangerous because it is frequently organised, well resourced, and reinforced by automated technology. (Ireton and Posetti 2018)

Fake news or organised disinformation is not confined to any one country, age group, or education level, although it is well-accepted that older people are more likely to believe or share fake news stories. Another important global and multilateral publication that puts fake news in perspective is the European Union's Independent and High-Level Group's report of 2018. Titled 'A Multidimensional Approach to Disinformation', the report on fake news and online disinformation says:

> We define it as false, inaccurate, or misleading information designed, presented and promoted to intentionally cause public harm or for profit. The risk of harm includes threats to democratic political processes and values, which can specifically target a variety of sectors, such as health, science, education, finance and more. It is driven by the production and promotion of disinformation for economic gains or for political or ideological goals, but can be exacerbated by how different audiences and communities receive, engage, and amplify disinformation. (European Union 2018)

Social Dilemma, a Netflix documentary, dramatises the evil effects of the mind manipulation perpetrated by algorithm-based artificial intelligence. It presents an elaborate exposé by former employees of social media companies who left their jobs for ethical reasons (Netflix 2020). It shows how these companies—which includes Google, Facebook, and Twitter (now 'X')—sell their 'users' as 'products' to advertisers and how their business model of virality and addiction allows fringe groups of racists, conspiracy theorists, and lynch mobs to disseminate fake news with impunity. The documentary discusses the financial gains of data mining and surveillance capitalism for the digital media giants, at enormous cost to social harmony and democracy around the world.

One feature of fake news is that it is often more believable than real news. Cognitive neurologist Julian Matthews explains that fake news works by distorting our memories through misattributions, frequent repetitions, and selective exposure, leading to a 'collective misremembering' of facts that are further reinforced by our own bias (Matthews 2019). A group of investigators at the Massachusetts Institute of Technology (MIT), who studied the spread of news on Twitter (now 'X') between 2006 and 2017, which comprised 126,000 cascades of news stories, found that

> Falsehood diffused significantly farther, faster, deeper, and more broadly than the truth in all categories. The effects were most pronounced for false political news than for news about terrorism, natural disasters, science, urban legends, or financial information. Controlling for many factors, false news was 70% more likely to be retweeted than the truth. (Vosoughi, et al. 2018)

No wonder, then, that the production, distribution, and marketing of false news makes for serious business, which P. N. Howard (2020) describes as part of a big 'lie machine', whose efficiency is improving by the day, much to the delight of the dictators and rabble-rousers.

Politicians are aware of the power of lies, perhaps instinctively, without these elaborate studies. There are dozens of successful populist leaders, like Recep Tayyip Erdogan in Turkey, Donald Trump in the US, and Jair Bolsonaro in Brazil, to name just a few, who trample on political dissent or accuse the media of lying, particularly when the news does not suit them. Wardle, et al. (2018) emphasise that fake news has become 'an emotional, weaponised term used to undermine and discredit journalism', which has its own political implications. 'In India, the government's relationship with the press has gone well beyond condemnation, with Modi opting to amend accreditation guidelines in order to weed out "fake news," exacerbating self-censorship,' says a report in *The Atlantic* (Serhan 2020). The ruling Bharatiya Janata Party (BJP), which had the first-mover advantage on social media prior to India's 2014 elections, also commands an impressive force of social media savvy volunteers. A report in the *Hindustan Times* stated that in 2019, the BJP leadership worked on creating three WhatsApp groups for each of India's just under one million polling booths, targeting over 700 million people (Uttam 2018). 'There is an army of volunteers whose job is to sit and forward messages,' said an article in *Time* magazine, quoting a Fellow at the Reuters Institute at Oxford University, which tracks some of these activities (Perrigo 2019).

The use of fake news cuts across political ideologies. Today, every political party is 'reasonably well-invested in the fray' on virtually all social media platforms, including Twitter (now 'X') (Pal and Panda 2019). As such, India figures high on the list of countries where the use of online fake news is rampant. A Microsoft report titled 'Digital Civility Index on Safer Internet Day' found that in 2019, almost two out of three Indians (more than 64 per cent) encountered fake news online, which was the highest among the twenty-two countries studied. India's digital ad-spend is also quite high and rising. In the 2019 Indian elections, the total ad-spend on digital advertising alone was expected to be in the range of around $2 billion, roughly a jump of around 150 per cent from the 2014 elections, with Facebook taking the lion's share (Chaturvedi and Laghate 2019). By law, all candidates and parties are mandated to disclose their spending on media management, including on social media, and on digital advertisements, but most get away because the law is hardly enforced.

Politicians have always used rumours and smear campaigns in elections, but fake news holds a special attraction because it reaches millions of people within seconds. And that is precisely why it needs the whole society's attention. We need to be more worried today because this is by far the most effective device to manipulate minds, in order to spread hatred, polarise people, and engineer riots and conflicts. Its sinister effect was made clear after the exposure of Cambridge Analytica, which hijacked and harvested the personal data of millions of Facebook users for political advertising and electoral manipulations as far back as 2013. The exposure involved the leak of more than 100,000 documents relating to work in sixty-eight countries, which was used to manipulate voters on an industrial scale (Cadwalladr 2020). Today, armies of hyperactive techies, overnight bloggers, and Twitter (now 'X')/Instagram influencers follow this example by micro-targeting individuals with tailor-made disinformation. The use of troll factories (or troll farms), particularly by the right-wing parties, in the national elections in India in 2014 and in Brazil in 2018 is well-documented, even though the laws and regulatory agencies still have a lot of catching up to do. *The Great Hack*, a 2019 Netflix documentary on Cambridge Analytica, exposes its hijack of the 'Brexit' campaign in the UK and the 2016 US elections, among many other elections worldwide, particularly in the Global South.

A 2019 Oxford University study examines cyber troop activity in seventy countries, including India, where it tracked political parties which used multiple teams ranging in size from fifty to around 300 to target voters with manipulated media (Bradshaw and Howard 2017). The study is part of Oxford University and its Internet Institute's Computational Propaganda Research Project. What makes these operations complex is the fact that these cyber troops (or troll farms/

factories) work with 'private industry, civil society organisations, Internet subcultures, youth groups, hackers' collectives, fringe movements, social media influencers and volunteers who ideologically support their cause' (ibid.). In another seminal study, part of the same Oxford project, Samantha Bradshaw and Phil Howard (2017) compared cyber troops across twenty-eight countries, along with their communication strategies. They found that all authoritarian regimes have social media campaigns to target their own audiences, for which they use anything from their military units to private strategic communication firms.

In India, the shadowy inner working of the BJP's cyber troops, as part of its IT operations, has been largely a secret affair, except for chance exposures when a disillusioned state IT head or a volunteer quit in apparent disgust. Sadhvi Khosla, a young entrepreneur who operated out of the party's Delhi office and whose story has been recounted by journalist Swati Chaturvedi (2019), gave an account of around 200 people working in the party's IT cell in 2014, mainly trolling opposition leaders and critical journalists on the party's 'hit-list'. Once 'blessed to be followed by the PM', Khosla said that including many other locations, the operation had nearly 2,000 people on the rolls' (ibid., Chapter 2, 'The BJP Connection'). After the book was published, the author herself was trolled extensively and issued threats of rape and reprisals. We are given a picture of thousands of paid and unpaid volunteers acting in unison, literally at the command of the party's social media management teams. Independent voices with a good number of followers are the most sought after (as potentially paid trolls) by both the BJP and the Congress (Kohli 2013). It is common for the typical nationalist troll to target journalists with abuse and rape threats, and attack anyone questioning or opposing party leaders. Bradshaw and Howard (2017) have offered a discussion of the activities of India's cyber troops indulging in both positive (pro-government, nationalistic comments) and negative (harassment, trolling) interactions with users.

Shivam Shankar Singh, a former associate of Prashant Kishore, India's best-known poll consultant and strategist and founder of the cash-rich political consultancy group I-PAC, gives a lucid account of his first-hand experience of being part of the BJP's well-oiled election machinery and social media operations in Manipur and Tripura. He was later also part of the Congress party's campaign in Punjab. Singh explains that every party tries to create fake news to their advantage and reach as many voters as possible, although his book shows that the BJP has a clear edge over their rivals and that its success with WhatsApp groups is steeped in anti-minority rhetoric (Singh 2019, 83–84). It seems that given a chance, politicians in the Congress, India's own Grand Old Party (GOP), would love to replicate BJP's success story. Singh illustrates how senior leaders of the Congress used the services of political image builders and spin doctors to mount an impressive social media campaign to win state elections in 2017. What separates the BJP from rivals is its ability to use hate speech to polarise people in order to reap electoral advantages. BJP's social media head, Arvind Gupta, insists that its operations are run by volunteers: 'We are a set of passionate volunteers. Because they (the Congress) are late in the game, they are paying people money. It is a fight between money and passion' (ibid.).

Hate Speech: Combining Propaganda with Prejudice

Indian elections are turning into do or die battles. Political parties and candidates spend ridiculously more than their capacity and risk losing everything if they lose an election. Cambridge Analytica experiments have shown that the strategy of winning elections is a capital-intensive mix of art, science, and management. Technology makes it possible to micro-target audiences really fast with customised packages of incitement and divisive politics. Hence, for maximum effect, hate speech is often combined with fake news on digital media platforms. The biggest irony is that polarising tactics work almost always, despite the electorate knowing the real motives of the actors involved.

Compared to paid news and fake news discussed above, the issues involving hate speech are more multifaceted and intractable. Hate speech is yoked to free speech; this becomes a problem when attempting to control the former. Preventing hate speech may therefore translate into restricting freedom of expression and curtailing minority rights, which is akin to a cure that is worse than the disease. Conventional censorship is not only ineffective, but it is also counter-productive because a ban may harm more genuine people than troublemakers. And that is why seasoned politicians often get away with using sophisticated signs and symbols that convey the most unreasonable of messages. They can stir old prejudices with a clever use of dog whistles to allege discrimination. Hate speech, therefore, does the near impossible—make the powerful sections, like upper-caste Hindus in India or the whites in the US—believe that they are being pushed around, and that the disadvantaged are being appeased at their expense.

Language employing coded and double meanings has been defined as a central feature of hate speech by the Dangerous Speech Project (DSP), which tracks (dangerous) hate speech around the world. 'The speaker is therefore capable of communicating two messages, one understood by those with knowledge of the coded language and one understood by everyone else' (DSP n.d.). The other features are allegations of threats and harassment faced by women/girls of the group; dehumanisation of the enemy; allegations of mortal threats; and suggestions that the target group might damage the purity, integrity, or cleanliness of the audience group (ibid.). The DSP description can be applied almost entirely to India's right-wing trolls, who label minorities as impure, dehumanise them as butchers and terrorists, and accuse them of targeting Hindu women through '*love jihad*' a term popularised by trolls and signifying a war being waged on Hindu women. The terms 'hate speech' and 'dangerous speech' might overlap but, according to the DSP team, dangerous speech may more easily incite or condone violence against another group.

In a 2019 TED talk, Carole Cadwalladr, a British writer and investigative journalist who exposed the Facebook-Cambridge Analytica scandal, explained how technology-enabled subversion of democracy combines with fear and hate. In her talk, titled 'Facebook's Role in Brexit—and the Threat to Democracy', she stated that technology platforms are sowing hate and fear all across the world for profit, and that technology is disrupting well-established electoral laws. Sharing parts of the painstaking investigation and insider revelations brought out in her research, she said:

> … this company which worked for both Trump and Brexit had to profile people politically in order to understand their individual fears, to better target them with Facebook ads. And it did this by illicitly harvesting the profiles of 87 million people from Facebook. (Cadwalladr 2019)

Social media platforms have provided enabling environments to (*i*) create fear and hatred on an industrial scale; and (*ii*) seriously disrupt free and fair elections. In Myanmar, where Facebook played a central role in inciting sectarian hatred and communal violence, leading to the murder of thousands of innocent people and the displacement of over 700,000 to neighbouring Bangladesh alone, the company agreed that it had failed to prevent its platform from being used to incite 'offline violence'. A report commissioned by Facebook after the UN accused it of being 'slow and ineffective' stated that the platform had created an 'enabling environment' for the proliferation of human rights abuse (BBC 2018). The report further stated that Facebook would have to get it right before the 2020 elections, and that there was 'more to do' on this front (ibid.). However, the company did not exactly swing into action even after making this admission.

In India, the role of Facebook in the spread of both fake news and hate speech during elections is now common knowledge. The scandal was exposed by *The Wall Street Journal* in a series of articles in and after August 2020. One article mentioned a letter written by Facebook's employees to its top management, demanding more transparency and a review of how the company handled hate speech and toxic content by prominent politicians (Purnell and Horwitz 2020). The company had earlier acknowledged that its then Social Policy head in India, Ankhi Das, had 'raised concerns about political fallout from banning Hindu nationalist figures over hate speech and incitement to violence against Muslims'. The letter, written by the company's Muslim employees, said: 'Many of us also believe our organizational structure combining content policy and government affairs under the same umbrella is fundamentally flawed' (ibid.). The *WSJ* article quotes an employee as saying: 'People's lives are at risk in India and we are acting like the public comments from our leadership were harmless.' Obviously, the global digital giant was flouting its own pledge to remain neutral during elections around the world for financial gains.

Journalists in India have often accused Facebook of selectively censoring political content 'by temporarily suspending accounts, labelling news as "spam", and not permitting news organisations to promote their articles' (Karan 2018). This is more likely to happen with news organisations that are either independent or not perceived as pro-ruling party, and appears to be a technology-enabled sleight of hand. The *WSJ* further exposed Facebook's partisan public policy by sharing some posts by its India head of Public Policy and her operations:

In one of the messages, Ankhi Das, head of public policy in the country, posted the day before Narendra Modi swept to victory in India's 2014 national elections: 'We lit a fire to his social media campaign and the rest is of course history.'

'It's taken thirty years of grassroots work to rid India of state socialism finally,' Ms. Das wrote in a separate post on the defeat of the Indian National Congress party, praising Mr. Modi as the 'strongman' who had broken the former ruling party's hold. Ms. Das called Facebook's top global elections official, Katie Harbath, her 'longest fellow traveler' in the company's work with his campaign. In a photo, Ms. Das stood, smiling, between Mr. Modi and Ms. Harbath.' (Horwitz and Purnell 2020)

Facebook's questionable role in the Indian elections is a classic case of convergence of demand and supply of disinformation, facilitated keenly by the social media platform. As argued by Samuel Woolley and Katie Joseff (2020), behind the flood of fake news and malicious propaganda is a 'demand for disinformation which is tied to the psychology of information consumption and opinion formation'. The inventory of the authoritarian lie machines is growing in India, along the lines as argued by Howard (2020), in partnership with political surveillance initiatives. The supply side of fear and disgust is best illustrated by the BJP supporters' favourite forum, the NaMo App, which follows a Twitter (now 'X')-like ecosystem and has been downloaded over 10 million times, mostly by cadres and supporters, and ardently promoted by some BJP-ruled state governments which pre-installed the App on smartphones distributed for free (and also preloaded by the private telecom company Reliance Jio on its low-cost phones) (Bansal 2019). 'This use of state apparatus to promote the app makes the NaMo App different than privately owned social media companies like Facebook and Twitter' (ibid.). This also makes it easy for supporters of the party to supply disinformation at will to the millions of beneficiaries of free phones. Such a demand and supply of disinformation may be unethical, but it is not entirely illegal.

Controlling hate speech is therefore not just a matter of legislature or administration. It also depends on the level of ethics in politics, the integrity of the electoral process, and the state of harmony (and polarisation) in a society. It also has a lot to do with the power of the opposition and the legal remedies available to common people. A White Paper on the subject prepared by the International Foundation for Electoral Systems (IFES 2018) states that 'Electoral integrity will be contingent upon a system that effectively integrates morals, ethics, and laws'. The Justice Srikrishna Commission, which was appointed in India in 2017 to propose data protection guidelines, has suggested that the data fiduciaries (or collectors) of political parties must stay within the ambit of the law and should come under parliamentary oversight (Drishti n.d.).[2]

Conclusion

The idea of examining paid news, fake news/disinformation, and hate speech provides us with a unique opportunity to study the news manipulation industry in the framework of safeguarding elections and democracy. Quite often, a blanket ban is proposed as an easy solution for large-scale information deception, but historically, bans and censorships have created more problems than solutions. The need, therefore, is to constantly measure the ability of democracy's checks and balances against the challenges posed by technology, with the participation of all stakeholders. So far, Germany is the first among very few countries to enact a strict Networks Enforcement Act (NetzDG) against the spread of fake news (or hate speech), which requires social networks to maintain a procedure for tackling complaints about illegal content. The law imposes heavy penalties on national or global digital platforms if they are found to be carrying 'unlawful content', and if such content is not removed within twenty-four hours of being reported. Hence, the emphasis is on the fast removal of content reported as objectionable. The problem with a system like the NetzGS is that it sidesteps public authorities and the judiciary and puts the sword of virtual censorship in the hands of the same digital platforms that are accused of facilitating disinformation or hate speech for profit.

In India, such arbitrary methods have proved to have limited efficacy at best, and are counter-productive at worst. The troll factories of the fake news industry have quickly learnt to report the handles or posts of their opponents and of the fact checkers who expose them. (Facebook prides itself on using eight fact-checking partners in India, but it has been charged that most of these have barely covered BJP-led misinformation [Chaudhuri 2020].) A damning internal memo written by a fired Facebook data scientist, Sophie Zhang, is full of 'concrete examples' in which presidents and prime ministers and national political parties in many countries have been found to be operating fake accounts or coordinated campaigns to influence elections by abusing 'our platforms on vast scales' (Silverman, et al. 2020). This converts cyberspace into an ideological turf of war. Many studies have suggested increased media literacy and prompt fact-checking as long-term solutions to information manipulation. These definitely have a long-term impact on the manipulated ecosystem of information, but they tend to work better for those who admit that there is a problem called 'fake news'. They have a very limited impact on the silent majority, which uncritically consumes fake news emerging from their intimate news sources, such as friends and family. Fact-checking can also be ideologically gamed to be more effective against certain kinds of posts, while ignoring others.

All this shows that news manipulation has grown into an unchecked and well-organised industry today, akin to advertising or public relations. Just like paid news, fake news too is transacted mostly through illegal, shadowy, and unaccounted for funds. It makes a particularly lethal combination when mixed with the colossal business of conducting election campaigns. In India, the 2019 elections cost around $8.7 billion (CMS 2019), which means that the global digital platforms have a lot to gain from advertising alone. In terms of volume, this is just under the size of India's spending on all forms of advertising for the year, which is around $9.5 billion (Rs 69,690 crore) (ibid.). Going by prevailing industry practices, it is not unusual for advertising companies to bend their policies just a little to accommodate their big advertiser clients. No wonder, then, that their business development and public policy teams almost always work in tandem, often reporting to the same bosses.

A more worrying part of such humongous election expenditure, including on information deception, is that it legitimises the parallel economy of slush funds, tax havens, and shell companies. The Panama Papers, a collaborative exposé by the International Consortium of Investigative Journalists (ICIJ), gave us an idea of how the rich and the powerful of the world park their money in offshore companies. The ICIJ database contains over 785,000 entities in more than 200 countries and territories (ICIJ n.d.). *The Indian Express*, ICIJ's Indian collaborator, has listed over 500 offshore companies, foundations, and trusts from India (*The Indian Express* 2017). The way in which these companies operate—and get around national laws and regulators—is simply breathtaking. The sheer scale of operations requires definite political links, which defiles and discredits the institution of both democratic and corporate governance.

A stable and strong liberal democracy will, therefore, have to safeguard elections and financial governance from these fundamental issues and simultaneously counter the politics of hate. Larry Diamond (2008) points out that despite competitive elections, many societies were experiencing 'abusive police forces, domineering local oligarchies, incompetent and indifferent state bureaucracies, corrupt and inaccessible judiciaries, and venal, ruling elites contemptuous of the rule of law and accountable to no one but themselves' (ibid., 292). This applies to almost all democracies, albeit to varying degrees. But conversely, an atmosphere of better participatory governance with higher standards of transparency and accountability will have a positive and long-term impact on governance, business ethics, and the rule of law, provided the battle is fought by multiple institutions and stakeholders in all democratic countries.

Ahead of the 2019 elections, several of India's well-known civil society organisations and former Chief Election Commissioners urged the ECI to make it mandatory for political parties to disclose their official handles on digital platforms, the names of their marketing companies and paid consultants, and their digital spending (Sam and Guha-Thakurta 2019; see especially the Annexure). They appealed to political parties to recognise the threat posed by money power in the elections and evolve a consensus to enact an appropriate legislation to cap the expenditure of political parties in elections (Marechal and Biddle 2020).

The issue at hand goes much beyond certain vested interests gaming the system. 'It's not just the content, but tech companies' surveillance-based business models that are distorting the public sphere and threatening democracy,' explains Ranking Digital Rights (RDR), a consortium of activists, researchers, and civil society watchdogs working to promote freedom of expression and privacy on the internet (Marechal and Biddle 2020). RDR's study questions the use of content-shaping and content-moderation algorithms by digital companies to argue that 'instead of seeking to hold digital platforms liable for content posted by their users, regulators and advocates should instead focus on holding companies accountable for how content is amplified and targeted' (ibid.). It recommends enforcing corporate transparency and the rights of national regulators over digital companies, as well as upholding the standards of citizens' privacy and human rights.

The insidious news operations will always thrive on democracy's weaknesses and its inability to catch up quickly with changing realities on the ground. For instance, elections have become do or die battles where all means are justified as permissible. Those manipulating information in elections are able to stir up raw emotions and justify them along the old fault-lines of society. However, stable democracies can neutralise old hostilities through fraternity and constitutional values. It is clear that all politicians or political parties will never have the same degree of respect or commitment for civil liberties, freedom of speech, and minority rights, but democracy's independent institutions will have to rise to the occasion when someone crosses the line. A good example is the Supreme Court verdict in 2024 striking down as unconstitutional the Electoral Bonds Scheme which legalised political corruption at the cost of the voters' right to information.[3] In India, the post-liberalisation State is retreating from key areas of economy and governance, leaving huge gaps for regulators in almost all sectors—from telecom to real estate, and from corporate hospitals to private universities. While the media and the cultural industry are no exceptions, they are unique due to the profound influence they wield over ideas, attitudes, and opinions. The real challenge, therefore, is to evolve participatory ways of real-time monitoring and to enforce a combination of regulations and ethical norms which are not coercive, and which do not compromise the individual's privacy and the freedom of expression.

Notes

1. The Press Council of India formed the sub-committee by exercising the powers conferred on them under Sections 8(1) and 15 of the Press Council of India Act, 1978.

2. See also https://prsindia.org/policy/report-summaries/free-and-fair-digital-economy (accessed February 2025).

3. See https://www.scobserver.in/cases/association-for-democratic-reforms-electoral-bonds-case-background/amp/ (accessed February 2025).

Select References

Association for Democratic Reforms (ADR). 2019. 'Analysis of Criminal Background, Financial, Education, Gender and Other Details of Winners'. Press Release, 25 May. Available at https://adrindia.org/content/lok-sabha-elections-2019-analysis-criminal-background-financial-education-gender-and-other (accessed November 2024).

Bansal, S. 2019. 'Narendra Modi App Has a Fake News Problem'. *HuffPost*, 27 January. Available at https://www.huffingtonpost.in/entry/narendra-modi-app-has-a-fake-news-problem_in_5c4d5c86e4b0287e5b8b6d52 (accessed November 2024).

BBC. 2018. 'Facebook admits it was used to 'incite offline violence' in Myanmar', 6 November. Available at https://www.bbc.com/news/world-asia-46105934 (accessed November 2024).

Bradshaw, S., and P. N. Howard. 2017. 'Troops, Trolls and Troublemakers: A Global Inventory of Organised Social Media Manipulations'. Working Paper 12. Oxford, UK: Computational Propaganda Research Project. Available at http://comprop.oii.ox.ac.uk/wp-content/uploads/sites/89/2017/07/Troops-Trolls-and-Troublemakers.pdf (accessed November 2024).

———. 2019. 'The Global Disinformation Disorder: 2019 Global Inventory of Organised Social Media Manipulation', Working Paper 2. Oxford, UK: Computational Propaganda Research Project.

Cadwalladr, C. 2019. 'Facebook's Role in Brexit—and the Threat to Democracy', TED Talk. Available at https://www.ted.com/talks/carole_cadwalladr_facebook_s_role_in_brexit_and_the_threat_to_democracy?language=en#t-1620 (accessed November 2024).

Cadwalladr, C. 2020. 'Fresh Cambridge Analytica leak "shows global manipulation is out of control"'. *The Guardian*, 4 January. Available at https://www.theguardian.com/uk-news/2020/jan/04/cambridge-analytica-data-leak-global-election-manipulation (accessed November 2024).

Centre for Media Studies (CMS). 2019. 'Poll Expenditure: The 2019 Elections'. A CMS Report. Available at https://cmsindia.org/sites/default/files/2019-05/Poll-Expenditure-the-2019-elections-cms-report.pdf (accessed November 2024).

Chaturvedi, S. 2019. *I Am a Troll: Inside the Secret World of the BJP's Digital Army*. New Delhi: Juggernaut Books.

Chaturvedi, A., and G. Laghate. 2019. 'Social media alone to corner Rs 12,000 crore in political ad spends'. *The Economic Times*, 23 January. Available at https://economictimes.indiatimes.com/news/politics-and-nation/social-media-alone-to-corner-rs-12000-crore-in-political-ad-spends/articleshow/67649833.cms (accessed November 2024).

Chaudhuri, P. 2020. 'Most Facebook fact-checking partners in India fail to fact-check BJP-led misinformation'. *Alt News*, 25 October. Available at https://www.altnews.in/most-facebook-fact-checking-partners-in-india-fail-to-fact-check-bjp-led-misinformation/ (accessed November 2024).

Cobrapost. 2018. 'Operation 136: Part 1', 26 March. Available at https://www.cobrapost.com/blog/Operation-136/1029 (accessed November 2024).

Dangerous Speech Project. 'Frequently Asked Questions'. Available at https://dangerousspeech.org/faq/ (accessed November 2024).

Diamond, L. 2008. *The Spirit of Democracy: The Struggle to Build Free Societies*. New York: Times Books, Henry Holt and Company.

Drishti. n.d. 'Justice BN Srikrishna Committee Submits Data Protection Report'. Available at chrome-extension://efaidnbmnnnibpcajpcglclefindmkaj/https://www.drishtiias.com/pdf/justice-bn-srikrishna-committee-submits-data-protection-report.pdf (accessed November 2024).

European Union. 2018. 'A Multi-Dimensional Approach to Disinformation'. Report of the Independent High Level Group on Fake News and Online Disinformation, Publications Office of the European Union. Available at https://op.europa.eu/en/publication-detail/-/publication/6ef4df8b-4cea-11e8-be1d-01aa75ed71a1 (accessed November 2024).

Government of India. n.d. 'Justice B. N. Srikrishna Report', Ministry of Home Affairs. Available at https://www.mha.gov.in/about-us/commissions-committees/ccsap-justice-retd-b-n-srikrishna-report (accessed November 2024).

The Hoot. 2017. 'The BCCL Empire – Towering over the Competition', 21 August. Available at http://asu.thehoot.org/media-watch/media-business/the-bccl-empiretowering-over-the-competition-10255#:~:text=BCCL's%20profits%20also%20dwarfed%20print,crore)%20for%20the%20ABP%20group (accessed November 2024).

Horwitz, J., and N. Purnell. 2020. 'Facebook Executives Supported India's Modi, Disparaged Opposition in Internal Messages'. *The Wall Street Journal*, 30 August. Available at https://www.wsj.com/articles/facebook-executive-supported-indias-modi-disparaged-opposition-in-internal-messages-11598809348 (accessed November 2024).

Howard, P. N. 2020. *Lie Machines: How to Save Democracy from Troll Armies, Deceitful Robots, Junk News Operations, and Political Operatives*. New Haven: Yale University Press.

International Consortium for Investigative Journalists (ICIJ). n.d. 'Offshore Leaks Database' Available at https://offshoreleaks.icij.org/search?c=IND (accessed November 2024).

International Foundation for Electoral Systems. 2017. 'Countering Hate Speech in Elections: Strategies for Electoral Management Bodies'. A White Paper from the International Foundation for Electoral Systems. Available at https://www.ifes.org/publications/countering-hate-speech-elections-strategies-electoral-management-bodies (accessed February 2025).

The Indian Express. 2013. 'Paid news, decline role of editors a major threat to media, says Hamid Ansari'. PTI, 15 June. Available at https://indianexpress.com/article/political-pulse/paid-news-decline-role-of-editors-a-major-threat-to-media-says-hamid-ansari/ (accessed November 2024).

The Indian Express. 2017. 'Pulitzer Prize for Panama Papers Investigation'. New Delhi, 12 April. Available at https://indianexpress.com/article/india/pulitzer-prize-for-panama-papers-investigation-indian-express-4609712 (accessed February 2025).

International Foundation for Electoral Systems. 2018. 'Countering Hate Speech in Elections: Strategies for Electoral Management Bodies'. An IFES White Paper, 8 January. Available at https://www.ifes.org/publications/countering-hate-speech-elections-strategies-electoral-management-bodies (accessed February 2025).

Ireton, C., and J. Posetti (eds). 2018. *Journalism, Fake News and Disinformation: A Handbook for Journalism Education and Training*. UNESCO Series on Journalism Education, UNESDOC Digital Library. Available at https://unesdoc.unesco.org/ark:/48223/pf0000265552 (accessed November 2024).

Karan, K. 2018. 'Journalists say Facebook is "censoring" political content in India ahead of 2019 elections'. *Scroll.in*, 31 October. Available at https://scroll.in/article/897879/journalists-say-facebook-is-censoring-political-content-in-india-ahead-of-2019-elections (accessed November 2024).

Kohli, K. 2013. 'Congress vs BJP: The curious case of trolls and politics'. *The Times of India*, 11 October. Available at https://timesofindia.indiatimes.com/india/Congress-vs-BJP-The-curious-case-of-trolls-and-politics/articleshow/23970818.cms (accessed November 2024).

Marechal, N., and R. E. Biddle. 2020. 'It's Not Just the Content, It's the Business Model: Democracy's Online Speech Challenge', A Report from Ranking Digital Rights, 17 March. Washington, DC: New America and Open Technology Institute. Available at https://www.newamerica.org/oti/reports/its-not-just-content-its-business-model/ (accessed November 2024).

Matthews, Julian. 2019. 'A cognitive scientist explains why humans are so susceptible to fake news and misinformation'. NiemanLab, 17 April. Available at https://www.niemanlab.org/2019/04/a-cognitive-scientist-explains-why-humans-are-so-susceptible-to-fake-news-and-misinformation/ (accessed November 2024).

Microsoft. 2019. 'Microsoft Releases Digital Civility Index on Safer Internet Day'. *Microsoft Stories India*, 5 February. Available at https://news.microsoft.com/en-in/microsoft-digital-civility-index-safer-internet-day-2019/ (accessed November 2024).

Mudde, C., and C. R. Kaltwasser. 2017. *Populism: A Very Short Introduction*. Oxford, UK: Oxford University Press.

Mudgal, V. 2011. 'Rural Coverage in Hindi and English Dailies'. *Economic and Political Weekly* XLVI (35), 27 August.

———. 2015. 'News for Sale: Paid News, Media Ethics and India's Democratic Public Sphere', in S. Rao and H. Wasserman (eds), *Media Ethics and Justice in the Age of Globalization*. London: Palgrave Macmillan.

Netflix. 2019. *The Great Hack*. A Netflix documentary film, directed by Karim Amer and Jehane Noujaim, and co-written by Karim Amer, Erin Barnett, and Pedros Kor.

———. 2020. *Social Dilemma*. A Netflix documentary film, directed by Jeff Orlowski, produced by Larissa Rhodes, and co-written by Davis Coombe, Vickie Curtis, and Jeff Orlowski.

Pal, J., and A. Panda. 2019. 'Twitter in the 2019 General Elections: Trends of Use Across States and Parties'. *Economic and Political Weekly* 54 (51), 28 December. Available at https://www.epw.in/engage/article/twitter-2019-indian-general-elections-trends-use (accessed November 2024).

Parliament of India. 2013. *Presentation of the 47th Report of the Standing Committee on Information Technology (2012-13) on the Subject Issues Related to Paid News, relating to Ministry of Information and Broadcasting*. Available at https://eparlib.nic.in/handle/123456789/743621?view_type=search (accessed November 2024).

Perrigo, B. 2019. 'How Volunteers for India's Ruling Party are Using WhatsApp to Fuel Fake News Ahead of Elections'. *Time*, 25 January. Available at https://time.com/5512032/whatsapp-india-election-2019/ (accessed November 2024).

Press Council of India. n.d. 'Sub Committee Report on Paid News'. Available at chrome-extension://efaidnbmnnnibpcajpcglclefindmkaj/http://keralamediaacademy.org/wp-content/uploads/2015/02/PCI-Sub-CommitteeReport-on-Paid-News.pdf (accessed November 2024).

Purnell, N., and J. Horwitz. 2020. 'Facebook's Hate-Speech Rules Collide with Indian Politics'. *The Wall Street Journal*, 14 August. Available at https://www.wsj.com/articles/facebook-hate-speech-india-politics-muslim-hindu-modi-zuckerberg-11597423346 (accessed November 2024).

Sainath, P. 2009. 'It is shameful to misguide people'. *The Hindu*, 23 December. Available at https://www.thehindu.com/opinion/columns/sainath/lsquoIt-is-shameful-to-misguide-peoplersquo/article16836001.ece (accessed November 2024).

Sam, C., and P. Guha Thakurta. 2019. *The Real Face of Facebook in India: How Social Media has Become a Propaganda Weapon and Disseminator of Disinformation and Falsehood*. New Delhi: AuthorsUpFront.

Serhan, Yasmeen. 2020. 'The Trump-Modi Playbook'. *The Atlantic*, 25 February. Available at https://www.theatlantic.com/international/archive/2020/02/donald-trump-narendra-modi-autocrats/607042/ (accessed November 2024).

Silverman, C., R. Mac, and P. Dixit. 2020. 'I Have Blood on My Hands: A Whistleblower Says Facebook Ignored Global Political Manipulation'. *BuzzFeed News*, 15 September. Available at https://www.buzzfeednews.com/article/craigsilverman/facebook-ignore-political-manipulation-whistleblower-memo (accessed November 2024).

Singh, Shivam Shankar. 2019. *How to Win an Indian Election: What Political Parties Don't Want You to Know*. New Delhi: Penguin India.

Tavernise, S., and A. Gardiner. 2019. '"No One Believes Anything": Voters Worn Out By a Fog of Political News'. *The New York Times*, 18 November. Available at https://www.nytimes.com/2019/11/18/us/polls-media-fake-news.html (accessed November 2024).

The Times of India. 2013. 'BJP's Gopinath Munde openly admits to flouting election expense norms', 2 July. Available at https://timesofindia.indiatimes.com/edit-page/BJPs-Gopinath-Munde-publicly-admits-to-flouting-election-expense-norms/articleshow/20864385.cms (accessed November 2024).

Uttam, Kumar. 2018. 'For PM Modi's 2019 campaign, BJP readies its WhatsApp plan'. *Hindustan Times*, 29 September. Available at https://www.hindustantimes.com/india-news/bjp-plans-a-whatsapp-campaign-for-2019-lok-sabha-election/story-lHQBYbxwXHaChc7Akk6hcI.html (accessed November 2024).

Vosoughi, S., D. Roy, and S. Aral. 2018. 'The Spread of True and False News Online'. MIT Initiative on the Digital Economy Research Brief. Available at http://ide.mit.edu/sites/default/files/publications/2017%20IDE%20Research%20Brief%20False%20News.pdf (accessed November 2024).

Wardle, C., et al. 2018. *Information Disorder: The Essential Glossary*. Boston: Shorenstein Center, Harvard University.

Woolley, S., and K. Joseff. 2020. 'Demand for Deceit: How the Way We Think Drives Disinformation', Working Paper, January. Washington, DC: International Forum for Democratic Studies, National Endowment for Democracy. Available at https://www.ned.org/wp-content/uploads/2020/01/Demand-for-Deceit.pdf (accessed November 2024).

Flowering of India's Democracy

Wajahat Habibullah

Prime Minister Jawaharlal Nehru's political odyssey had convinced him that, 'The questions that a country puts are a measure of that country's political development. Often the failure of that country is due to the fact that it has not put the right question to itself' (Nehru 2004, 260–261). The Constitution, with its 73rd and 74th Amendments, sought to turn this conviction into reality through institutionalising public participation in governance, which was carried to its logical conclusion with the right to ask questions being made a statutory right with the passage of the Right to Information Act 2005.

The greatest challenge to independent India, recognised by the Congress government under Indira Gandhi, who understood the urgent need to address it and made it the pivot of her 1971 election triumph with the slogan *garibi hatao*, was India's unacceptable level of poverty. Yet, despite this resolve, programmes designed to create employment that would generate income for the rural poor were delayed because funds were not released by the state governments to the districts.

Even where funds were released, implementation was poor, with complaints of underpayment of wages and leakages. These problems were typical not only of many programmes which the Central government funded, but also of those that fell in the areas reserved for the state governments, and which had to be implemented by the state and district machinery. The Central government would release funds to the state governments, but it had little control over how these funds were spent.

It was shortly after his visit to Odisha's tribal districts of Kalahandi and Phulbani in 1985 that Prime Minister Rajiv Gandhi made his oft-quoted observation that out of every rupee spent by the government to help the rural poor, only 15 paise actually reached the target. But this observation rested not on Gandhi's assessment of corruption levels in government, which many construe as the reference, but on his realisation of the massive expenses involved in servicing a bureaucratic structure to administer poverty alleviation measures. An empirical study undertaken a few years thereafter, supervised by the well-known economist Kirit Parikh, later Member of the Planning Commission, to calculate the percentage of funds spent on the Public Distribution System (PDS) that actually reached the poor, came up with 16 paise as the best estimate, remarkably close to Gandhi's assessment.

Cutting Edge of Governance

The face of governance before the common citizen was distant and inaccessible. In his term as prime minister, Gandhi sought means to ensure public participation in governance. He turned first to the district administration and the office of the Collector, which he considered the cutting edge of the administration. He toyed with the idea of smaller districts, under the mistaken impression that this might lead to ease of access for the otherwise excluded, until he realised that the answer lay in involving the public itself in the delivery of service. In a series of meetings culminating in 1988 with District Collectors in different parts of the country, meant to elicit their views on this issue, Gandhi urged the District Collectors to speak freely and share their views on how the system could be strengthened. He also asked if Panchayati Raj Institutions (PRIs) should be given constitutional status. Many District Collectors were in favour of such a Constitutional Amendment. A draft Constitution Amendment Bill passed by the Lok Sabha failed in the Rajya Sabha, and led to the announcement of the 1989 elections. The succeeding National Front government cobbled together after the elections was also unable to muster the necessary support, leaving it to the Congress-led government, headed by Narasimha Rao, which came to power in 1991, to bring the necessary amendments to the Constitution. The meetings with Collectors, followed by a conference of chief ministers in 1988, became the launching pad that concluded with the 73rd and 74th constitutional amendments, supported by a majority of chief ministers, that crowned local government with constitutional fiat.

Making Democracy Real

Rajiv Gandhi's field visits and the feedback from the concurrent evaluation of the twenty-point programme that targeted poverty helped to convince him that the government's rural development programmes would not eliminate poverty without much greater local partnership and ownership. It became increasingly obvious to him that robust PRIs would be the means to bring this about. The Balwant Rai Mehta Committee had made elaborate recommendations in 1957 for the creation of a three-tiered structure, with the Gram

Panchayat at the village level, the Panchayat Samiti at the block level, and the Zilla Parishad at the district level. Some states had put these structures in place, but because there was no compulsion to hold regular elections, and neither was authority decentralised, the system had flagged. Article 40 of the Constitution enjoined the state to organise and empower village panchayats, but this was only a nod to Mahatma Gandhi's commitment to the ideal of Purna Swaraj through Gram Swaraj—total freedom by local self-government—and hence was only part of the Directive Principles of State Policy, which stated: 'The State shall take steps to organise village panchayats and endow them with such powers and authority as may be necessary to enable them to function as units of self-government.' Babasaheb Ambedkar, the father of the Constitution, was, while introducing the Draft Constitution for a second reading, condemnatory of village self-government: 'What is the village but a sink of localism, a den of ignorance, narrow mindedness and communalism? I am glad that the Draft Constitution has discarded the village and adopted the individual as its unit.'

What Ambedkar had observed was doubtless true of his time, and part of the detritus of colonial exploitation. As the executor of plans for rural development, the government had in 1952 instituted the Community Development Programme. Blocks were established as units of development administration, each with a Block Development Officer (BDO) assisted by Village Level Workers (VLW), who exercised financial authority. Among them were many who fed off this rich financial repository and satisfied the corrupt elements in an ever-hungry political structure, and then went on to become powerful political leaders. This led to the introduction of the Balwant Rai Mehta Committee. Erudite jurist L. M. Singhvi, while reviewing the possible consequences of the Committee's report, recognised that the 'lack of public involvement and participation began to be perceived as an impediment in the successful implementation of the Community Development and National Extension Service Programmes'.[1] Yet, the post of the BDO was to persist, and this institutional framework was to become the nemesis of democracy at the grassroots. Rajiv Gandhi credited his grandfather Jawaharlal Nehru with laying the foundation of parliamentary democracy. He believed that he needed to do more to make democracy a reality.

Panchayati Raj

Rajiv Gandhi often lamented that the total number of elected representatives in India, including both Members of Parliament (MPs) and Members of Legislative Assembly (MLAs), was about 60,000, and thus they were accessible to only a few influential members of the public. For the majority of India's (then) 800 million, access was only through the bureaucracy. To explore alternatives, a Committee on Revitalisation of Panchayati Raj Institutions for Democracy and Development was set up in 1986, under the Chairmanship of L. M. Singhvi, the eminent jurist. Panchayat elections had not been conducted for many years, and the system had effectively been undermined by local elites. As noted by Singhvi, according to a Committee set up by the Planning Commission, which presented its report in December 1985, a three-tier system had been adopted in twelve states and one Union Territory, and a two-tier system existed in four states and two Union Territories. The electoral system also varied from state to state. In the design of structures, electoral procedures, powers, and functions, there was considerable variation in the panchayat institutions of the states. At that time, there were more than 217,300 village panchayats in the country, covering over 96 per cent of about 5.79 lakh inhabited villages and 92 per cent of the rural population. There were about 4,526 Panchayati Samitis of different nomenclatures at the block, taluka, or tehsil level, and about 330 Zilla Parishads covering about 76 per cent of the districts in the country; each Zilla Parishad had an average of 13–14 Panchayati Samitis and about 660 Gram Panchayats. The Singhvi Committee Report, after somewhat ruefully recounting the debate in the Constituent Assembly that ruled out mandatory Panchayati Raj, recommended that the PRIs be given constitutional status assuring free, fair, and regular elections overseen by the Election Commission of India, and legal protection from executive subversion through the institution of a Panchayati Raj Judicial Tribunal in each state, with access to adequate financial resources.

As the officer monitoring the PM's Twenty-point Programme since the days of Mrs Gandhi's government, I had, as Joint Secretary in the Prime Minister's Office (PMO) in 1985–1986, been assigned the task of processing the PM's new vision of decentralised governance through the instrument of the Panchayati Raj. The PM had come to the conclusion that this was the best institutional mechanism with which to bring rural India within the ambit of governance. He was of the idea that essential to democracy in India was a third tier of elected government at the basic level of administration, which would give a voice to all sections of the people. This was to be in addition to the tiers of democracy represented by the Union and state governments. It would involve a substantial change in the system of district administration as it had evolved over the centuries, centred on the District Magistrate/District Collector, who controlled the district administration and was not accountable to any local elected body. This was in fact a legacy of the Mughal administration, adapted by the British to better serve their imperial interests and replicated across Britain's vast empire. Although panchayats existed at the time, they were concerned with narrow, local issues (thus provoking Ambedkar's scathing comment). The Collector was responsible only to the state government, and while he might respond to the demands of the elected MP and a few elected MLAs, he was not answerable to any other elected representative. An elected local government was designed to effectively turn the district administration into an executive responsible to a local elected legislature.

What was contemplated then was a dramatic change, both in the concept and form of governance. From being a means to perpetuate imperial rule, governance was to develop into a means of seeking and managing equitable economic growth. Yet, the bureaucratic infrastructure remained relatively constant and grounded in mistrust. The reason for this mistrust can be found in the legacy of governance in India, stemming directly at the district level from the Mughal period,[2] adapted and extended with an archaic Secretariat system in the colonial period, and then becoming an elitist structure informing both systems which continues, despite Panchayati Raj, to subsist to this day.

The old structure needed to be replaced. But while change was indeed in the offing, there was no political or even administrative consensus on the objectives to be met. Participation in governance is too often seen as a struggle for sharing power. But governance must be distinct from the exercise of power and must comprise an assurance of security of life and property, both of which are predicated on the security of the nation, as conceived not by the security forces or the bureaucracy, but very clearly by the people of India themselves, whose concerns must be addressed by these instruments of governance. If this is understood, it is easier to see that what was being sought was a new threshold in India's form of governance.

What, then, were to be the future prospects? Gandhi certainly saw the bureaucrat of the future as a facilitator, and because of their wide-ranging field experience, as a potentially effective manager; hence his repeated outreach to field officers, which strengthened this view. For this to actually happen, however, an action plan is required to combine effective administration with a responsive administration— an action plan designed to deliver what the people, and not the bureaucracy, identified as their need. There is a general consensus that good governance must be participatory, transparent, and accountable (Morris 2002, 19). As I have sought to explain, the system, thanks to perceptions enshrined in the Official Secrets Act 1923 (not yet abrogated even as I write), was firmly grounded in mistrust. If governance was to be participatory, the public was required to be a participant.

Rajiv Gandhi believed that restructuring the system of government in this way would make the administration much more responsible to the elected representatives and would increase local ownership of and participation in development programmes. The consequence was the decentralisation of governance through the 73rd and 74th Amendments of 1993 to the Constitution, making Panchayat Raj, an instrument of local self-government, a constitutional imperative, and thereby making every registered voter a legislator for their own village through the gram sabha (the village community), or township through the municipality. This was built upon to ensure accountability and transparency in India's governance along with one of the world's strongest laws on the subject, the Right to Information Act 2005. This Act was initiated in 2004 by the Manmohan Singh government, complying with an election pledge of the Congress-led UPA, following on the demand initiated by activists like Aruna Roy of the MKSS, who had been nurtured by Rajiv Gandhi's legislation on citizens' rights.

Addressing the challenge of social inclusion continues. A reproduction of a letter I received over email on Friday, 13 April 2012, will, I hope, demonstrate the access to authority that a Muslim villager, described in the Planning Commission's report as among the excluded, enjoys today, like every Indian.

To,
The Chairman
National Commission for Minorities
New Delhi

Sub: PM's New 15-point programme is not properly inforced in Bihar state[3]

Sir,
I humbly submit that the PM's New 15-point programme is not properly implimented in letter and spirit as per guidelines.

Infect there is no such committees are constituted neither in the state lavel nor in district level for the benifits of the minority communities.

As because it has been initiated by the P.M.O, the govt of Bihar is not seriously intrested to implement the same on political bias perhaps. The govt of Bihar issued a notification No.456 dated 17/07/2007 in this regard without proper and propertionate representation of the minorities. According to the Govt's notification No 456 dt.17/07/2007 only the govt. officials of the concerning departnment are included in such committees since last 5 years.

Hence virtually there is no progress at all in this regard.

I therefor request your kind honour to look after the same as it will change the face and status of the minority people at large economically, educationaly and moraly.

Thanks,
Your's Faithfully

Section 243(d) of the Constitution of India specifies that Panchayat means 'an institution (by whatever name called) of self-government', constituted under Article 243(b) for the rural areas. Drafted assiduously under supervision, first by Mani Shankar Aiyar in the PMO and thereafter by Meenakshisundaram, who like me was from the IAS batch of 1968, part of the same Andhra Pradesh cadre as Prime Minister P. V. Narasimha Rao, the objective behind the Narasimha Rao government bringing this amendment was to give voice to the voiceless in governance. Key to the effective inclusion of even the most far-flung and isolated communities in governance is the Gram Panchayat or the village council, which can prove to be the repository for scheme information, citizen surveys, fiscal information, etc. The Government of India has for decades been the world's largest investor, in terms of its Gross Domestic Product (GDP), in poverty eradication. Panchayati Raj Institutions, more than any other instrument of the State, were specially designed to include individual citizens in rural areas in aspects of governance. Gram sabhas, designed to be the font of the country's legislative framework, transform every citizen into a legislator.

While helping to educate the public on the benefits provided by the government, Gram Panchayats can in turn educate the government on the aspirations of residents of villages by implementing these benefits in a manner best suited to their aspirations. But this can happen only with the devolution of functions, funds, and functionaries by state administrations. Although clearly enunciated in policy, such devolution has been patchy, thus making panchayats today not institutions of 'self-government' as envisioned in Article 243 of the Constitution, but organs of the state administration and a conduit for development finance. Nevertheless, as the third level of representative government, this body can become the service provider (that Rajiv Gandhi had dreamt of) for over-the-counter services, certificates, taxation, billing, licenses, ration cards, and a host of other such services at the grassroots. In order to keep the citizenry informed, this third tier of government can work with citizens as a group (gram sabhas) and citizens as individuals, whose concerns and questions could also be appropriately addressed with reference to the relevant authority. This would ensure efficiency and better feedback and accountability, a convenience both to the citizen and to government, thus ensuring a smooth devolution of administrative authority that will include the citizen in the process of decision-making.

Why did this new threshold, with the public leading development instead of the bureaucracy, not materialise? In the 1970s, the Union government created the Small Farmers Development Agencies (SFDAs), which were meant to channel Union budget money directly to districts, and thence to the Blocks, bypassing state budgets. The government genuinely felt that this was necessary for the efficient implementation of poverty alleviation programmes, initiated after the elections of 1971, in order to prevent delays and diversions of Union government funds by state governments, and to overcome the yearly lapsing of unspent funds channelled through state treasuries. These SFDAs, then, were special service vehicles designed for a specific purpose. As pointed out by T. R. Raghunandan, a dynamic IAS officer from the Karnataka cadre who was to serve as Joint Secretary when Mani Shankar Aiyer was Minister of Panchayati Raj and I was the Secretary, in a note of 4 August 2018, this tendency to create special purpose vehicles for ring-fencing Union government funds mushroomed in the years subsequent to the constitutional amendments, with the active encouragement of IAS officers in line departments in states, who teamed up with their counterparts in the concerned Union Ministries to create direct fiscal transfer systems that bypassed state budgets.

The SFDAs morphed into the District Rural Development Agencies (DRDAs) in 1979. As T. R. Raghunandan said,

> These were powerful district-level societies that channelised funds for flagship Government of India programmes such as IRDP, JRY, and suchlike. The only state that did away with DRDAs was Karnataka; this happened because the Secretary of the RDPR department in Karnataka. Dr. S.S. Meenakshisundaram, who sent the proposal for abolishing the DRDAs and merging them with the Zilla Parishad, became the Joint Secretary in the Ministry of RD subsequently and approved his own proposal.

While serving in Narasimha Rao's PMO, Meenakshisundaram was instrumental in finalising the Bill that brought in the 73rd and 74th Amendments.

Once the panchayats (at all three levels) were mandated through the 73rd Amendment, it quickly became clear that the DRDAs were now obstructing the growth of the former by encroaching into the constitutionally and legally devolved powers of the Zilla Parishads. Yugandhar, the then Secretary of the Ministry of Rural Development (MORD), saw much sense in the merger of DRDAs with the ZP, and moved papers to do so, which included the abolition of a scheme to fund DRDAs. However, the then Minister Sundarlal Patwa, was persuaded by his private secretary, an IAS officer, to not only continue the DRDAs, but to also enlarge the allocations to them and force states such as Karnataka (which had abolished DRDAs) to revive them, on paper at least, so that the state could be eligible to receive funds from the Union government. A letter from Sunderlal Patwa to the state ministers became a lifeline for state RD departments that wanted to wrest back the space they had so reluctantly conceded to ZPs.

The Union Ministry of Panchayati Raj, set up in 2004 under the ministership of Mani Shankar Aiyar, in which I was appointed First Secretary, did what it could to do away with the DRDAs, but the MORD, larger, more influential, and with a bigger budget, did not relent. Some of the justifications that Raghunandan heard in those days from officers in the MORD (not ministers) were blatantly in favour of protecting the domain of the District Collector. One officer from the UP cadre told him that the DRDAs were necessary in UP to enable the DCs to maintain law and order. Apart from the access that district-level IAS officers had to generous allocations from the Union government, the DRDAs also provided them with flexibility to invest these funds in banks and earn interest. Audit reports showed that these interest funds were used to build luxurious quarters and buy air-conditioners and vehicles, which the officers would not have otherwise been able to afford, as state government rules allowed little luxury. That, Raghunandan holds, was 'the real reason' why DRDAs were continued. Even the raisins and cashew nuts offered in district meetings were supplied by the DRDA!

Due to this duplication of development planning and implementation, both of which were originally intended as part of the province of the panchayats, Raghunandan recalls that the Ministry of Panchayati Raj worked with the then Planning Commission, headed at the time by Montek Singh Ahluwalia, to ensure that district development plans were based on the plans initiated by, and at the level of, panchayats. A direct transfer of funds targeting development under the poverty alleviation programmes was instituted. The Ministry of Rural Development had in the meantime set up a Committee headed by V. Ramachandran, to look into the role and relevance of the DRDAs following the enactment of the 73rd Amendment. The Committee recommended the abolition and merger of DRDAs with the ZPs. The then Minister. Jairam Ramesh, passed the orders. But the file was held up in the Ministry, which steadfastly resisted implementing the order till the government changed.

This should answer the question as to what became of Rajiv Gandhi's vision of instituting local self-government. The Father of our Nation, Mahatma Gandhi, had this dream for India upon winning freedom:

> Independence must begin at the bottom. Thus, every village will be a republic or Panchayat having full powers. It follows therefore, that every village has to be self-sustained and capable of managing its affairs even to the extent of defending itself against the whole world. (Gandhi 1959, 8–9)

But as I write, the DRDAs are alive and kicking. Chairpersons of ZPs have been co-opted to chair or participate in DRDA meetings, but their accounts are separate from the ZP accounts. The PRIs have no independent structure of authority or finance, or indeed an executive accountable to it that would enable them to be the institutions of self-government that the Constitution mandates.

Raghunandan concludes,

> The Union Government has now started a movement called the Gram Swaraj Abhiyan. The idea is to inject directly to the Gram Panchayats, programme thrusts and funds of the Union Government. More than 800 Officers of the Union Government, which include a large number of IAS officers, have been allocated to districts, to deal directly with district collectors and implement schemes directly. There is also plenty of pressure on these officers to promote amongst people the impression that these schemes are all directly due to the munificence of the Prime Minister. The DRDA is a vital link in this direct stream of programme management. This approach is a travesty of federalism. While there are political motives behind such approaches, IAS officers have responded to moves towards such centralisation with enthusiasm and have filled in the detail.

The Right to Information

As mentioned earlier, the natural corollary to placing the people's needs at the centre of governance is the right to information, a reality today in our country, constituting as it does a major leap in evolving towards full democracy. As the Right to Information Act, 2005 celebrated its fifteenth year, there was much heated discussion, often emotional, of the benefits it has brought, as well as the challenges it has forced the government, and indeed the nation, to confront. 'Scams' centering on government initiatives had agitated both the government and the public in the opening years of the past decade, leading to a universal clamour for an effective ombudsman, a 'Lokpal'. This can be said to have been among the causes for the discomfiture in the national elections of 2014 of the very government that piloted the Act. The government that succeeded it avowedly retained the credo of transparency and accountability and sought to distinguish governance from government. The prime minister's promise in the 2014 campaign was maximum governance with minimum government, and thus a promise of increased participation of the people in governance through the slogan, '*Sabka saath, sabka vikas*' ('Together with all, development for all').

Yet there is a growing feeling that governments have been tardy in promoting transparency and accountability, a feeling exacerbated by the restrictions necessitated by COVID-19. This has been accompanied by positions in Information Commissions being left vacant, with some states being reduced to having single Information Commissioners or none at all, and the Central Information Commission being repeatedly left headless. This is despite the PM announcing, in the 2014 Annual Convention of Information Commissions, that his government intended to use this law to monitor its own functioning. In the words of Barack Hussein Obama, who spoke of his 'profound national commitment to ensuring an open Government' on assuming charge of the Presidency of the United States, in his inaugural speech in the East Room of the White House on 28 January 2009, 'At the heart of that commitment is *the idea that accountability is in the interest of the Government and the citizenry alike*' (emphasis mine). It is for the citizenry to decide how true the government has been to its promise through the use of the innovative concept of social audit.

It is universally accepted that the essence of government in a democracy must be transparency, with every organ of government, be it executive, judiciary, or legislature, being answerable to the citizen. Hence the Father of the Nation, when describing his vision of self-governance for India, described it as follows: 'The real Swaraj will come not by the acquisition of authority by a few but by the acquisition of capacity by all to resist authority when abused' (Gandhi 1925, 41).

India's Right to Information Act, 2005 therefore declares that democracy requires an informed citizenry and transparency of information, both of which are vital to a government's functioning and also crucial to containing corruption and holding governments and their instrumentalities accountable to the governed. This is a universal truth of particular relevance to India. Seen in this light, the RTI is an instrument that has the potential to strengthen governance immeasurably. In the words of Kofi Annan, the seventh Secretary-General of the United Nations,

> The great democratizing power of information has given us all the chance to effect change and alleviate poverty in ways we cannot even imagine today. Our task, your task ... is to make that change real for those in need, wherever they may be. With information on our side, with knowledge of a potential for all, the path to poverty can be reversed.[4]

Democracy has indeed been challenged by what can only be described as a violent insurrection by those we know as Maoists, and then by sections within the government itself in an effort to promote authoritarianism. But it is my conviction that this has happened because the pace of economic progress in India, spectacular though it might have been before descending into its present regression, has been anything but uniform, either amongst different sections of the Indian community, or even region-wise within states. Those who have felt deprived will feel even more so when they see before their own eyes the fruits of prosperity in their own neighbourhoods, which are not theirs to share or to enjoy. This will come from among those citizens who have never had the opportunity to hold the government accountable.

In conclusion, any commentary on the enforcement of the RTI Act, 2005 must place such a review in perspective, bearing in mind the remarks of Justice Mathew on behalf of the Bench, oft quoted in judicial circles while debating the law:

> In a government of responsibility like ours, where all agents of the public must be responsible for their conduct, there can be but few secrets. The people of this country have a right to know every public act, everything that is done in a public way, by their public functionaries ... to cover with veil of secrecy the common routine business, is not in the interest of public. (*State of UP vs Raj Narain* [1975] 4 SCC 428)

This mirrors the observation of that great American apostle of democracy, Justice Brandeis, when he observed that 'sunlight is the best disinfectant'. It is only when that sunlight shines into every crevice of governance that we can finally declare our RTI Act to have been a success. Till that day, we must persevere in our quest to make governance ever more participative, and more inclusive, which is the essence of democratic governance.

Notes

1. L. M. Singhvi Committee Report 1986, under the head 'Integrated Vision of Democracy'. Available at https://unacademy.com/content/railway-exam/study-material/polity/characteristics-of-the-l-m-singhvi-committee/ (accessed February 2025).

2. The position of Collector, as the name implies, was instituted under the title *Amal Guzar* by Raja Todar Mal, head of Mughal imperial finance in the sixteenth century, to collect land revenue, the mainstay of the Empire's finance.

3. The spellings and syntax used in the email have been preserved verbatim and not corrected in order to uphold the original voice of the letter's author.

4. UN Press Release SG/SM/6268, 23 June 1997.

SELECT REFERENCES

Gandhi, M. K. 1925. 'What Swaraj Means to Me'. *Young India*, 29 January.

———. 1959. *Panchayat Raj*, compiled by R. K. Prabhu. Ahmedabad: Navjivan Publishing House.

Morris, Sebastian. 2002. *The Challenge to Governance in India*, India Infrastructure Report. New Delhi: Oxford University Press.

Nehru, Jawaharlal. 2004. *An Autobiography*. New Delhi: Penguin.

13

WHEN WE THOUGHT WE HAD ALL THE ANSWERS, HINDU SUPREMACY CHANGED THE QUESTIONS[1]

MOYUKH CHATTERJEE

While the list of what ails the world's largest democracy (India) and the world's oldest democracy (the United States) is a long one, I will focus on a style of politics that seems not to be working, and even backfiring at times in both democracies. I will call this the 'politics of exposure'.[2] What is the politics of exposure and why is it not working anymore? It is the hopeful assumption that the exposure of violence by State and non-State actors against minorities within liberal democracies would lead to public outrage. Instead of public condemnation, however, the exposure of violent politics and hate speech in many parts of the world has galvanised a new supremacist politics and a new global right.

Consider two examples where the politics of exposure did not take off.

First: The publicly televised proceedings that led to the first impeachment of President Donald Trump in 2019. A stream of witnesses testified how President Trump had broken precedent and used his office to blackmail a foreign power to dig up damaging information on his political opponent. The Democrats used the impeachment to reveal a plethora of scandalous details about Trump's behaviour in office before the press. Diplomats and bureaucrats, in their precise spare language, revealed that everyone in Trump's closest circle knew what was going on. There was nothing to expose because President Trump was not even trying to hide it.

I listened to the live radio telecast of the impeachment proceedings on VPR (Vermont Public Radio) and waited hopefully for the arrival of some clinching evidence that would reveal the emperor's new clothes. Surely, this public trial full of facts and documents would convince Trump supporters that a great betrayal of presidential power had taken place. But the proceedings were polarised along Party lines—the Republican Party was happy that the proceedings revealed the 'witch hunt' against Trump. The polarised proceedings retained the garb of procedural democracy: the question-and-answer format, the equal division of time to both sides, and even though things got heated during the proceedings, thankfully no one threw a chair or microphone at their opponent. And yet public polls showed that the so-called 'exposure' had no adverse effect on Trump's image among his supporters. Yes, he would eventually be impeached, but my point is that there was no general anti-Trump mood among the wider public. It was partisan all the way down. Exposure did not persuade anyone, it simply fortified already existing divisions. Exposure also did not neutralise Trumpism. The Democrats had hoped that revealing the dark deeds of a regime and its leader would unravel its power and popularity. Instead, it became the launching pad for Trump's re-election campaign.

Second: The aftermath of the anti-minority violence in India in 2002. The entire country and the world witnessed the attacks on Muslims. National and international media, human rights organisations, NGOs, and civil society groups exposed the attacks on Muslim life and property. Films, special issues of magazines, investigative journalism, and first-person testimony exposed the inaction of the government to prevent the attacks on Muslims. Television channels showed images of policemen watching factories being looted and burned. Photographs of burned bodies and torched neighbourhoods were displayed on television and newspapers. There was widespread outrage and protests against the pogrom outside the state of Gujarat. But the strategy to 'expose' these attacks as an exceptional case of hatred did not address the pogrom as an outcome of a long process that touched upon all aspects of Gujarati society—public culture, popular history, electoral politics, segregated neighbourhoods—which ultimately created the Gujarati Muslim as a permanent outsider.

The then state machinery weaponised the exposure of violence. The human rights struggle and the fight for justice were framed by Hindu nationalists as a conspiracy against Gujarat, against Hindus, and against India. Like the impeachment of Trump, the media was split in Gujarat. The Gujarati vernacular press had backed the government's inaction, spread rumours, and fuelled the fire. An editor of a leading Gujarati newspaper told a fact-finding committee that Gujarati papers were pro-Hindu because the English media sided with Muslims (Patel, et al. 2002). The public exposure of the attacks on Muslims simply reinforced the polarisation of Gujarat along the axis of Hindus *versus* Muslims.[3] The new triumphant Hindu majority created by the violence voted for the Hindu nationalists after the pogrom, and have stood by them in many subsequent elections. With the benefit of hindsight, we can now say that the pogrom launched the career of several politicians, and aided the arrival of Hindu supremacy as a form of governance.

The politics of exposure is failing in both democracies because it assumes 'the people' as a fixed category, in existence before acts of public anti-minority violence. It also assumes that the exposure of complicity, corruption, and violence would lead to predictable passions like outrage and disgust; however, in the polarised media environment in democracies like India and the US, whilst there is outrage in liberal circles, there is also celebration and solidarity being formed through acts of violence against minorities.

Where do we go from here? Should we simply abandon exposing the violence and join the ranks of the meek and unconcerned? That is not my point at all. But when the politics of exposure produces diminishing and even counterproductive results, is it justifiable to keep doing the same old thing and expect different results? Should we not pause and reconsider our strategy, the materials we are working with, and the questions we ask ourselves and others? I offer three ways in which Hindu supremacy is leading us to ask new questions about politics and society in India. But first, let me step back and show that the simultaneous rise of Hindu and White supremacy is also an opportunity to revisit our assumptions about democracy and violence in India, and also beyond.

For far too long, Europe and North America have been the yardstick to discuss democracy, the State, and the nature of politics elsewhere (Chakrabarty 2008). By this, I mean that politics in India is usually compared to North American democracies on an evolutionary scale. Postcolonial democracies fill what the anthropologist Michel-Rolph Trouillot called 'the savage slot'. This means that Western democracy is defined against so-called fragile and failing States in the Global South. African democracies have failed, and Asian democracies are flawed. This way of understanding democracy persists because politics in the West is considered disconnected from its colonial past and present. The subjugation and extermination of Native American people and the legacy of slavery forms the 'historical' context, and is disconnected from the State-sanctioned dispossession of indigenous people, police violence against African-Americans, and the growing Islamophobia in all parts of Europe.

The rise of Trumpism and Brexit—to name only two prominent events—have removed the veil off the idea that Western democracies stand separate from majoritarian politics in other parts of the world. Insofar as Trump has placed White supremacy at the heart of American politics and his style of functioning[4] is familiar to citizens of 'weak' democracies like India, this is a good opportunity for us to bring together knowledge, scholarship, and activism, which have been artificially separated. Like Trump, the Hindu supremacist government in India is helpful for us to move past Indian exceptionalism—the false idea that India is somehow immune to the form of authoritarian rule and supremacist statecraft that reigns in Pakistan, Sri Lanka, and Myanmar. Let us see then what comes into view when we move away from the politics of exposure and try to compose a story about our shared global present.

From Ideology to Passion

The story of the demolition of the Babri mosque in Ayodhya, Uttar Pradesh on 6 December 1992 is often told as a narrative of crisis. On one momentous day, Indian secularism came crashing down because State officials stood by as Hindu supremacists destroyed a mosque. But the destruction also created something more than the electoral success of the Hindu nationalist political party, the Bharatiya Janata Party (BJP). What it created is most vivid in the photographs of the demolition that capture the moments before and after the attack. The photographic record of the demolition of the mosque tells us a story that goes beyond the cliché of catastrophe (Jain 2020). There is a photograph that reveals a large group of men atop a small hill, using rocks to rehearse the assault on the mosque a day before it was razed to the ground. In another photograph, a policeman has joined a crowd of *karsevak*s (workers) in shouting slogans. Then, there are those better-known photographs of political leaders and future ministers sitting across the mosque, waiting for the show to begin.

All this is to say that the photographs document the atmosphere—festive and triumphant—that transformed the destruction of the mosque into something more than mere destruction. We know what the crowds were bringing down, but what were they replacing it with? Mass, public, anti-Muslim violence could be used to produce a new solidarity between State actors (like the police and politicians) and Hindu supremacist groups. The demolition was an infrastructural success—iconography, songs, posters, bricks, pickaxes, and hammers were procured, distributed, and used to create the right atmosphere for the destruction. It brought together young men from across north India, ready to sacrifice their lives to undo a perceived wrong. Hindu supremacy was interwoven with the ordinary life of democratic politics—a gathering of citizens around a public issue.

And even those far from the ruins of the Babri mosque were not immune to the message. My next-door neighbour and friend in Delhi, an affable family man with a young daughter, handed us a present in the aftermath of the demolition of the mosque. It was a keychain. The keychain had the Hindu symbol of Om on one side and the message *'Garv se kaho hum Hindu hain'* ('Say with pride, you are a Hindu') on the other.

The ideological dimensions of Hindu supremacy are well-known and documented. But the focus on ideology is misleading. What such a focus misses are the passions of Hindu supremacy, and how they are entangled with the passions of democracy, and its promise of public participation in the life of the nation. The gist of our liberal critique of Hindu nationalism, which we repeat endlessly in front of the camera and in outraged editorials, is this: Hindu supremacy and democracy are incompatible because democracy is about plurality and diversity, whereas Hindu supremacy is about violence, homogeneity, and intolerance. But this ignores an important paradox. In analysing what they call 'New Hindutva', Hansen and Roy point out that Hindu nationalism, in its new avatar, 'simultaneously advances and violates ideas and practices of popular and constitutional democracy' (Hansen and Roy 2022, 2). What is lost in the binary of violence *versus* democracy is the question of participation: What words, technologies, and images allow the passions of Hindu supremacy to spread *across* region, caste, class, and language in India?

This is not a new question. What we in India call 'communalism' is better understood as a variant of far-right ethnic supremacist movements that have been popular in Europe since the nineteenth century (Leidig 2020). In the colonial period, this form of politics was used by a range of actors to shape a public (Freitag 1989) and create a people. The demolition of the Babri mosque was a sign that Hindu supremacy is more than electoral politics. Put differently, songs, images, and symbols, *and* shovels and pickaxes and hammers destroyed the mosque that day. The demolition was an effect of a network of words, images, media, and passions that set the stage, created the right mood, and produced a collective. Yes, it was illegal, but that is not why it was dangerous. If we keep our focus squarely on the law and the State, we will not understand why those who destroy mosques and lynch people from the minority communities receive a hero's welcome by their neighbours when they are released from prison on bail. The question of passion becomes even more pertinent in the present when the message of Hindu supremacy is disseminated on new and old media—television, WhatsApp, Twitter (now 'X'), YouTube—and produces publics that cannot be localised to a stable space and time, like Ayodhya.

The question, then, is not the older one of how Hindu nationalists can get away with breaking the law, but rather one of how they are able to turn Hindu supremacy into a viral phenomenon. How are they able to bring people together (and also, when do they fail to do so) and create a mood of victimhood, jubilation, pride, anger, and disgust that pervades contemporary India? What is it about the message of Hindu supremacy that makes it *persuasive* to large numbers of people across the social divisions of caste, language, class, region, and gender?

FROM FRINGE TO FABRIC

Hindu supremacy is no longer a 'fringe' phenomenon in India. Whether it is the German Ambassador visiting the Rashtriya Swayamsevak Sangh (RSS) and calling it the 'world's largest voluntary organization' (Bhatia 2019), or the ability of the RSS to get an ex-President to address its members (Kak Ramachandran 2017), our present moment is characterised by the hyper-visibility of Hindu supremacy in public life (Chatterjee 2023). From the WhatsApp messages that ascribe all the ills of modern India to Jawaharlal Nehru's treasonous politics, the public movement to rename Indian cities with 'Hindu' names, to the movement to prevent girls and young women in hijab from attending schools and colleges, it is uncontroversial to say that the space occupied by the RSS is no longer that of a few men dressed in khaki shorts doing morning exercises in the neighbourhood park.

Hindu supremacy was always a war waged for the total transformation of Indian society, which is only possible by capturing public attention, taking over public space, and gaining public legitimacy. The goals of Hindu supremacy are not limited to the career of the political party, the BJP. Rather, for Hindu supremacists, the State is a means to an end. If Hindu supremacy is no longer a fringe aspect of Indian society and politics, and neither does it stand in opposition to the State anymore, then what is it? It is slowly becoming a part of the fabric of everyday life in India. I borrow the idea of fabric from the German philosopher Ludwig Wittgenstein, who suggested that our doubts and certainties about the social world are not isolated facts, but part of a larger weave and comprise a form of life.[5] By 'form of life', I mean ideas of what counts, who counts, what is reasonable, what is open to suspicion, and what must be outside doubt. To understand the transformation of the fabric of Indian society, we must look beyond violence and elections. Despite electoral wins and losses, we are being trained in the language of Hindu supremacy, and it is happening in public, in malls, on the television, in schools and colleges, and on WhatsApp.

Seen in this light, Hindu supremacy is not concerned solely with the old questions around winning and losing elections, or communalism *versus* secularism, but is focused on creating a shared outlook about minorities and statecraft between Indians across caste, class, language, and region.

I would like to suggest that this is an experiment, one that we have seen before. Many will remember the laboratory of Hindutva — Gujarat. What were the experiments conducted in Gujarat after the pogrom in 2002? The pogrom did not end with attacking Muslims; it served as a catalyst for Hindu nationalists to weave Hindu supremacy into the language of the judges, journalists, public officials, artists, and writers. Soon it became a part of everyday life in Gujarat. The pogrom was the beginning of the creation of Muslims as a permanent minority (Mamdani 2020). All life in Gujarat would be organised along the lines of the majority *versus* the minority. In this sense, the vast infrastructure of Hindu supremacist organisations across the length and breadth of the country are not mere war machines. As I have shown elsewhere (Chatterjee 2018), the everyday life of Hindu supremacy in India goes beyond the pogrom; it works in the background of electoral politics to produce new crises, new attachments, new feelings.

The work of Hindu supremacy in India can no longer be reduced to the institutionalised riot system (Brass 2011). Instead, there is a wider struggle over public space (the construction of temples, memorials, statues, and the segregation of Muslims), public culture (campus life, banning the hijab, renaming cities), and everyday governance (to directly or indirectly influence local police, courts, and administration).

Over the past decade, I have realised that the challenge posed by the Gujarat pogrom in 2002 was not about exposing the horror of a state that facilitated a massacre of its own citizens, but to show how that violence became a catalyst for a new form of life—Hindu supremacy. How did Hindu supremacy in Gujarat become politics-as-usual? In this sense, the Gujarat model of governance is not a gimmick, but a world-making project; it is a project where anti-Muslim politics is fused with neoliberal policies, not as two separate entities moving on two parallel tracks but as part of a single shiny world. Gujarat is a reminder that Hindu supremacy can happily coexist with welfare schemes for the poor, mega infrastructure projects like the Sabarmati Riverfront, and heritage tourism that glorifies religious syncretism in the past even as the government actively polarises people along religious lines in the present. This is possible when the question of Hindu supremacy is open and public, and even minorities are forced to participate in it, for the sake of their lives and livelihood.

From Hollow Democracy to Democracy's Hollow

In a recent editorial in the *Hindustan Times*, Sonia Gandhi, the erstwhile leader of the Congress Party, which is currently facing an existential crisis following multiple defeats in national and regional elections, argued that 'India's hard-won democracy is being hollowed out' by the NDA government at the Centre (Gandhi 2020). Her critique of the government is familiar: stifling dissent, and the use of federal agencies to target the political opposition. While based on real and alarming facts about Indian politics, the idea that Hindu nationalists are hollowing out democracy is not helpful because Hindu supremacy is advancing in India through the infrastructure of courts, media, and electoral politics.

Rather, it is the nature of democracy to be 'hollow'. Perhaps it is even its strength, insofar as the struggle of democratic politics is a struggle between different actors to fill democracy's hollow. What is special about the current regime, then, is not that it is anti-democracy; Hindu supremacists are the first to defend elections, the Constitution, the independence of the courts, the value of the media, and the vigorous participation of the public in all things related to the State. The current Hindu nationalist regime is actually revealing the dark side of democracy, its underbelly, its potential to become, in the words of Alexis de Tocqueville, the tyranny of the majority.

Hindu supremacy is an attempt to capture democracy and its infrastructure (courts, media, elections, public culture) to fill the hollow inside democracy with the thoughts and images of a godlike leader and forms of anti-Muslim violence (like mob lynching and attacks on minorities), which can create a new permanent majority. B. R. Ambedkar had pointed out a crucial difference between political majorities, which are malleable, and communal majorities, which are permanent. The renaming of cities and streets, the construction of monuments and statues, and the new language of the State is placing Hindu supremacy at the heart of Indian democracy.

The ambition of this new politics is to produce a simple equation: Modi=Hindu=India=Nation=People. Once this equation becomes popular, anyone against Hindu supremacy is in danger of being pitted against the People/Nation. This strategy has worked in Gujarat. The rest, as we know, is history.

Beyond Indian Exceptionalism

There is something puzzling about how the world views India. Most publications that take stock of the current crisis of democracy across the world typically do not include India in the same list as countries where authoritarian rule is normalised, like Turkey, Brazil, the Philippines, and Hungary. This is the power of Indian exceptionalism—the idea that India's political history and cultural norms are somehow immune to the kind of ethnic majoritarianism flourishing in its neighbourhood in countries like Pakistan, Myanmar, and Sri Lanka. This is unhelpful because it isolates Hindu supremacy from supremacist movements elsewhere, like the US (White supremacy) and Sri Lanka (Sinhalese Buddhist supremacy).

The impression one gets from reading the mainstream media in Europe and the US is that Hindu supremacy in India is simply a rightward shift in Indian politics, the victory of one political ideology over another. If that were indeed the case, we could return to our old questions: How did secular India become so intolerant? When will the pressures of the economy force Hindu nationalists to adopt more moderate politics?

Even though these are important questions, they are firmly ensconced within the idea of Indian exceptionalism. It is this exceptionalism that leaves us baffled when we realise that every domain of contemporary life in India—architecture, education, cinema, culture, space, and media—is undergoing a radical transformation in which difference, debate, and resistance is becoming dangerous, futile, and irrelevant. In this context, we have no choice but to accept that Hindu supremacy has taken the shape of a State-sanctioned social and political movement in India. This means that we must begin the urgent task of learning from authoritarian transformations taking place in other parts of the world (like

Turkey and the US) and from places where majoritarianism has stabilised into an ordinary form of life and politics (like Sri Lanka). What experiments in participatory democracy—whether in the form of public protests, processions, public hearings, rallies, reading groups, associations at the neighbourhood level—can resist, stall, or interrupt the process of Hindu supremacy? How do we engage with large sections of Indian society—uncles, aunts, teachers, colleagues, and friends—who are increasingly attracted to and spreading Hindu supremacist messages and sentiments? How can we build coalitions between existing collectivities like the Dalit movement, feminist activists, student groups, and environmental groups? These are some of the questions posed by the rise of the new global right in India and beyond.

Notes

1. My title is inspired by the Russian Artist Collective, Chto Delat's installation titled, 'When we thought we had all the answers, life changed the questions'. In their art, they pose questions about forms of resistance to authoritarian politics in contemporary Russia. For more, see https://vimeo.com/151924730 (accessed December 2024).

2. I develop this concept, especially in the way it pertains to India, in Chatterjee (2019, 2023).

3. Raju Solanki exposed the hollowness of the Hindu-Muslim binary, showing the overwhelmingly large number of Dalits and lower castes imprisoned by the police in the aftermath of the riots. See Solanki (2013).

4. I have in mind things like the open intimidation of political opposition, threatening violence and chaos if challenged, the incitement to hatred, the closing of borders, and the demonisation of Mexicans, Muslims, and women.

5. For a discussion of this concept, see Grayling (2001, 97).

SELECT REFERENCES

Bhatia, Sidharth. 2019. 'The Cruel Irony of the German Ambassador's Visit to the RSS Headquarters'. *The Wire*, 20 July. Available at https://thewire.in/world/german-ambassador-walter-lindner-rss-headquarters (accessed December 2024).

Brass, P. R. 2011. *The Production of Hindu-Muslim Violence in Contemporary India*. Washington, DC: University of Washington Press.

Chatterjee, Moyukh. 2018. 'The Ordinary Life of Hindu Supremacy: In Conversation with a Bajrang Dal Activist'. *Economic and Political Weekly* 53 (4) (27 January). Available at https://www.epw.in/engage/article/ordinary-life-hindu-supremacy (accessed December 2024).

———. 2019. 'Beyond the Politics of Exposure: Notes on Violence and Democracy from the South'. *Violence and Democracy* 44–47, British Academy Report.

———. 2023. *Composing Violence: The Limits of Exposure and the Making of Minorities*. Durham: Duke University Press.

Chakrabarty, D. 2008. *Provincializing Europe: Postcolonial Thought and Historical Difference*. Princeton, NJ: Princeton University Press.

Freitag, S. B. 1989. *Collective Action and Community: Public Arenas and the Emergence of Communalism in North India*. Berkeley: University of California Press.

Gandhi, Sonia. 2020. 'Indian Democracy is Being Hollowed Out'. *Hindustan Times*, 26 October. Available at https://www.hindustantimes.com/analysis/indian-democracy-is-being-hollowed-out/story-AvED52JaiKrJxBk2NI4kWN.html (accessed December 2024).

Grayling, Anthony C. 2001. *Wittgenstein: A Very Short Introduction*. Oxford: Oxford University Press.

Hansen, T. B., and S. Roy. 2022. 'What is New about "New Hindutva"?', in Thomas Blom Hansen and Srirupa Roy (eds), *Saffron Republic: Hindu Nationalism and State Power in India*. New Delhi: Cambridge University Press

Jain, Praveen. 2020. 'Unseen photos of how Babri Masjid demolition was planned and executed in 1992'. *The Print*, 5 August. Available at https://theprint.in/in-pictures/unseen-photos-of-how-babri-masjid-demolition-was-planned-and-executed-in-1992/474297/ (accessed December 2024).

Kak Ramachandran, Smriti. 2017. 'RSS Chief Mohan Bhagwat Meets President Pranab Mukherjee'. *Hindustan Times*, 17 June. Available at https://www.hindustantimes.com/india-news/rss-chief-mohan-bhagwat-meets-president-pranab-mukherjee/story-WoseSq5RehtiwPc5J2RqjK.html (accessed Decdmber 2024).

Leidig, Eviane. 2020. 'Hindutva as a Variant of Right-Wing Extremism'. *Patterns of Prejudice* 54 (3), 215–237.

Mamdani, M. 2020. *Neither Settler nor Native: The Making and Unmaking of Permanent Minorities*. Boston: Harvard University Press.

Patel, A., D. Padgaonkar, and B. G. Verghese. 2002. *Rights and Wrongs: Ordeal by Fire in the Killing Fields of Gujarat*. New Delhi: Editors Guild Fact Finding Mission Report.

Solanki, Raju. 2013. 'Blood under Saffron: The Myth of Dalit-Muslim Confrontation'. *Round Table India*, 22 July. Available at https://www.roundtableindia.co.in/blood-under-saffron-the-myth-of-dalit-muslim-confrontation/ (accessed December 2024).

Trouillot, M. R. 2003. 'Anthropology and the Savage Slot: The Poetics and Politics of Otherness', in *Global Transformations: Anthropology and the Modern World*, 7–28. New York: Palgrave Macmillan.

A Coda

Aruna Roy

Theory to Practice

The concepts—and names—of democracy and the constitution as a form of government originated in ancient Athens in 508 BCE. Democratic theory has battled different practices, from the days of the Greek city-states to contemporary democracies. The electoral system guarantees a basic political uniformity. Democracies continue to experiment with ways in which the complex process of governance addresses the delivery of equality in access and the use of power within theoretical frames. Theories contribute by capturing the essence of practice, and organising it into a pattern to allow other cultures and countries to draw their own lessons. The making of a policy or a law from sound practice enables a structure that can be used by different communities, systems, and governments to revive, reform, and change governance to deliver.

Democratic participation has to be understood in the context of the increasing movement of democratic leadership towards centralisation, despotism, and dictatorship, and in particular, its importance in putting an ethical and decentralised system into place, thereby building systems of transparency and accountability. Democracies also face crises in the takeover by theocratic systems. These crises then become the grounds for arguments for inequality.

Power, both economic and political, is getting concentrated into smaller units of control, leading to arbitrary decision-making. Such decision-making in a democratic structure is threatening the world with environmental hazards, injustice, and inequality. This challenges a fundamental tenet of democracy—the participation of the people.

The chapters in this volume have analysed how such a concentration of power can be countered theoretically by people's action. Given the perception that all theory begins with a cognitive understanding of reality, the invocation with which this volume begins reflects this basic connect.

Notes on the Contributors

MOYUKH CHATTERJEE is a Lecturer in the Department of Social Anthropology, University of Edinburgh. He is the author of *Composing Violence: The Limits of Exposure and the Making of Minorities* (2023). His work on law, violence, and justice has appeared in the *American Ethnologist, Law, Culture, and the Humanities, Distinktion: Journal of Social Theory*, and *Economic and Political Weekly*.

PEARL ELIADIS is Associate Professor (professional) at the Max Bell School of Public Policy at McGill University and a full member of the Centre for Human Rights and Legal Pluralism at the Faculty of Law. She is a lawyer in private practice as well, working mainly with governments and multilateral institutions as a senior advisor and consultant, and her research interests include the role of national institutions, human rights, and the relationship between law and public policy.

WAJAHAT HABIBUILLAH, a former civil servant of the J&K IAS cadre, was also India's first Chief Information Commissioner and Chair, National Commission for Minorities. He has served in different parts of the country and in Washington, D.C. He is the author of *My Kashmir: The Dying of the Light* (2011) and *My Years with Rajiv: Triumph and Tragedy* (2020). He works with NGOs on human rights, democratic functioning, and the need for bureaucratic accountability in a democracy.

JOHN HARRISS is Professor Emeritus of International Studies at Simon Fraser University, Vancouver, and currently an Adjunct Professor at Queen's University, Kingston, Ontario. He continues to study social and political change in India, and to take a keen interest in trends in international political economy.

PATRICK HELLER is the Lyn Crost Professor of Social Sciences and the Director of the Saxena Center for Contemporary South Asia at the Watson School for International and Public Affairs at Brown University. He holds a joint appointment in the Department of Sociology. Heller's main area of research is the comparative study of social inequality and democratic deepening, with a focus on India, Brazil, and South Africa.

T. M. THOMAS ISAAC is a two-time finance minister in the Government of Kerala, an academic and development activist focussed on development alternatives, democratic decentralisation, co-operatives, and public finance.

LUCILE MARTIN has worked as a development practitioner for the past fifteen years, in both civil society and public institutions, including in Afghanistan between 2012 and 2019, and in 2022–2023. Her research interests include governance, cultural transfers, gender and state/civil society relations.

PAULA MARTINS is Policy Lead and Programme Manager at the Association for Progressive Communications - APC. She engages in digital and human rights policy processes at the global level and helps to shape APC's responses to emerging tech policy trends. She is currently a doctorate candidate at the Faculty of Law, McGill University, and a fellow with the Centre for Protecting Women Online at Open University.

VIPUL MUDGAL heads Common Cause, known for its high-impact PILs and reports on police accountability. He has served as the Editor of *Hindustan Times* in Jaipur and

Notes on the Contributors

Lucknow, Regional Editor of *Asia Times* in Bangkok, and as a BBC journalist in London and Delhi. His work is on the intersections of media, democracy, and political violence.

PRABHAT PATNAIK has taught at the University of Cambridge, UK, and at Jawaharlal Nehru University, New Delhi, where he currently holds the title of Professor Emeritus. His publications include The Value of Money (2008), Re-envisioning Socialism (2011), A Theory of Imperialism (with Utsa Patnaik, 2016), Capital and Imperialism (with Utsa Patnaik, 2021) and Beyond Liberalism (2024).

OTSI'TSAKÉN:RA (CHARLES PATTON) retired from teaching Kanien'kéha (Mohawk language) immersion in Kahnawá:ke. He now attends conferences in Montreal to open the gathering, using these words to bring all minds together as one. He is involved in repatriation of Kanien'kéhá:ka (Mohawk Nation) ancestral remains and ceremonial objects that are being held in museums and universities in Montreal, is continually involved in Kanien'kéhá:ka ceremonies, and works with Kahnawá:ke schools.

SUCHI PANDE is Scholar in Residence, Accountability Research Center, School of International Service, American University, Washington, D.C.

NANDINI RAMANUJAM is a Full Professor (Professional) at Faculty of Law, McGill University, where she co-directs the Centre for Human Rights and Legal Pluralism. Her teaching and research interests include law and development, the rule of law, economic justice, food security, as well as the exploration of interconnections between field-based human rights work and theoretical discourses.

VIVEK RAMKUMAR is Chief of Staff at Amnesty International USA. He is responsible for operationalising AIUSA's strategic framework and for overseeing the operational heartbeat that helps ensure organisational effectiveness. Prior to joining AIUSA, Vivek worked at the International Budget Partnership for more than seventeen years, progressing to the position of Senior Director of Policy. He also worked in India as a community organiser with the MKSS.

ARUNA ROY is a sociopolitical activist and co-founder and working member of the Mazdoor Kisan Shakti Sangathan (MKSS) since 1990. She previously worked with the SWRC Barefoot College (1975-83), and prior to that, was in the Indian Administrative Service from 1968 to 1975. She was presented with the Ramon Magsaysay Award for community leadership in 2000.

INAYAT SABHIKHI is an organiser and researcher with over a decade of experience with social movements in India and the United States, related to social welfare, the right to information, and platform accountability.

SOHINI SENGUPTA is Assistant Professor at the Tata Institute of Social Sciences, Mumbai. Her work centres on the ways in which social policies and practices intersects with the beings and doings of indigenous tribal peoples, women, and digital communities, to shape their livelihoods, cultures and identities.

RAJESH VEERARAGHAVAN is an Associate Professor, School of Foreign Service, Georgetown University. His research focuses on the politics of technology and development, particularly how marginalised communities engage with digital systems in agriculture, welfare, and governance. He is the author of *Patching Development: Information Politics and Social Change in India* (2021) and co-founder of the non-profit Digital Green.

SHIV VISVANATHAN is currently Professor at Jindal Global Law School, Sonipat and Director, Centre for the Study of Knowledge Systems, O.P Jindal Global University. An interdisciplinary thinker and prolific writer, his wide interests range from cognitive justice, urban studies, the sociology of corruption and ethics, the sociology and philosophy of science, history of technology and traditional knowledge, social movements, globalisation, to the culture and politics of ecology. He is the author of *Organizing for Science* (1985), *A Carnival for Science* (1997), and *Theatres of Democracy* (2016).

Index

Constitution of Afghanistan
1964 116
2004 115, 116
   declaration of a state of
     emergency 115
2014 Annual Convention of
   Information Commissions
   280
2018 UNESCO report 243
   Journalism, Fake News and
     Disinformation 243
2019 TED talk 251
   'Facebook's Role in
     Brexit—and the Threat to
     Democracy' 251
2020 World Economic Outlook
   193

Access to Information Law 124
Accountability 19, 23, 25–27,
   56, 63, 79–80, 99–104,
   110–111, 116, 120, 123, 127,
   140–143, 149, 159, 170, 194,
   196, 198, 200, 202, 210, 221,
   223, 228–229, 257, 273, 275,
   280, 299
   bureaucratic 27, 99
   continuous 25, 26
   democratic 103, 111

social 210
Action plan 68, 273
Activism 166, 230, 288
Administration
   district 267, 271–272
   state 275
Administrative Reforms
   Committee (ARC) 62, 65
Aesthetics 184, 189
Afghan civil society 102, 119
Afghanistan, Islamic Republic
   of 99–104, 106–110, 114–116,
   119, 122–127
   2019 presidential election
     106
   adoption of the new
     Constitution in 2004 107
   armed conflict 102
   citizens 104
   women 122
   collapse of the 105–106, 120,
     126
   COVID-19 in 100–101, 106,
     108, 114
   cultural change in 109
   democratic initiatives 100
   Emergency Committee
     for the Prevention of
     COVID-19 116

Index

governance mechanisms in 101
High-Level Emergency Committee 115
implications for participatory democracy in 102
migrants 103
National Unity Government 109
participatory democracy in 102
peace in 106
post-pandemic future of 101
presidential decree 115
sanitary, humanitarian, and economic crises 102
social and economic conditions 103, 111
State-Civil Society Relations under the 109
Taliban administration 109, 111
Taliban takeover 105, 111, 117, 120, 122
Afghanistan, Government of the Islamic Republic of 99–104, 106–110, 114–116, 119, 122–127
Afghanistan Independent Human Rights Commission 122
Africa 6, 21, 40, 44, 198
African-Americans 42, 287
Agency(ies) 23, 26, 51, 60, 77, 84, 88, 102, 140, 145, 149, 151, 156–157, 168, 175–176, 195, 198, 208, 210, 238, 242, 247, 294

Age of reaction 5, 17–18, 28
Agriculture xiv, xvii, 64, 68, 171, 177–178, 186, 188
Ambedkar, Babasaheb B. R. xvi, xvii, 20, 269, 271, 294
American
 democracy 3
 political parties 207
Annan, Kofi, the seventh Secretary-General of the United Nations 281
Anti-capitalism 39, 43
Anti-corruption 109, 192
Anti-dam movement 171
Anti-democratic practices 221
Anti-poverty programmes 60
AP Exata 77, 78
Appellate Tribunals 63
Approaches 52, 56, 67–68, 101–102, 118, 121–124, 127, 142, 149–151, 153, 200, 279
 experimental 121
 Gandhi's 153
 human rights-based 101–102, 122–123
 multi-sectoral 68
 participatory 101–102, 123, 149–150, 151
Artificial intelligence 86, 244
Association for Democratic Reforms (ADR) 203, 240
Atlantic, The 75, 246
Audit(s) 7, 23–27, 51, 64, 109, 140–142, 154, 158, 170, 184, 195–198, 208, 210–211, 238, 242, 247, 277, 280, 294
 agencies 195, 198
Authoritarian
 regimes 3, 248

rule 18, 100, 152, 288, 295
Authoritarianism 4, 42, 53, 86, 99, 281
  rise and spread of 4, 99
Autocracy(ies) 3, 42, 237
  electoral 3, 42
Autonomy 17, 51, 63, 65, 88

Babri mosque, Ayodhya, demolition of the 288–290
Balwant Rai Mehta Committee 268–69
Bangladesh 251
Bangladeshis 226
Basic services 56, 105
Below the poverty line 103
Beneficiary committees 56, 63, 67
Beneficiary selection 63, 66
Bharatiya Janata Party (BJP) 201, 203, 208–209, 240, 246, 248–249, 253, 255, 288, 291
Bhilwara Principles of Social Accountability 210
Big money, unaccountable 201, 208
Bihar 182, 274
Biotechnology 177, 188
Bolsonaro, Jair, Brazilian President 74, 76–79, 81–82, 85, 90, 245
  administration 74
  electoral campaign of 2018 74
  public relations strategy 81
  statements on the pandemic 76
  use of disinformation 74, 77, 82

Brazil xv, 4–6, 17, 22, 25, 42, 44, 72, 74–76, 78, 80–81, 90, 126, 152, 196–198, 245, 247, 295
  2011 Freedom of Information Act 79
  2018 Brazilian elections 75, 247
  2018 presidential elections 75
  COVID-19 health crisis in 76
  military dictatorship 74
  participatory budgeting model 196
  patterns of disinformation in 78
  Provisional Measure 928 80
  public participation in 197
Brazilian Access to Information Forum 80
Brazilian National Congress 77
Brazilian National Council for Human Rights 81
Brazilian Press Association 82
Brexit 19, 247, 251, 288
Britain 39, 271
Budget/Budgeting 6, 25, 43, 52–53, 56–57, 67, 120, 152, 191–92, 194–201, 276–277
Bureaucracy 9, 26–27, 56, 139, 227, 270, 272–273, 276

Cambridge Analytica 247, 249, 251
Campaign(s) xviii, 3, 7, 25, 43, 49–50, 56, 58, 62, 64–65, 68, 74–76, 83, 109, 143, 170, 202–203, 209, 212, 220–21,

224, 226, 230, 236, 239–240, 242, 247–249, 253, 255–256, 280, 285
  2014 election 280
  expenditure 236
  finance 202, 203, 242
  people's 7, 25, 65
  People's Plan/Planning 7, 43, 49–50
  social media 248–249, 253
Canada 1, 2, 36, 125, 192
Capabilities 23, 29, 87, 91
Capital xiv, 22, 31, 34, 38–39, 88, 207, 249
  concentration of 31
  private ownership of 34
Capital and labour 38–39
Capitalism xiii–xiv, 3, 5–6, 31, 34, 39–44, 147, 245
  neoliberal xiv, 3, 40, 42
Cases
  decentralisation experiment 53
  Kerala experiment 52
Caste xvi, 4, 21–22, 50, 147, 221, 250, 290–292
  upper- 221, 250
Censorship 82, 246, 250, 255
Central Information Commission 210, 280
Centralisation xvi, xvii, 5, 18, 36, 279, 299
Central/Union government 267, 276–277
Challenges xviii, 2, 5–7, 9, 19–22, 27–28, 40, 42, 51, 54, 61–62, 65–66, 80, 83–84, 86, 101, 109, 114, 117, 119–120, 127, 140–142, 144–145, 150, 155–156, 159, 168, 170–171, 175, 179, 182–183, 187, 192, 196–198, 211, 254, 258, 266, 273, 279, 293, 300
Child/Children 15, 64, 104–105, 176, 226
  development 64
  labour 105
  rights 104
Chile 6, 192
China 31, 106
Citizen/Citizenry 4–5, 18, 20–25, 27–29, 33–34, 37–38, 43–44, 54, 57, 63–64, 67, 72–73, 80, 84, 99–100, 102, 104, 106, 109, 116, 118, 124–125, 139–144, 147, 152–153, 156, 158–159, 166–167, 171–173, 176, 178, 187, 196–197, 199, 219–223, 227, 229, 258, 267, 273, 275, 280–281, 288–289, 293
  as a consumer of knowledge 166
  informed 4, 72, 144, 281
  marginalised 4, 139–42, 153, 156, 159
  participation 43, 84, 99, 125
  voices and needs of 102, 199
  vulnerable 106
Citizen's Charter 63, 67
Citizenship 17, 19, 31, 33, 52, 165, 167–174, 187, 190
  inventive 190
  performative acts/nature of 168, 170
  practice of 168
  quality of 52
  reciprocal richness of 169

values of 33
Citizenship Amendment Act
 (CAA) 19, 24
Civil society 2, 4, 17, 21–25, 27,
 38, 40–41, 52, 73, 76, 80, 82,
 88, 101–103, 106, 108–111,
 113–114, 116–125, 127, 140,
 142, 147, 159, 175–176, 198,
 228–229, 241, 248, 257, 285
  ability of 109, 116, 119
  groups 73, 82, 122, 285
  participation 25, 121
  representatives 117, 124
  role of 4, 101, 120
  subaltern 22
Civil society organisations
 (CSOs) 22, 24–25, 28, 76, 80,
 101–102, 106, 110–111, 113,
 117–121, 140, 159, 241, 248,
 257
Class(es) xvi, xviii, 4, 18–21,
 32, 39, 41, 59, 145, 147–148,
 169, 180, 192, 290–292
Climate change 83, 184
Coalition(s) 27–28, 38, 40, 75,
 296
Cobrapost 239–240
Coding Rights 82
Collective action 28, 52, 73
Commission for Bimolecular
 Engineering 185
Commitment(s) 24, 26, 34, 117,
 122, 258, 269, 280
Committee on Decentralisation
 of Powers 62, 64
Committee on Revitalisation of
 Panchayati Raj Institutions
 for Democracy and
 Development 270

Communalism 269, 290, 292
Communication 8, 74, 78, 86,
 88–89, 144, 152, 156, 171,
 173, 175, 184, 204, 220–221,
 223, 228, 248
  strategies 74, 78, 248
Communist Party of India
 (Marxist) (CPI[M]) 22
Community(ies) xiii, xvi–xvii,
 6–7, 34, 50, 60, 63, 66,
 102–103, 116, 118–119,
 121–122, 124–127, 149–150,
 171–174, 180, 182, 184, 188,
 191, 195, 197, 199–200, 207,
 220, 222, 226, 244, 269–270,
 273–275, 281, 290, 299
  impacted 6, 195, 200
  international 102, 122, 127
  local 103, 125, 197
  marginalised 116, 125, 149
  micro-targeting of 220
  organisations 60, 66
  vulnerable 118, 121, 124,
   226
Company(ies) 32, 84, 178,
 202–203, 205, 207–209,
 211–212, 229, 238–240,
 242, 244–245, 251–253,
 256–258
  annual profit and loss
   statements 203, 205, 211
  domestic 203, 205, 212
  foreign 202–203, 205,
   207–208, 212
  media 238–240, 242, 244,
   253
  private 229, 240
  shell 203, 205–256
  social media 244, 253

Congress party 241, 249, 253, 293
Consensus 8, 68, 144, 152–153, 257, 272–273
Consent 8, 147, 149, 156, 243
Conspiracy 83, 85, 89, 245, 286
  theories 83, 85
Constituent Assembly 271
Constitutional
  bodies 116
  guarantees 113
  normative pretensions 25
  oversight 202
  protections 20, 118
  provisions 108
  requirements 99, 107
  values 258
Constitutional Amendments 23, 50–51, 268, 276
  73rd amendment 50–51, 266, 268, 273, 277–278
  74th amendment 50–51, 266, 268, 273, 277
Constitutional democracy 23, 290
Constitution of Afghanistan 107, 115
  Article 79 107–08, 115
  Article 89 108
  Article 121 107
  Article 143 108
Constitution of India 23, 50–51, 62–64, 201, 203, 268–269, 273–278
  amendments to the 23, 50, 62–64, 201, 203, 268, 274, 276
  Article 40 269
  Article 243 274–275

Containment measures 103, 115
Contemporary democracies 21, 299
Content 73, 75–78, 83–84, 86–87, 90, 169, 208, 220–221, 228–230, 238, 243, 252, 254–255, 257
  curated 220
  discriminatory and harmful 87
  divisive 84
  illegal 254
  moderation 86, 90, 228
  political 252
  social media 229
  sources of 230
  'viral' 221
Contestation 54, 140, 156, 159–160
Controversy(ies) 75, 78, 176–177, 181, 185–186, 227
  periodic 227
  technological 176, 181
Co-optation 81, 159
Coordination 36, 43, 88, 90, 110
  failures of 36
Corruption 5, 24, 61, 67, 76, 102, 109, 116, 143, 159, 169, 192–193, 209, 242, 258, 267, 281, 286
Counter-narratives 73, 88
Countries/States
  actions 140–141
  apparatus 42, 52
  democratic 52, 141, 257
  fragile 114, 287
  machinery 26, 27

power xv, 41, 210
powerful 42, 73
responsibility 79, 226
vulnerable 103
COVID-19 pandemic xvii, 5–6, 8, 31–37, 40, 42, 74, 76–82, 89–91, 100–108, 110–111, 113–121, 123, 125–127, 191–193, 200, 204, 220, 226, 280
  consequences of the 33, 193
  crisis 35–36, 76, 78, 80–81, 89, 106, 121, 200
  deaths 79, 90
  emergency measures 100–101
  governance 102, 111, 114
  impact of the xvii, 76, 81, 104, 117
  lockdown 32, 115, 226
  political manipulation of 106
  quarantine 5, 77, 116
  restrictions 115–16, 280
  spread of the 76, 79, 89, 115, 119
Crimes 67, 115, 220, 229
Culture(s) 2, 77, 110, 119, 152, 171–174, 286, 293–295
  public 286, 293–294
Cyber
  attacks 89, 229
  troops 247–248
Cyberspace 223, 255

Dalit(s) 2–3, 42, 211, 296
Dangerous Speech Project (DSP) 250–251

Data 78–79, 103, 125, 143, 172, 194, 199, 223, 245, 247, 254–255
Decentralisation xvi–xviii, 23, 43, 50–54, 57–62, 64–68, 74, 273
  democratic 50–51, 54, 57–58, 60, 62, 65–66
  forms of 23, 52
  programme 50, 53
Decision-making 20, 25, 29, 43, 49–50, 57, 102, 110, 119, 150, 173, 189, 195, 198–200, 223, 275, 300
  process of 20, 275
  public 49, 119
Delegitimisation 90
Delhi High Court 201, 203
Deliberation(s) 1, 3, 18, 26, 49–50, 54, 66, 83, 85, 142, 151–56, 198, 219, 229
Deliberative spaces 156–58
Democracy(ies) xiii–xviii, 1–9, 17–28, 34, 36–44, 49, 52–53, 55–57, 72–74, 85–86, 88, 90–91, 99, 101–103, 107, 109, 114, 116–117, 119, 121, 125–127, 143–144, 149, 151–152, 154, 165–166, 169–171, 173–174, 179–180, 185, 189–190, 197–198, 201, 208, 210, 219–223, 229–230, 236–237, 239, 242, 245, 251, 254, 256–258, 270–271, 279–282, 284–290, 294–296, 299–300
  crisis of 221, 295
  deepening of 42–43
  deliberative 57, 151–52, 154

electoral 5, 18, 20, 44
foundations of 5, 28
liberal 3, 5, 42, 256
local 23, 25
practitioners of 2, 237
Democratic
authority 18–19
deepening 20–21, 42
deficits 101, 115
governance 7, 100, 282
institutions 5, 7, 53, 73, 83, 90, 100, 106, 221, 236–37, 243
participation 5, 45, 117, 220
political collectivities 38–39
practice 28, 198, 221
processes 22, 72, 74, 83, 99, 117, 223
society 6, 34, 40, 44
space 54, 68, 85
structures 44, 300
systems 117, 196, 199, 237
theory 2, 4, 7, 198
Democratisation 51, 54, 90, 153, 169, 219
Department of Public Policy (DAPP) 75, 77
Despotism 23, 299
Detention 116, 119, 122
arbitrary 116, 122
Development 1, 21, 23, 31, 37–38, 40, 44, 51–56, 61, 64–66, 86, 99, 109, 118, 120–121, 123, 127, 139–140, 143, 149–151, 172, 175, 196, 210, 220, 256, 266, 268–270, 273, 275–278, 280
Dialect(s) 169, 176–177, 180–181

Dialogue 1–3, 8, 90, 173, 179, 181–182, 189, 227
Dictatorship 74, 299
Digital
age 75, 87
platforms 236–237, 243, 255–257
technology(ies) 32, 86–87, 223
Digital democracy 219
Digital media 230, 235, 237, 245, 250
Digitalisation 86, 222
Disaster(s) 58, 68, 108, 144, 171, 184, 245
management 58, 68
natural 108, 245
Discrimination xvi, 41, 67, 113, 123, 125, 250
Disinformation and misinformation 4–5, 74–79, 82–84, 86–88, 91, 220, 224, 235–236, 243–244, 247, 253–255
use of 74–75, 77, 82
Dissent 2, 4–5, 8, 49, 155, 182, 237, 245, 294
political 237, 245
Distortion 73–74, 151
District Rural Development Agencies (DRDAs) 65, 276–79
abolition and merger of 278
Distrust 74, 87, 223, 226
Diversity 54, 87, 173, 176–178, 181, 188, 289
Dominant groups 19, 24
Donations 201–203, 205, 207–211

anonymous 202–203
by foreign companies 207
political 202–203
private 208
Donor(s) 52, 102, 104, 109–110, 120, 126, 201–202, 206–209, 212
  foreign 52, 201, 206, 212
  international 104, 120
Drinking water 60, 68

Economic
  consequences 126, 193
  crisis xiv, 104
  democracy 36
  gains 244
  groups 21
  growth 31, 272
  life 117
  trends 5, 34, 42
Economy(ies) xvii, 19, 21, 34–39, 42, 105, 168–69, 171, 186, 193, 256, 258, 295
  capitalist 37, 42
Ecuador 6, 192
Editorial
  discretion 238
  freedom 242
  space 238
Editors' Guild of India 242
Education 23, 25, 33, 44–45, 56, 59, 61, 67, 104–105, 123–124, 152, 169, 194, 207, 244, 295
Election Commission (EC) 64, 202–203, 211, 236, 240, 271
Election(s) 3–4, 23–25, 44, 49–50, 64, 73, 75–76, 90, 106, 121, 199, 201, 208–209, 212, 220–222, 225–226, 235–237, 239–241, 243, 246–247, 249, 251–258, 266, 268–271, 273, 276, 280, 285–286, 292–294
  campaigns 212, 226, 256, 285
  expenditures 208, 256
  free and fair 237, 251
  national 208, 240, 247, 253, 280
  Panchayat 270
Electoral
  accountability 19
  bonds 202–203, 205, 208–211
  gains 7, 239
  politics 286, 290, 292, 294
  system 22, 270, 299
Electoral democracy 5, 18, 20, 44
Emergency(ies) 36, 81, 89–90, 100–103, 107–108, 111–116, 120, 124–125, 193, 200
  formal state of 108, 112
  legislation 100, 107–108, 115
  measures 100–101, 112, 124–125, 193
  responses 111
Employment 32, 40, 77, 170, 266
Empowerment 51–52, 60, 139, 142, 151, 156, 184
Engagement 21, 24, 72, 84, 90, 102, 111, 118, 120, 123, 125, 127, 159, 166, 185, 192, 195, 198–200
  modes of 102, 120, 125, 127
Environmental
  concerns 100

hazards 300
   sustainability 36
Epistemic
   brokerage 177, 181
Epistemology 171, 174, 189
Equality xvii, 6, 8, 18–21,
   34, 49, 109, 122, 152, 167,
   169–170, 299
   political 18–21
Equity 8, 33, 52, 109
Ethics 170, 174, 177, 179,
   181–182, 184, 189, 254, 257
Europe 21–22, 39, 287, 290,
   295
   post-World War II 21
   socialist parties in 22
European Union 25, 244
European Union's Independent
   and High-Level Group's
   report of 2018 244
Exceptionalism 288, 295
Expenditure(s) 33, 36, 58, 191,
   202, 208–209, 211, 236, 240,
   256–257
Exploitation xvi, 49, 104, 143,
   145, 147, 150, 269

Facebook 32, 75–76, 78, 84–85,
   224–226, 245–247, 251–253,
   255
   partisan public policy 252
   questionable role in the
     Indian elections 253
Fake news 75–76, 82, 85,
   235, 237, 243–247, 249–250,
   252–255
Fake news and hate speech 252
Farmers 124, 189, 228, 241
Fascism xv, xvii, 5, 17

Finance xvi, 33, 50, 62, 65, 201
Finance Bill 201
Financial
   authority 269
   crisis of 2008 35
   gains 245, 252
   governance 256
   institutions 35, 200
   procedures 66
   repository 269
   transaction 243
Fiscal
   deficits 37
   exemptions 81
   policy 6
   transparency code 196
Five-Year Plan 54, 60, 62
   13th Plan 60
   Ninth Plan 54, 62
Flexibility 33, 200, 277
Folklore 171, 180, 184, 189
Food 1, 11–13, 32, 44–45, 103,
   105, 168–69, 177, 182, 187,
   227
   insecurity 103, 105
Foreign Contributions
   Regulation Act (FCRA) 201,
   203–205, 210
Foreign funding architecture
   205, 206
Forest Rights Act of 2006 45
Formal electoral democracy 5,
   18
France xv, 6, 192
Fraternity 20, 258
Freedom of Information Act
   79–80
   restrictions imposed on the
     80

Freedom(s) xv, 5, 8, 29, 34–35, 37, 43, 49, 64, 82, 86, 87, 91, 112–114, 117–118, 167, 222, 228–230, 242, 250, 257–258, 269, 278
  absolute 64
  democratic 43, 230
  fundamental 118
  of association and assembly 114
  of expression 8, 49, 82, 86, 113–114, 117, 228, 250, 257–258
  of information 79–80, 91
  of speech 229–230, 258
Fundacao Getulio Vargas DAPP (FGV DAPP) 75, 77
Fund/funding xvi, 50, 52, 54, 57, 65, 118, 120, 143, 186, 191, 195, 197, 200–206, 208–212, 256, 266–267, 275–279
  Central/Union government 267, 276
  devolution of 50, 54, 57
  foreign 201, 204–06
  government 205, 276
  judicious use of 200
  political 209–12
Fundraising 205, 208–209

Gandhi, Indira 266
  garibi hatao 266
Gandhi, Mahatma 153, 269, 278
  ashram 153–154, 179
  commitment to the ideal of *Purna Swaraj* 269
  deliberative process 153

Gandhi, Rajiv, Prime Minister of India 267–268, 270, 273, 275, 278
  assessment of corruption 267
  vision of instituting local self-government 278
Gandhi's model 153
Gandhi, Sonia 27, 293
Gender xvi, 67, 105, 225
Germany xv, 36, 254
Girls 105, 122, 250, 291
Global
  digital platforms 236, 256
  disinformation disorder 236
  governance gap 100
  growth rate 193
Globalisation 19, 36, 51
Global South 19, 247, 287
Governance 7, 20, 44, 53, 62, 64–65, 91, 99–102, 108, 111, 113–114, 117–124, 126–127, 139, 144, 158, 169–171, 223, 256–258, 266–267, 271–275, 279–282, 286, 293, 299
  effective 118, 223
  good 108, 114, 119–20, 123, 127, 273
  participatory approaches to 101–02
Government of Brazil 74, 80
Government of India 228, 275–76
Government(s)
  actions 79, 107, 142
  authoritarian 4
  budgets 191, 195
  competence of 36
  directives 228
  importance of 119

investments 58, 194
local 23, 54–55, 63, 111, 268, 272
records 141–142, 145–146, 156
representatives 110–111, 120
restructuring the system of 273
ruling 205, 209, 211
state 58, 65, 227, 272, 278
United Progressive Alliance (UPA) 25, 45, 273
Gram Swaraj 269, 279
Grants 58, 65, 143, 204, 210
  discretionary 65
  non-plan 58
  subcontracting 204
Gross Domestic Product (GDP) 33, 275
Gujarat 286, 292–94

Habermasian public sphere 152–153, 158
Haiti 6, 192
Hate speech 87, 228, 235–237, 249–252, 254–255, 284
Hatred xiv, xv, 4, 247, 251, 286
Health 23, 25, 36, 44, 56, 58–59, 61, 73, 76, 79–80, 89–90, 100–102, 104–105, 108, 112–115, 117, 119–120, 123, 166, 169, 171, 191, 193–194, 221, 244
  concerns 120
  crisis 76, 79, 89–90
  emergencies 108, 113
  infrastructures 102
  services 59, 104
  system 58, 105
Healthcare 32–33, 36, 40, 58, 68, 105, 207
  coverage 33
  pre- and post-natal 105
  public provisioning of 40
Hegemony 20, 147
Hidden transcripts 146, 154–155
Hijab 291, 293
Hindu
  agenda 239
  majority 286
  nationalism 289–290
  nationalists 286, 290, 292, 294–295
Hindustan Times 225, 246, 293
Hindu supremacist(s) 288–289, 292, 296
  messages and sentiments 296
  organisations 292
Hindu supremacy 286–287, 289–296
  hyper-visibility of 291
  passions of 289–90
Hindu, The 204, 241
Hindutva xv, 20, 240, 290, 292
Hospitals 37, 56, 64, 258
Households 33, 60, 103–105
Housing 44, 60
Human
  capabilities 29
  suffering 5, 33, 226
  welfare 34
Humanitarian
  aid 105
  organisations 115
Human rights
  abuse 251

committees 125
fundamental 237
implications 101
international law 108, 116, 127
monitoring and reporting 126
norms 102, 113, 122
violations 122, 126
Human Rights Watch 105, 117, 122
Hungary xv, 198, 295
Hunger xiv, 32, 178, 186, 238

Identity(ies) 41–42
  -based groups 147
  exclusionary 42
  nationalist 17
  struggles 88
Ideology(ies) 147, 179, 246, 288–289, 295
  nationalist 179
  political 246, 295
  power of 147
Immigrants 19, 222
Impeachment 75, 82, 237, 284–286
Incentives 40, 206–208
Income 36, 40, 85, 202–204, 207–208, 211, 240, 266
  basic 36, 40
  minimum 40
  per capita 240
  sources of 202
India
  1971 elections 266, 276
  1989 elections 268
  2009 parliamentary election 240–241
  2014 national elections 246, 253
  2019 national elections 208, 240, 246, 256–257
  Congress government 266
  cyber troops 247–48
  Hindu supremacist government 288
  Manmohan Singh government 273
  Narasimha Rao government 274
  national elections in 247
  National Front government 268
  NDA government 294
  per capita income 240
  political development 266
  political history 295
  public participation in 197, 266
  RTI struggle in 168
  social audit model 197
  UPA government in 25, 45
Indian
  democracy 222, 294
  elections 246, 249, 253
  exceptionalism 288, 295
  media 239
  politics 294–295
  society 49, 291–292, 296
  trade union federations 40
Indian Express, The 242, 256
Indian National Congress (INC) 201, 203, 253
Indigenous people 2–3, 287
  forcible dispossession of 3
Inequality(ies) 5, 20, 31, 33, 100, 104–105, 125–127, 146,

149–151, 156, 193, 195, 221–222, 300
  reduction of 222
  structural 125, 146, 149
Inequities 58, 104, 127, 193
Infodemic 89, 229
Information xv, 3–4, 24–25, 45, 72–75, 77, 79–80, 82–91, 105, 109–110, 118, 120, 124–125, 139–151, 155–160, 166–175, 181, 186, 189, 195, 200, 205, 209–212, 219–220, 225, 229, 235–237, 242–245, 253–256, 258, 266, 273, 275, 279–281, 285
  access to 109–110, 124, 140, 143, 146, 149, 156, 159, 173
  as a public good 91, 170
  deception 243, 254, 256
  disorders 3–4, 73, 75, 86–87
  manipulated 236–37
  official 80, 124
  provision of 145–146, 149
  requests 79–80
  role of 74, 143
Information and communication technologies 88–89
Information and social change 140
Information and State 141
Infrastructure 52, 58, 123, 125, 127, 272, 292–294
Innovations 34, 43, 174, 180–181, 183, 185, 189, 199
Institutional
  design 26, 202, 208
  framework 66, 270

integrity 210
mechanism 271
reforms 28, 142
Institutions xvi, 5, 7, 17–18, 35, 49–53, 61–62, 73–74, 76, 79, 83, 85, 90, 100, 102, 106, 108, 114, 118, 122, 140, 147, 153, 158–159, 166–167, 178–181, 187, 189, 195–197, 200, 204, 219, 221, 223, 236–237, 243, 256–258, 268, 270–271, 274–275, 279
  financial 35, 200
  formal or informal 108
  government xvi, 7, 195
  oversight 195–197
Integrity 109, 178, 210, 222, 250, 254
Interest groups 24, 178, 188
Intermediary(ies) 4, 140–141, 149–150, 155–160, 228
  role of 4, 141, 159
  third-party 158
International Budget Partnership (IBP) 194–195, 199
International Consortium of Investigative Journalists (ICIJ) 256
International Covenant on Civil and Political Rights (ICCPR) 108, 112–113, 116
  Article 4 108, 112
International human rights 108, 112–113, 116, 118, 122, 127
Internet
  access to the 85, 89, 120
  emancipatory power of the 86

governance of the 91
ownership and regulation 86
proprietary standards and
   platforms 87
use 85, 89
user-mediated 219–220, 226
Invention(s) 171, 179, 183
Invocations 2, 8, 300
I-PAC 249
Iran 103–104, 106
Iraq 6, 192

Jan sunwai 170, 181
Job(s) 11, 32–33, 244, 246
Journalism 243, 246, 286
Journalist unions 242
Judiciary(ies) 17, 80, 83, 107, 236, 255, 257, 280
   composition and functioning of the 107
   corrupt and inaccessible 257
   independence of the 17
Juggernaut 184, 188
Justice 5–6, 8, 20, 38, 74, 126, 165, 187–188, 191–192, 195, 200, 222, 254, 282, 286
   access to 126
   fiscal 6, 195, 200
Justice Srikrishna Commission 254

Karnataka 276–277
Kerala xvi, xviii, 1–2, 7–8, 22, 25, 38, 41, 43, 49–62, 65, 67
   achievements in decentralisation 61
   achievements in training 57
   decentralisation programme in 50, 53
   decentralised planning in 67
   Left in 51, 53
   local governments in 50
   non-Left governments in 53
   People's Campaign for Decentralised Planning 25
   poverty ratio in 61
   public health system in 58
   social infrastructure crisis in 52
Kerala Municipality Act of 1994 62
Kerala Panchayati Raj Act of 1994 62
Kerala PPC 53, 55–56
Knowledge xviii, 7, 89, 99, 141, 154, 165–67, 171–89, 220, 239, 250, 252, 281, 288
   forms of 173–174, 179
   politics of 171, 180
Knowledge and democracy(ies) 174, 179
Knowledge and technology 180–181, 184
Knowledge Panchayat(s) 165, 175–176, 179, 182–183, 187
   role of the 167
Kudumbasree 60, 67
Neighbourhood Groups (NHGs) 60–61, 66

Labour 27, 32–33, 38–40, 104–105
   low-skill 33
   manual 39
   market 33
   organisations 39

Land 23, 60, 68, 143, 172
  management 23
  records 143
Languages 1, 52, 56, 124, 166, 174–177, 180–181, 183–184, 188, 225, 241, 250, 285, 290–292, 294
  diversity of 176
  oral 175–176
Law xv, 5, 17, 20, 27, 50–51, 61–63, 86, 99, 108–110, 112–113, 116, 123–124, 127, 141–142, 171, 177, 201, 203–204, 209–211, 223, 228, 230, 246–247, 251, 254, 256–257, 273, 277, 280, 282, 290, 299
  enforcement agencies 210
  international 99, 228
Learning 61, 75, 169–170, 184–185, 295
  process 169–170
Lebanon 6, 192
Legal
  frameworks 26, 86, 102
  standards and principles 87, 114
  statutes 230
Legality 112–113, 116
Legislation 7, 25, 27, 63, 79, 100, 107–110, 115, 141, 171, 257, 273
  emergency 100, 107–108, 115
Legislations 25, 27, 79, 100, 107–108, 110, 115, 141, 171, 257, 273
  anachronistic 63
  rights-based 7

Legislative
  amendment 62
  framework 111, 275
  oversight 100, 113
  privilege 210
Legitimacy 4, 20, 29, 42, 104, 110, 112, 126, 196, 221, 227, 291
  assessment of the 112
  crisis of 221
  normative 20
  public 291
Legitimation, crisis of 222
LGs 53, 55, 58–61, 63–65, 68
  finances for the 65
  leadership of 64
  legal entitlement of 63
  performance of the 61
  resolutions of the 63
Liberal democracy index 42
Liberalism 34
Liberty(ies) 20, 33, 100, 258
Lie(s) 67, 74, 159, 235–236, 245, 253
  machines 236, 253
  power of 245
Linguistic Survey of India 175
Livelihoods 31–32
Living
  conditions 222
  standards 40, 61, 193
Local
  planning 66, 67
  self-government xvi, 7, 269, 273, 278
Local governance 7, 65
Local governments 50–51, 53–54, 61, 64, 68
  allocation to the 54

Majoritarianism 5, 182, 189, 295–296
Majority versus the minority 292
Malfeasance 24, 63
Manipulated information, features of 236–237
Marginalisation 58, 123, 126
Marginalised
 groups 140, 146, 149, 151, 154, 158
 people 99, 116
 populations 139
 voices 155
Market economy 34–35, 38
Marketing 208, 221, 223, 238, 245, 257
Market(s) 19, 32–36, 38–40, 42, 52, 86, 228–229, 239, 243
 fundamentalism 35–36, 39, 42, 86
 stock 32, 239, 243
 suppression of 35
Mazdoor Kisan Shakti Sangathan (MKSS) 24–25, 156–170, 189–190, 197, 273
McGill University's Institute for the Study of International Development (ISID) 1, 99, 109–110, 116–119, 124–126
Media xv, 4, 73, 75–78, 81–86, 89–90, 122, 147, 191, 208, 219–224, 226–230, 235–251, 253, 255, 258, 285–287, 290, 294–295
 attacks on the media 81
 campaigns 239, 248
 coverage 191, 236
 functions of the 236

 international 285
 management 247–48
 national 285
 organisations 239
 regional 241
 social 83, 224, 228, 230, 251
Mediation 152, 155, 178, 181
Members of Legislative Assembly (MLAs) 270, 272
Memory 166, 168, 174–175, 181, 189
Microsoft 32, 246
 'Digital Civility Index on Safer Internet Day' 246
Micro-targeting 220, 247
Migrants 101, 103, 117, 119, 226
Ministry for Health, Government of Brazil 80
Ministry of Health and Family Welfare, GoI 59
Ministry of Home Affairs, GoI 204, 205
Ministry of Panchayati Raj, GoI 277–78
Ministry of Public Health, Afghanistan 114
Ministry of Rural Development (MORD), GoI 277
Minorities xiv–xv, 3, 41, 116–117, 125, 180, 222, 225, 249–251, 258, 274, 284–287, 290, 292–294
 ethnic 3
 groups 116–117, 125
 violence/attacks against 204, 287
Mobilisations 27, 40, 44, 53–54, 58, 107, 140–141, 155

abusive 107
from below 27
political 140–141
social 54
through a third party 155
Modi, Narendra, Prime
  Minister of India 36, 246, 253,
  294
Money 19, 26, 36, 201, 203,
  205, 208–209, 212, 236–238,
  240, 249, 256–257, 276
Monitoring 26, 66, 119, 126,
  258, 271
Movements 2, 5–6, 15, 22–25,
  27–28, 35, 37, 39–41, 44,
  50–51, 53–54, 56, 58, 72–75,
  85, 87–88, 91, 105, 113, 115,
  140–141, 155–156, 158, 160,
  165–171, 177–178, 186–187,
  189, 210–212, 248, 279,
  290–291, 295–296, 299
  agrarian 22
  caste 22
  grassroots 140
  people's 5, 210–212
  protest 35, 41, 44, 166
  social 22–24, 40, 50, 53–54,
    72–73, 75, 87–88, 91,
    155–156, 160, 177–178,
    211
  supremacist 290, 295
Municipality(ies) 53, 62, 67,
  273
Muslim(s) 226, 227, 252, 273,
  285–286, 289, 292–294
  attacks/violence against,
    252, 286
  refugees 226
Myanmar 251, 288, 295

Namboodiripad, E. M. S. 49,
  51
Narasimha Rao, P. V., Prime
  Minister of India 268, 274,
  277
National
  borders 222
  economic growth 31
  economy 105
  government 126, 199
  legislation 25
National Advisory Committee
  (NAC) 25, 27
National Food Security Act,
  2013 45, 227
Nationalism 4, 20, 45, 207,
  289–290
  diasporic 4
  majoritarian 45
National Rural Employment
  Guarantee Act (NREGA) 27,
  45, 141–142
Nehru, Jawaharlal, first Prime
  Minister of India 266, 270,
  291
Neighbourhood 60, 63, 184,
  291, 295–296
Neoliberalism xiv, 33, 35
Networks 5, 22, 60, 75–76, 78,
  84, 87–89, 103, 110, 117–118,
  121, 144, 187, 254, 290
News xv, 4, 75–77, 79, 82, 85,
  225–227, 230, 235, 237–247,
  249–250, 252–256, 258
  fake 75–76, 82, 85, 235,
    237, 243–247, 249–250,
    252–55
  investigative 239
  online 226, 246

paid 235, 237–238, 240–243, 250, 254–255
   stories 238, 244–245
Non-government organisations (NGOs) 52, 110, 147, 154, 159, 181, 285
Non-profits 201, 204–205, 207
   foreign contributions to 204
Non-profit sector 204
Non-state actors 73, 284
North America 3, 198, 287

OAS Inter-American Commission on Human Rights 82
Obama, Barack Hussein, US President 280
Occupations 32, 37, 39, 121
   paid service 37
   professional 32
   service 37, 39
Official Secrets Act 1923 273
Ombudsman 63, 67, 280
One person, one vote 3, 19
Online harassment 81, 83
Open budget/budgeting 195, 200
   international norms and standards on 195
Openness 140, 142, 151
Opportunity(ies) 19, 21, 23, 25, 28, 72, 90, 103, 121, 123, 152, 154, 192–193, 228, 254, 281, 287–288
   equal 152
   political 28
   socialisation of 21
Opposition party(ies) 202, 205, 210–212, 225–226

Oppression xiii, xvi, 146
Orality 168, 174–175, 180
Organic intellectuals 140, 147–148
Organization for Economic Cooperation and Development (OECD) 21, 196
Organization for Islamic States 106
Oversight Commission on Access to Information in Afghanistan 109–110
Oversight committees 125–126

Paid news 235, 237–238, 240–243, 250, 254–255
Paid news and fake news 250
Pakistan 103–104, 288, 295
Panchayati Raj 7, 49, 62, 268, 270–272, 275–278
   constitutional amendments 23
Panchayati Raj Institutions (PRIs) 268, 271, 279
Panchayats xvi, 54, 67, 165, 167, 175–185, 187–189, 269–271, 273–275, 278–279
   orality of the 180
Parliamentary Investigative Commission (*Comissão Parlamentar Mista de Inquérito* [CPMI]) 77–78, 82
Parliament of India 7, 243
Participation 3–7, 18, 21–22, 25–29, 34, 40, 43, 45, 49–50, 52–56, 58, 63, 66–67, 72–73, 82–84, 90, 99, 114, 117–119, 121, 123–126, 149–151,

155–156, 165, 170–172, 178, 192, 195–200, 211, 219–220, 222–223, 254, 266–267, 269, 273, 280, 289–290, 294, 299–300
  benefits of 199
  condemnation of 151
  direct 53, 55–56
  forms of 126
  importance of 150
  in democratic processes 72, 99
  in development programmes 273
  in grama sabhas 58
  in policy processes 121
  in public decision-making 49
  means of 34
  mechanisms for 198
  modes of 6, 155
  opportunities for 72
  people's 63
  PPC 50–51, 53–57, 60–61, 65–66, 68
  public 6, 90, 121, 192, 195–99, 266–67, 289
  role of 150
  scale and quality of 66
Participation and democracy 3
Participation and power 28
Participatory
  decisions 26
  forums 24, 25
  governance 113, 257
  inputs 22, 26
  mechanisms 141, 151, 159
  processes 100, 159
  spaces 23–26

Participatory Budgeting (PB) 53, 56
  Latin American 55, 56
Participatory democracy xv–xvi, xviii, 1–2, 5, 18, 20–22, 27–28, 38, 72, 99, 101–103, 107, 109, 114, 117, 119, 125–126, 154, 201, 208, 210, 296
  alternative model for 154
  aspects of 208
  form of 18
  implications for 102, 201
  repercussions for 101
  understanding of 22
Payments 27, 237, 241
  surrogate forms of 237
Peace 13–14, 103, 106, 111, 117–118, 121, 179, 240
  processes 103, 106, 111, 117–118, 121
People's Plan Campaign (PPC), Kerala 50–51, 53–57, 60–61, 65–66, 68
  achievements of the 57
  design of 54
Persuasion 220, 223
  campaigns of 220
Philippines, the 19, 198, 295
  extra-judicial killings in the Philippines 19
Planning and implementation 7, 66, 278
  architecture of 58
  campaign-based 56
  decentralised 7, 67
  from below 58
  local 66–67
  micro-level 67

phase of 55
strategic 109
Planning Commission 267, 270, 273, 278
Plan(s) xvi, xviii, 1, 49–50, 53–56, 58, 60–63, 65, 67–68, 269, 273, 278
  annual 61
  devolution of funds 65
  district-level guidelines 68
  funds xvi, 65
  implementation 56
  local 53–54
Plurality 8, 17, 166, 177, 188–190, 289
PM CARES fund 204–205, 210
Polarisation 74, 76–77, 83, 90, 230, 239, 254, 286
  communal 239
  political 90
Policy(ies) xiv, 6, 24–27, 31, 33, 35–36, 38, 74–75, 84, 100, 110–111, 117–126, 150, 158, 171, 175, 188, 191–193, 196–199, 208, 212, 220, 222–223, 228–229, 252–253, 256, 269, 275, 293, 299
  considerations 120
  determination of 212
  development 150
  effective and inclusive response 6
  measures 193
  objectives 120
  process(es) 110, 117–118, 121, 175
  public 25, 125, 197–198, 220, 223, 252–253, 256

public participation 192
welfare 38
Política 79–80, 82
Political
  action 149, 156, 160
  actors 22, 220, 230
  agency 140, 151, 156
  campaigns 224, 230
  contestation 54, 140
  control 87
  crisis/crises 74, 106, 117
  democracy 88
  demonstration 167
  economy 19, 168–169, 171
  elites 193, 222
  fallout 252
  formations 53
  gain 74, 77
  leaders 37, 42, 225, 269, 289
  majorities 294
  movement 6, 44, 295
  outcomes 235
  participation 3, 28
  processes 223, 244
  representatives 219–220
  rivals 220, 239
  will 50, 54
Political party(ies) 27, 41, 45, 51, 64, 201–203, 205, 207, 210–212, 221, 225–226, 236, 240–241, 246–247, 254–255, 257–258, 288, 291
  annual income statement 202
  foreign contributions to 202, 204
  funding architecture 205–206, 212
  funding for 202, 210

Politicisation 5, 17, 158–159
Politics 2, 5, 19, 21, 34, 38–39, 83–84, 87–88, 139, 151, 154, 166, 171, 180, 184–185, 189, 208, 219, 222, 250, 254, 256, 284, 286–288, 289–296
  democratic 21, 38–39, 289, 294
  majoritarian 288
  of exposure 5, 284, 286–88
  populist 222
  supremacist 284
Poor 32–33, 44, 49, 52, 58, 61, 99, 104, 116, 124, 126, 139, 150, 152, 154, 170, 222, 266–267, 293
  involvement in decision-making 150
  marginalisation of the 58
  rural 266–67
  urban 104
Populism 72, 90, 237
  authoritarian 90
Porto Alegre, Brazil 56, 152
Poverty 60–61, 67, 103, 139, 193, 198, 220, 238, 241, 266–268, 275–276, 278, 281
  eradication of absolute 67
  global 193
  rate 103
Poverty alleviation 67, 198, 267, 276, 278
  efficient implementation of programmes 276
  interventions for 67
  measures 267
  programmes 276, 278

Power(s) xiv–xvii, 3–5, 7–8, 11, 14, 17–20, 23–25, 28, 31, 36, 39–43, 50–51, 57–58, 63–64, 84–88, 90, 99, 101, 106–107, 109, 116, 124, 140–142, 144, 146–147, 149–151, 153–154, 156, 158–159, 170–171, 173, 175, 178, 180–181, 197, 201, 203, 210, 221, 229, 236–237, 245, 254, 257, 268–270, 272, 277–278, 281, 284–285, 295, 299–300
  balance of 19, 39, 107
  centralisation of 5, 18, 36
  dynamics 144, 146
  imbalances 99, 116, 144, 146, 149, 153–54
  legislative 107
  political 19, 43
  separation of 17, 101, 107
  sharing 170, 272
Press Council of India (PCI) 238, 242–243
Prices 103, 170, 192, 239
  announcement of 170
  fuel 192
  marked-up 170
Pride 207, 227, 289, 291
Prioritisation xiv, 55, 120
  democratic procedure for 55
Prisoners 101, 115
Private
  parties 202, 243
  sector 58
  spaces 154–155
  testimonies 154
  treaties 238–239, 243
Privatisation 32, 39, 52, 86–87

INDEX 327

Productivity 34, 178, 181, 188, 189
Projects 5, 7, 20, 28, 40–41, 43, 52–53, 55–56, 67–68, 74, 111, 125, 143, 171, 173, 184, 187, 248, 293
  formal proposals 55
  implementation of the 56
  integration of the 68
  social-sector 52
Propaganda 84–85, 91, 236–237, 247, 249, 253
  computational 91, 236–237, 247
Protest(s) 6–7, 24, 35, 40–41, 44, 73, 153–154, 166–167, 170, 189, 191–193, 228, 286, 296
Public
  action 9, 49, 141
  affairs 18–20, 28, 90
  attention 24, 81, 291
  bodies 79–80
  budgeting 192, 197
  concern 72, 225, 227
  debate 73–74, 83, 89, 224
  deliberation 85, 153
  discourse 219, 226–227
  engagement 21, 24, 195, 198–200
  exposure 155, 286
  forums 141, 156, 241
  funds 191, 195, 200
  good 26, 87, 91, 154, 170
  hearing(s) 141–142, 145, 154–155, 197, 296
  information 73, 79, 82
  institutions 74, 83, 195
  meetings 155, 240
  policy(ies) 25, 74, 125, 191, 193, 197–198, 220, 223, 252–253, 256, 296
  protests 191, 193, 296
  sector 52, 103
  services 23, 32, 39–40, 44
  sphere 24–25, 72, 84–85, 87, 89, 144–145, 152–153, 155–156, 158, 236, 257
  works 56, 66–67
Public Distribution System (PDS) 227, 267
Public health 36, 58–59, 79, 90, 100, 112–113, 117, 119–120, 193
  care 36
  crisis 79
  emergency 120
  guidelines 90
  strategies 119
Public participation 6, 90, 121, 192, 195–199, 266–267, 289
  challenges to 198
  in budgeting 192, 196–197
  in governance 266–67
  meaningful and inclusive mechanisms of 192

Racism 191, 195, 200
  institutionalised 191
  systemic 200
Rajya Sabha 241, 268
Redeployment 64–65
Reforms 24, 28, 44, 50–51, 54, 60, 62, 64–65, 109, 114, 124, 142–143, 202–204, 209, 299
  administrative 54
  finance 203
  land 60

legal 109
legislative 124
radical local-level 50
transparency 143
Regulatory
  environments 119
  structures 25
Relations 3–4, 23, 28, 33, 75, 81, 87, 100, 102, 107, 109, 111, 116, 122, 125, 139–142, 156, 166, 174–175, 179, 185, 187, 207, 246, 255
  participation and power 28
  science and innovation 185
Reporters Without Borders (RSF) 81
  2020 World Press Freedom Index 81
Representation xv, 4, 19, 22, 125, 144, 165, 170–173, 181, 184, 189, 219, 274
  behavioural demands of 171
  equal 144
Representative democracy xv, 40, 55
Repression 21, 159
Reprisals 122, 248
Resistance and opposition 18, 34, 37, 41, 73, 87, 90, 99, 146–147, 153, 166, 202, 205, 210–212, 223, 225–226, 248, 254, 291, 294–295
  Gandhian model of 153
  subtle forms of 146
Resources xvi–xvii, 4, 21–22, 24, 26, 43, 51, 55–56, 64, 89, 104–105, 116, 120, 123, 171, 173, 198, 204, 207, 209–210, 220, 229–230, 240, 271

financial 55, 64, 271
human 204
misappropriation and mishandling of 104
natural 171
Revenue(s) xvii, 33, 42, 58, 154, 193
Rights and obligations
  associational and political 23
  basic 104, 117
  citizens' 273
  civil 38
  constitutional 21, 106
  cultural 123
  democratic 49
  economic 6, 40, 44–45, 114, 116
  fundamental 100, 113, 116, 126
  infringements 113
  minority 250, 258
  of access to public information 79
  of the future 178
  political 38
  social 21, 38, 40, 44–45, 114
  statutory 266
  to access government information 141
  to ask questions 266
  to education 44
  to equality 170
  to expression 90
  to freedom of association and assembly 114
  to health 44
  to information. 90
  to liberty 100
  to life 100

to opinion 90
to participate 49, 54
to question 170
to security 100
to stand for public office 209
to vote 209
Right to Education Act of 2009 45
Right To Information (RTI) Act, 2005 25, 281–82
Riots 247, 293
Rule of law 5, 17, 20, 108, 112–113, 123, 127, 223, 257
  politicisation of the 5, 17
Ruling party(ies) 205, 207, 209–210, 252–253
  advantage to the 209–210
Rural areas 50, 274, 275
Rural India xvi, 238, 271
Russia 106, 198

Satyagraha 153
Scandinavia 6, 38–39, 41, 44
Scheduled Caste/Scheduled Tribe (SC/ST), reservations for 50
School Education Quality Index 59
Schools 33, 59, 64, 105, 115, 143, 291–292
Scrutiny 18, 55, 140, 142, 159, 195, 202, 204–205, 208, 210, 222
  institutional 210
  legislative 205
  public 202, 204, 208
Secularism 288, 292
Security 32–33, 40, 100–101, 115, 124, 177, 179, 272

Self-government xvi, 7, 269, 273–275, 278–279
  local xvi, 7, 269, 273, 278
Sen Committee 57, 62–63
Services 23, 32, 39–40, 44, 52, 56, 59, 104–105, 110, 194, 249, 275
  basic 56, 105
  essential 194
  standards of 63
Shari'a 109, 116
  Taliban's interpretation of the 109
Social
  change 86, 88, 140, 143, 148–149, 158
  contract 33, 167, 175
  democracy 6, 37, 39, 41
  groups 28, 44, 147, 230
  harmony 236, 245
  inequalities 126, 151
  issues 85, 144, 152
  life xvi, 67
  means 34, 41
  movements 22–24, 53, 72–73, 75, 87–88, 156, 160, 177–178, 211
  networks 75, 254
  support 118, 121
Social audit/auditing 7, 24–25, 27, 56, 63, 67, 109, 140–141, 154, 158, 197, 211, 280
  minimum standards for 211
  participatory mechanism of 141
Social democratic
  development 38
  parties 39, 41

politics 38
programme 45
Socialism xiii, 34, 37, 53, 57, 253
  21st-century 57
  emergence of 53
Social media xv, 75–78, 82, 84–86, 89–90, 220–224, 228–230, 236–237, 243–244, 246–249, 253
  platforms 77, 85, 89, 221, 229–30, 246
  use of 75, 230
Society(ies) 2, 4, 6, 17, 20–25, 27–28, 31–32, 34–35, 37–38, 40–44, 49, 52–53, 57, 73–74, 76, 80, 82, 86–88, 100–103, 106, 108–111, 113–114, 116–125, 127, 140, 142, 144–145, 147, 159, 167–168, 173, 175–176, 180, 191, 193, 198, 222, 228–229, 236, 241–242, 244, 247–248, 254, 256–258, 276, 285–287, 291–292, 296
  capitalist 145, 147
  democratic 6, 34, 40, 44
  unequal 28, 144
Solidarity 5, 34, 39, 41, 43, 90, 104, 114, 127, 182, 287, 289
Sortition 43, 44
South Africa 6, 40, 44, 198
Sovereignty 21, 23, 26–27
  chain of 26, 27
Speech 21, 87, 90, 152, 155, 158, 168, 222–223, 228–230, 235–237, 249–252, 254–255, 258, 280, 284

free 228–229, 236–237, 250
hate 87, 228, 235–237, 249–252, 254–255, 284
Sri Lanka 288, 295–296
Standing committees 64, 243
State and citizens, gap between the 199
State and civil society 109, 118, 120, 127
State and society linkages 38, 44
State Bank of India (SBI) 202, 205, 210–211
Statecraft 288, 292
State Finance Commission (SFC) 65
Storytelling 166, 168, 171–172, 189
Struggle and conflict 3, 5, 18, 34, 38, 40, 42–45, 49, 78, 87, 89, 100–102, 106, 114, 116, 118, 121, 127, 168–171, 212, 272, 286, 293–294
Subaltern voices 24, 146
Subsidiarity 49, 52, 63
Supreme Court of Afghanistan 80, 83, 107
Surveillance 36, 89–90, 220, 245, 253, 257
Swaraj 184, 269, 279–280

Taliban 105–106, 109, 111, 116–117, 120, 122, 126
  surrender of national army troops to the 106
  willingness and ability of the 117
Taliban and the United States 106

Tax xvii, 33, 36, 192, 196, 203, 256
  burdens 192
  collections 196
  havens 203, 256
Technology(ies) 32, 75, 82, 85–89, 148, 165–166, 180–184, 188, 199, 223, 229, 244, 251–252, 254, 290
  assessment 181
  automated 244
  bias of 182
  distributive effects of 183
  forms of 165
  nuances of 183
  representation of 181
Tension(s) 4, 19, 41, 111, 143, 159
  civil society organisations and the government 111
  (electoral) representation and participation 4
Times Group 239–240, 243
Tocqueville, Alexis De 23, 294
Torture and slavery 104, 113, 122, 287
Trade unions 40–41, 147
Training 33, 55–57
  programme 55–56
Tribals/Tribes 2, 50, 61, 67, 175, 182, 227–228, 267
Troll/Trolling 220, 225, 247–249, 255
Trudeau, Justin 36
Trump, Donald, US President xv, 3, 19, 36, 90, 237, 245, 251, 284–286, 288
  assault on immigrants 19
  impeachment of 284, 286
  presidency 3
  re-election campaign 285
Trumpism 285, 288
Turkey xv, 198, 245, 295–296
TV Senado 78
Twenty-point programme 268

Uganda 142, 194
Uncertainty(ies) 82, 103, 177, 188, 222, 226
Unemployment xiii, 79, 226
  rates 79
Unions 22, 27, 39–41, 147, 242
United Kingdom (UK) 31–32, 36, 39, 44, 247
United Nations (UN) 59, 61, 89, 104–106, 112–113, 117–119, 121–122, 228, 251, 281
United Nations (UN) Human Rights Committee 112–113
United Progressive Alliance (UPA) 25, 45, 273
United States (USA) xv, 3, 5, 17, 22, 31–33, 36, 39, 42, 44, 90, 106, 109, 198, 205, 207–210, 219, 225, 237, 245, 247, 250, 280, 284, 287, 295–296
Universal franchise 208–209

Village panchayats 269–70
Violence 5, 17, 27, 67, 83, 101, 105–106, 155, 179, 225, 251–252, 284–287, 289–290, 292–294
  anti-minority 285, 286
  anti-Muslim 289, 294
  communal 251

exposure of 284, 286
gender-based 105
outsourcing of 5, 17
sexual 105
Violence versus democracy 290
Voiceless 2, 6, 274
Voices 14, 24, 26, 37, 86–87, 102, 110, 125, 127, 146, 150–151, 155, 165, 178, 180, 184, 188, 193, 199, 219–224, 226, 229–230, 248, 271, 274
diverse 199, 219
popular 220, 222
Volunteer Technical Corps (VTC) 55, 66
Vote 3–4, 18–19, 23, 207–209, 211–212, 240
buying 240
legitimacy of the 4
Voter suppression 21, 22
Voting 22–23, 64, 168, 207–208, 224
Vulnerability(ies) 103–104, 118, 125, 176
Vulnerable groups 101, 104, 126, 230

Wages 40, 103, 170–171, 267
Wall Street Journal (WSJ), The 81, 84, 252
War xiii, 17, 21, 34–35, 100–101, 108, 179, 251, 255, 291–292

Way of life 119, 169, 178
Wealth 19, 21, 31–33, 208
Welfare programmes 142, 227
WhatsApp 76–77, 192, 224, 246, 249–292
White supremacy 287, 295
Women 3, 15, 22, 27, 32, 41, 50, 60, 64, 67, 82, 101, 105, 117, 122, 182, 198, 225–226, 250–251, 291
empowerment 60
groups 22
organisations 41
reservations for 50
rights 122
tribal 182
violence against 67
Workers xiii, xviii, 22, 27, 32, 40, 56, 105, 124, 144–149, 154–155, 158, 226, 269, 288
World Bank 52, 103, 150, 172, 194
World Food Program 32, 103
World Trade Organization (WTO) 177–178, 186
World War II xiii, 34–35

X (Twitter) 75, 221, 223–228, 245–247, 253, 290

YouTube 75, 225, 290

Zilla Parishads (ZPs) 271, 277–278